SHAM

SHAM

In the Shadow of a Superhorse

by

Mary Walsh

Aventine Press

Cover Photo:
Sham is all alone coming to the finish line at Santa Anita Park,
winning by six lengths on February 2, 1973 with Laffit Pincay, Jr. up.
George Andrus, photographer.
Used by permission, courtesy of Bill Mochon Photography.

Author Photo:
Kyer Castlewood Portrait Arts, Used by permission.

Published by Aventine Press
1023 4th Ave #204
San Diego CA, 92101
www.aventinepress.com

ISBN: 1-59330-506-0

Printed in the United States of America

To those
Who tried their utmost
At something they strongly believed in
With their whole heart and mind
And gave it their absolute all
Only to find that it was not enough,
because they were in the wrong place in time.

Mary Walsh

Sham with his groom, Secundino Gato, in the paddock prior to the 1973 Santa Anita Derby. Copyright © Bill Mochon Photography. Used by permission.

CONTENTS

PART THREE

Second photo of Sham with his groom, Secundino Gato, in the paddock prior to the 1973 Santa Anita Derby. Copyright © Bill Mochon Photography. Used by permission.

INTRODUCTION

In the year 1969 at the Claiborne Farm breeding shed, two stallions standing stud played an important part in history. Under the care of Lawrence Robinson, the head caretaker of stallions at Claiborne since the 1950s, Pretense covered Sequoia, and Bold Ruler was bred to the Meadow Stable mare, Somethingroyal. In utero both mares amazingly passed on Princequillo's large-heart gene: one to Sham and the other to Secretariat.

I adored Sham's undying courage. That's why I felt the need to research his life and share my findings, all the while praising that unsung hero.

However, I also loved Secretariat. I even have a fine young equine grandson of his standing in my corral. Every morning and night, he nickers to me, reminding me of the greatness of a certain horse in a certain era.

Secretariat proved his greatness by racing against a total of one hundred and fifty-nine horses, beating all but seven of them to the finish line and one other by default. Everyone loved Secretariat, past and present. When they hear about him, such an incredible being piques people's interest. He was the greatest in equine perfection—no question about it. Upon his death, an autopsy revealed he had a heart two-and-a-half sizes larger than that of an average equine—just over twenty-one pounds. He was what the word *superhorse* was created for.

Then there was Sham. He, too, was great—not nearly as great as his illustrious rival, but, nevertheless, a great horse. He didn't have time to prove his greatness as champions before and after him did. He stood strong and relentlessly challenged Secretariat. Sham managed to beat the handful of horses that dared test their luck against Secretariat for the 1973 Triple Crown. Even Ron Turcotte, Secretariat's jockey, praised Sham.

When Turcotte was asked, "Who *did* Secretariat beat?" he unhesitatingly replied, "Sham. Three straight times."[1]

However, Sham's racing days were numbered by fate from the start. That's why I felt such a strong need to share his efforts with the world, to keep his memory alive. Though his heart was found to be twice the size of an average equine—nineteen pounds—his tremendous heart wasn't just in the physical sense of the word. It was in his nature. His greatness came from indomitable courage.

There was something special about his proud bearing and gentle eyes. He knew he was great and always gave his paramount effort, never quitting or tiring of being called second best.

PROLOGUE

Overview of a Racehorse

To become a champion, a racehorse must first possess a certain combination of precise mechanical movement, superior athleticism, a robust heart and lung capacity, and, most importantly, the will to consistently perform at its maximum potential.

Athleticism in the horse is undoubtedly influenced by muscular strength and skeletal build. Nature intended these structures to act together and influence movement in the legs and body. Researchers feel the equine brain sends initial movement signals, but nerve impulses to the spinal cord control motion after that point. The brain then concentrates on general surroundings and situations. If the brain is overloaded with both chores, the equine body cannot help but respond with signs of extreme exhaustion.

A galloping equine is truly awe-inspiring. Its graceful beauty captivates the eyes while its majestic speed fascinates the ears with a powerful melody. In a flat-out gallop, the hindquarters are of great importance in determining the speed of the individual horse and are often referred to as the *power train.*

A four-beat, free-flowing movement beginning with a powerful thrust of the inside hind leg and another push following that from the outside hind quickly transfers the movement forward to the receiving inside foreleg, which lands on the ground a microsecond before the leading outside foreleg. That creates an unmistakable *te-da-da-dum* sound. Then the equine's body seems to float gracefully above the ground for a moment of suspension while the hindquarters recoil below, preparing for the next powerful thrust. This is known as a *no-overlap pattern* granting a horse its own *action.*

The efficiency of this action is what allows a jockey to crouch in the stirrups, hovering above his flying mount, seemingly never moving, just floating. The shoulders lean into turns and are offset by the head and neck instinctively swinging out to maintain balance. With a rider on its back, an equine must adapt to certain changes to stay in perfect balance.

Through numerous years of research, many equine cardiology experts have determined that heart size can be an important indicator of superior performance at the racetrack. Known as the X-factor, the enlarged heart size is believed to be inherited from the dam's ancestry. Therefore, a dam may acquire the large heart X-gene from her sire and pass it on to her offspring. The average equine heart size is eight-and-a-half pounds. In general, a larger heart produces a stronger, more powerful beat. Experts assume that with the increased force a bigger heart provides, oxygen reaches the muscles more quickly and efficiently, and the body is rid of waste products faster.

The heart beats in unison with the rhythm of the gallop, sending oxygenated blood throughout the body processes. When hooves hit the ground, the used blood is forcefully pumped into the veins, back up the legs, through the body and back to the heart. This cycle is important for proper circulation. Meanwhile, the intestines and abdominal organs shift backward with the propulsion of the powerful hindquarters initiating the gallop, drawing air through the nostrils to the lungs like a suction pump. As the front legs grab up the ground, the hindquarters recoil and the abdominal mass thrusts forward, pushing air out of the lungs in perfect timing with the gallop. Each breath and heartbeat per stride processes oxygen and blood in huge volumes per minute.

Thoroughbreds are specifically bred for racing—with their long limbs, sleek frames, and the instinctive yearning to run, combined with the hardiness and stamina of their ancestral Arab origins. Not every Thoroughbred is equipped for the rigorous sport of horse racing. Over the years, experts have documented the winning percentages of young racehorses. They have concluded that only 69 percent would run a single race. Less than half would win once, and only 34 percent would ever win more than once. Only 3 percent would ever win a stakes race. With those shocking statistics, the perfect combination of breeding, balance, stamina, and will isn't always all it takes.

Every great champion racehorse needs a solid team to keep it on course. A jockey can be either an independent contractor or an employee of the trainer. He is responsible for the costs of his agent, valet and saddle. Jockeys receive about 10 percent of the purse money or winnings. The owner has immense responsibilities to deal with daily. Owners pay for purchasing horses, breeding, farrier and veterinary costs, the silks, entry fees, shipping expenses, mortality insurance on the horse, and—most importantly—a trusted trainer.

The trainer's responsibilities usually include each horse's specialized equipment including the bridle, some travel expenses, assistant trainer's salary, liability or health insurance, the groom, exercise rider and hotwalker, horse feed, supplements, office supplies, barn equipment and managing day rates. Through the twentieth century, the day rate for a horse's keep rose from single-digit costs to anywhere from $40 to $60 per day per horse. A trainer also receives a share of the winnings, usually 10 percent.

Since a trainer's responsibilities are enormous, he covets good staff, and if seasons force relocation he moves the entire operation with him to retain trusted help. Tight funds sometimes make it hard to manage health-insurance expenses, and horsemen's organizations have been established for that reason. A good trainer knows the utmost importance of quality care and feed for an equine and would never jeopardize a horse's health or performance by scrimping on its basic needs. That's why a trainer is very selective when choosing which horses to keep in the barn.

It's a game of chance all around. Anyone who becomes involved in horse racing knows that, or learns it very quickly.

ACKNOWLEDGMENTS

Special thanks to my family:

My husband, Gary, for verbally reading and rereading this manuscript at various stages; for his valuable, personal input, and for arranging our trip to California to complete my final research.

My son Mike, for reading, editing, and giving his personal views on the manuscript while in the midst of studying for his MCAT; for seeking information for me from his professors who'd been published; and most of all, for his heartfelt belief in me.

My sons Rob, Chris, and James for giving me special words of encouragement along the way.

Doris Friedmann, my mother, who, at the wonderful age of eighty-eight, has read and reread my manuscripts without losing interest during the numerous changes made along the way, and has reiterated her interest in my work many times.

Sue Fletcher, my sister, for traveling from her home in Ontario, Canada, to spend hours with me researching my project at the equine library in Arcadia, California; for spending a day at the Santa Anita Racetrack to get the feel of Sham's past victories and for photographing certain aspects for me that I would need to remember.

Special thanks to all the people who gave that extra effort to help with this project:

Especially the benefit I garnered from the expertise and knowledge of Keith Pearson, Ryan Ratliff and editor, Stephen Llevares.

Viola Sommer, Sham's owner, who graciously answered my questions concerning her racehorse and added her heartfelt memories of her special horse. Penny Chenery, Secretariat's owner, for taking the time to review my manuscript, discuss it with me, and add her valuable input. Without Penny, I may never have been introduced to Leonard Lusky, president of Secretariat.com.

Rudi Groothedde, managing editor of the *California Thoroughbred* magazine, whose leads, input, general help, and monumental expertise, were offered without reservation time and time again.

Vivian Montoya, librarian at the California Thoroughbred Breeders Association, who patiently helped my sister and me through a grueling day of nonstop research in her library; for going above and beyond the call of duty by unbegrudgingly staying past closing time as we frantically completed our work, and for following up by mail on missing information.

Bill Mochon of Bill Mochon Photography, North Hollywood, California. An outstanding gentleman who not only provided me with his most-prized possessions—magnificent photographs—but also went out of his way to obtain photographs I never would've otherwise found. At every turn, he showered me with good wishes for success.

William Nack, author, for answering my questions and giving me information and leads while on a very tight schedule of his own. Anne Peters, representative of *The Pedigree Post,* who gave me all my best initial leads for research along with all the information she could obtain herself. Sammie L. Justesen, agent, for her great input and encouraging words. Norma Vermeer, of the publicity and marketing department at Santa Anita Park, for her patience while answering my questions. Jerry Crowley and Domenico Caringella, security attendants at Santa Anita Park, for assisting us at the racetrack to achieve our goals. Tom Gilcoyne, historian, and Kate Cravens, curator, at the National Museum of Racing and Hall of Fame in New York for helping in the early stages of my research. Donna Freedman, freelance writer, Illinois, for general help and encouragement. Frances J. Karon, representative at Walmac International, for information I could not have found elsewhere.

Special thanks goes to Patti Cerda, of the NYRA, for solving my final stumbling block through Raul Garcia, who worked with Frank Martin and his staff so many years ago on the backstretch of Belmont Park.

PART ONE

CHAPTER ONE

The Belmont Stakes, Belmont Park, Elmont, NY
June 9, 1973

Under a sleek coat of seemingly jet-black hair, sweat formed in his pores, almost making him glisten like a piece of finely polished dark onyx. Sham, nervous, must have wondered what was expected of him, considering haunting recollections of the near past.

The irrepressible humidity, gusty winds, and broiling sun made the situation even more unbearable. The colt's eyes rolled, and the whites showed in trepidation as he tossed his head taking in the scene while the quickened thud of his heart sent a warning to his jockey.

Equine senses were sharp, and cascading spasms in taut tendons desperately played on nervous hooves. A shrieking bell tore at sensitive eardrums and a reverberating crash sent tremors through the ensnaring steel cages as the gates burst open. Instinctive fears awakened cramped muscles as they sprang to life, catapulting into motion like slingshots.

Sham was fit, but the recent racing timetable was harsh and unyielding on the colt's physical and mental well-being, and his fate was about to unfold. He and Secretariat broke clean, without faltering or colliding with unseen dangers like before.

With the first powerful push of coiled hindquarters, all five horses were free from the gates, and in two more, vying for the lead. They gained speed with quick, successive thrusts.

Completely out of character, both Sham and Secretariat were up front early and earnestly fighting for the lead at the break.

Over the loudspeaker, Chic Anderson's voice was cool. "And they're off. Looks like the early lead goes to My Gallant. Yes, My Gallant going for the lead with Twice a Prince on the outside. Secretariat away very well, has a good position on the rail and in fact is going up now with the leaders."[2]

Ron Turcotte guided Secretariat along the rail with the experience of a well-respected jockey, and Laffit Pincay Jr., with a reputation for being just as skilled, knowingly kept pace with Sham on the outside. Pincay was focused on the task he had been sent to accomplish that day. Frank "Pancho" Martin's resolute instructions were to challenge Secretariat from the start, and Pincay had every intention of obliging the trainer.

Chic's voice increased in tempo. "They're moving for the first turn. It is Secretariat. Sham on the outside is also moving along strongly. And now it's Sham. Sham and Secretariat are right together into the first turn. My Gallant has third behind them, then it's Twice a Prince and the trailer is Pvt. Smiles as they go by the turn. Those two together, Sham on the outside. Sham getting a head in front as they move around the turn with Secretariat second, then there's a large gap—make that eight lengths, back to My Gallant in third and Twice a Prince fourth, and Pvt. Smiles is still a trailer."[3]

Pincay saw his chance to take the lead from Secretariat and his colt obligingly flew into first place. The pace was sizzling hot as they fought with every ounce of strength. Pincay reveled in the realization that they were leading, with half Sham's body length commanding the front position.

Secretariat drove on steadily at Sham's flank, increasing his stride. Determined eyes casually met Sham's as Secretariat's powerful head and neck drew even. The two horses sped past in a whirlwind of dirt into the backstretch. They were in unison, matching stride for stride, blazing away unbelievable quarter fractions—23 3/5 at the first quarter, 22 3/5 to the half-mile, and then 23 3/5 for the three-quarter-mile split. The telemeter blinked 1:09 4/5 at that halfway point as Secretariat and Sham dueled for the fastest six-furlong clocking in Belmont history.

"They're on the backstretch. It's almost a match race now. Secretariat's on the inside by a head, Sham is on the outside. They've opened ten lengths on My Gallant who's third by a head with Twice a Prince fourth, then it's another eight lengths back to Pvt. Smiles who is trailing the field."[4]

It was a ludicrous pace, for a mile-and-a-half race—it couldn't be happening! All eyes were riveted on the two as they battled inches apart. Their bodies churned like two massive locomotives ripping holes in the wind, legs pumping like pistons, lungs bellowing like smokestacks and heads stretched out low to the track.

Pincay looked over at Turcotte with a feeling of foreboding.

Turcotte sat chilly, portraying the same lack of interest as his mount.

It almost appeared that the copper horse was quietly calculating some spectacular feat—an exploit of magnitudinous proportions. Secretariat was as cool as a vial of nitroglycerin. Flawlessly, he burst into overdrive like a time bomb. The mighty red horse had engineered a new gear ratio—a phenomenal dimension of speed—precise timing, perfect balance; a new efficiency requiring minimal power to deliver equal force. His hoofbeats sounded like a tribal drum pounding out a war chant. He was soaring!

Sham's body strained as he gave all he had. Bones and tendons violently writhed, while his heart pumped in staccato as he fearlessly kept up. His swollen nostrils, throat, and lungs sucked at the rushing air in loud, rhythmic snorts. The dark horse's powerful frame whirred like a turbine engine in top gear, churning red-hot.

Time seemed to stand still for Sham as his equine heart kept firing, driven by a diamond-tough will to succeed.

Up in the box seats of the grandstand, someone whispered with bated breath, "*Go for it, Sham....*"[5]

CHAPTER TWO

Claiborne Farm, Paris, KY
April 9, 1970

"Be prepared to get the vet," James Christopher, the Claiborne stable's foaling manager, said. Everyone, suddenly alerted to the new distraction and spurred into action again that morning, ran off in different directions, all knowing their jobs. Those were very familiar words during the spring foaling season at Claiborne Farm's stables where the broodmares spent the last trimester of their 320-day gestation period.

Darkness still filled the air outside where crickets played their endless melodies throughout the night and into the early morning hours. The days were unusually warm that past week. However, the early morning air was still crisp at two o'clock and James instinctively pulled his light jacket tighter across his chest.

After countless trips spent pacing her foaling stall, Sequoia, through with pawing the fresh straw to find a good place to birth her foal, lay down. The long hours of relentless circling were over. Worried snorts continuously came from her nostrils, and she turned her head back to view her aching belly as her contractions increased in severity and tempo. A small form began to take shape in the straw under her tail.

"Sequoia's already begun!" James growled. "The foal's already on its way! Quick, bring the disinfectant and supplies. I don't think this one's waiting. At least it looks like a normal birth."

Tired, he was relieved to see the tip of the foal's mouth alongside the front feet—both toe-down. Knowledgeable, James had seen just about every type of birthing imaginable. He knew the dangers of abnormal presentations such as hind feet first, or front feet first, toe up, and even front feet first, toe down with the head bent back. Those positions required special procedures to turn the foal. Locating the head in the mare's uterus and slipping an obstetrical chain over the foal's mouth and behind its ears was risky for both mare and foal.

"That's the way it goes," he muttered. "As soon as I take my eyes off her, she sneaks into a corner and hides." Even though he watched Sequoia carefully the past few nights, knowing the birthing signs all too well, he still hadn't been prepared for the speed with which that particular foal decided to enter the world.

As soon as the foal's delicate nose was visible, James knelt and gently cleared the mucus from its nostrils and mouth to ensure the oxygen path would be open when the placenta detached from the mare. James knew that during delivery the still-attached placenta would provide oxygenated blood until the foal was breathing on its own. If the placenta detached and was expelled too early, the foal's oxygen supply would be cut off, which could kill the foal from oxygen deprivation during birth or soon thereafter. The exertion of trying to stand would cause its oxygen-starved heart to fail.

Sequoia was a dark bay, a near-black beauty as dark as her sire, the famous French-bred racehorse Princequillo. Breeder Laudy L. Lawrence bred his dam, Cosquilla, to Prince Rose. In 1940, after the start of World War II, Lawrence shipped pregnant Cosquilla to Ireland, where Princequillo was born. Then, with Irish fears of German bombing, both mare and foal were sent overseas for safety.

Princequillo made his debut on American soil in July of 1942. Boone Hall Stable purchased him and he ran as a claimer. The horse was claimed for $2,500 by Hall of Fame trainer Horatio Luro, and under his guidance Princequillo broke the one-and-three-quarter-mile track record at Saratoga. The horse proved his worth at the track in the early 1940s with twelve wins and five seconds in thirty-three starts, earning over $96,000. Princequillo retired to stud at Ellerslie and became *chef-de-race* (I/S). He continues to be renowned as one of the most important large-heart stallions, historically holding the title as America's best long-distance runner. During his eight Leading Broodmare Sire titles, he gave America his gift by siring Sequoia and Somethingroyal.

Chefs-de-race (French for "chiefs of racing") are placed in male aptitudinal groups, namely Brilliant (B), Intermediate (I), Classic (C), Solid (S) and Professional (P)—Brilliant indicating their offspring excelled at short distances, all the way to Professional, excelling at the longest distances.

Losing more often than not in twenty-two racing starts, Sequoia never shared the same fame as her sire and was now testing her fame as a broodmare. Everyone hoped she would be a *blue hen* as she was first-generation offspring of The Squaw II, Bobinski family 9 *blue hen*.

Blue hens are broodmares recognized for founding dynasties amongst Thoroughbred lines by consistently giving superior foals, and the title honors them much the same as the official *chef-de-race* classification for stallions. These foundation mares are assigned Bobinski Female Family numbers and letters designating their group.

Sequoia's descendants were almost exclusively European, not having raced on American soil as she had. She was bred to Pretense, a very well known and impressive dark-bay stallion who ultimately raced his way to total career earnings of over $494,000 and future *chef-de-race* (C) honors. His racing career landed him thirteen wins and five seconds in thirty-one starts. Like Sequoia's, Pretense's ancestors were also predominantly European. They included the great winner of the English Triple Crown, Gainsborough *chef-de-race* (C), along with his chestnut son, Hyperion *chef-de-race* (B/C), who was Leading Sire six times and Leading Broodmare Sire four times in England, as well as the sire of twelve champions.

Sequoia was getting restless, and her breathing increased in tempo. After what seemed like seconds to the attendants, soft, welcoming nickers came from her throat, beckoning the newborn to her side. James treated the foal's navel with iodine to prevent infection, and then checked him carefully for birthing injuries or defects by softly running his hands and fingers over his entire body. Satisfied, James left the stall.

The mare washed her foal, enjoying the miracle of motherhood while securing that instinctive bond shared between newborn and mothers of all species. Sham's breathing became steady, and his blurry eyes began to clear and search for the source of his dam's soft, personal nickers.

Feeling as if her attentive licking had sufficiently opened the foal's air passageways, Sequoia struggled to pull her shaky legs beneath her and heaved herself to her feet, not wanting to lie down longer than necessary. After steadying herself, she aggressively shook her coat from head to tail. Particles of straw embedded in her hair and covering her back flew into the air.

Though the foaling lasted only ten minutes, she had been waxing for the past ten or eleven hours, and thick yellow colostrum still formed on the ends of her teats. To a newborn foal, colostrum means the difference between life and death and is produced by the mare for only twenty-four hours after giving birth. Instinctively, Sequoia knew her foal must be up on his feet, nursing and absorbing that colostrum. It would stave off any bacteria lurking in the new environment, ready to afflict him with life-threatening infection.

Her soft, beckoning nickers continued while his inquisitive ears flicked back and forth. Being prey animals, foals must be up and moving within hours of birth.

Sham was a striking foal. His coat was tinged with golden-brown baby down and a rich, dark forest brown underneath—a solid color without a trace of white. Even though he would darken as he matured, he would not turn black. He would be registered a dark bay.

Alert now, he constantly struggled to make his first attempts to stand. He curled his extraordinarily long front legs under his chest and awkwardly pushed up with his hind, which immediately made him flip forward or to the side. After many unsuccessful attempts, Sham finally hoisted himself up on all four legs and looked around in amazement at his new place in the world.

Sham's spindly legs wobbled one after the other while his head bobbed up and down. "*Huh, huh, huh…,*" Sequoia sent her message again. He soon ingrained her scent to memory, butted his soft nose at her udder, nuzzled a teat, and instinctively began suckling.

James, peering into the stall, breathed a sigh of satisfaction seeing all was going well. Sequoia's groom was busy the rest of the morning. He paid extra attention to the newborn's requirement for fresh, clean straw and watched his progress as the day went on.

Unbeknownst to Sham, only minutes after midnight on the chilly morning of March 30, 1970, and under golden halos cast from a moon so bright the stars seemed dull by comparison, the one who would strip him of any glory and chance at fame was born. Even the date seemed to signify greatness, coming just ten minutes past the birth date of the immortal Man o' War, fifty-three years prior. As yet unnamed, he was the son of acclaimed sire Bold Ruler and dam Somethingroyal.

While Bold Ruler stood stud at Claiborne, a client of A.B. (Bull) Hancock, Jr.—Ogden Mills Phipps of Wheatley Stable—owned him. Ogden's mother, Gladys Phipps, boarded her Thoroughbred stallions and mares at Claiborne for many years. Bold Ruler was Leading Sire seven years in succession from 1963 to 1969. The stallion earned *chef-de*-race (B/I) honors, but breeders were wary of his unproven success over long stretches. Through the years, Ogden had a foal-sharing agreement on Bold Ruler breedings with Chenery mares at Meadow Stable.

In 1947, Christopher Tompkins Chenery bought a mare that would earn the title of *blue hen* and ultimately provide his stables with the most notable Thoroughbred champion of the century. That prized mare was Imperatrice, a Bobinski family 2 *blue hen*, born in 1938 from a match between Caruso and Cinquepace. She was the dam of six stakes winners, including Scattered, Imperium, Squared Away, Speedwell, Yemen, and Imperial Hill, but her greatest claim to fame was her filly, Somethingroyal.

With such a royal pedigree and the champion beliefs of Thoroughbred breeding on his side, he was perfect. While that ten-day-old rival was blissfully asleep in his foaling stall at Meadow Stable, his soft breaths were tenderly monitored by his dam while she quietly rested in the straw at his side. Nights were cool since his birth, but nearly every dawn, a rich, golden sun would warm the day long into the afternoon.

Howard Gentry stepped out of the farm office and began his daily trek past the main barns and across to the foaling barn for one of his numerous daily visits. The farm manger for The Meadow, he was a very busy and well-respected man.

The night watchman, Bob Southworth, hadn't once woken him through the night, so he seemed full of energy that morning. Finally, he had a good night's rest. It seemed to him that spring season at the farm was always the busiest, most demanding time of year, and that spring proved no different.

"Hey, Mistah Gentry," Southworth said. "You look wide awake this mornin'. Wan' a coffee, anyway?"

It was always good to see Howard in the barns, knowing in case of emergency, he was the first person to be summoned.

"Even though things were pretty quiet last night, sure's shootin' that'll change," Southworth added, chuckling.

"Yeah," Howard replied. "I feel wide awake this morning, but I guess I could still use one. Thanks. I've come to see that big copper colt Somethingroyal dropped a little over a week ago. Think I'll move them to the outer barn today. Get 'em used to the halter and walks to the paddock. He'll benefit from a daily turnout with his dam."

Howard always took a special interest in starting the foals, but he knew the importance of letting them bond with their dams in the early days after birth.

"Oohwee! That shuh is one fine-lookin' foal," Southworth said. "He jus' looks too pretty to be anythin' on the track, that 'un."

"Yeah, but the Chenerys have great expectations for that colt. If he runs as good as he looks, he won't disappoint any," Howard knowingly replied.

Chris Chenery was battling Alzheimer's disease and could no longer manage the farm. Penny [Helen Chenery] Tweedy, mother of four, was the perfect solution. Her father had introduced her to horses at age five, which led to an equestrian prep school in Virginia and a degree from Smith College in 1943. Much like her father, Penny was vibrant and always ready for change.

Chris had instilled a determined ruggedness in his daughter's nature. She was self-confident and knew he had her back. Penny agreed to take over with little convincing.

Howard remembered the day Penny first came to see the foal. She kept a diary with her own personal observations of her horses. When she first came to see the beautiful red foal with three gleaming white socks, a star and unique blaze, her entry consisted of just one word, "Wow." To her, he would be fondly nicknamed "The Wow Horse."[6]

Howard's eyes focused on the chestnut foal looking back at him from its stall and said, "And I wonder what Pretty Boy has in store for us."

Instantly, Howard became lost in thought, reminiscing about the way that chestnut colt became the Chenerys'. *It had to be fate that in keeping with the foal sharing agreement between Chenery and Phipps, Somethingroyal and Hasty Matelda were sent to Bold Ruler at Claiborne for the 1968 breeding season.*

In the spring of '69, a colt and a filly were born. That summer, Somethingroyal was again bred to Bold Ruler but instead of Hasty Matelda, Cicada was sent as the second mare. The foal sharing agreement, decided by a coin toss, would dictate who had first pick of the two foals from that season and the loser would have first choice the following year.

Cicada, a champion filly at ages two, three and four, 1967 Hall of Fame inductee, and a leading money-earning filly, would prove to be a poor broodmare. In her total sixteen years of breeding, for ten seasons she was barren or lost her foal. With the date of the coin toss quickly approaching, it was already apparent that Cicada was barren, so the winner could choose only one of the three—the colt, filly, or unborn foal—leaving the loser with the other two.

In the fall of '69, with Bull Hancock as witness, Alfred Vanderbilt II, chairman of the New York Racing Association, flipped the coin. Phipps quickly called "tails." The coin fell tails-up giving him first pick. He chose Somethingroyal's 1969 filly, The Bride, who would later fail to place in her four lifetime starts.

Representing her father's interest, Penny left with Rising River, Hasty Matelda's colt who would never race, and the pregnant Somethingroyal.

Meanwhile, Sham dozed in the warm afternoon sun filtering through the open upper Dutch door of his stall at Claiborne as his dam peacefully stood watch over him.

It was a peaceful beginning for the two foals in comparison to the trials and tribulations of the nation. Indeed, a year of achievements; while the British-French *Concorde* reached speeds of 700 miles per hour in its first supersonic flight on the twenty-fifth of March, just six days later NASA's *Explorer I* satellite, pioneer for the Explorer spacecraft program, reentered the atmosphere. Everyone breathed a sigh of relief for *Apollo 13* astronauts Jim Lovell, Fred Haise and Jack Swigert on April 17, after the mission was aborted by an onboard explosion four days earlier.

Women were striking for equality in New York City. The Broadway musical *Hair* was a huge success in its second of four years, and the hippie movement continued to bring about constant concern with "love-ins" and drugs. The phenomenal era of Beatlemania was coming to an end. At a press conference on April 10, Paul McCartney shattered the music world with the release of his new solo album and his announcement that the Beatles had split up. Just prior to Christmas, the World Trade Center's north tower would be hailed the tallest building in the world at 1,368 feet.

Mostly, it would prove a trying year for Americans with the war in Vietnam. Massive protests across the United States followed the April 29 invasion of Cambodia to hunt the Vietcong. During a May 4 demonstration protesting the invasion, the Ohio National Guard shot and killed four students and injured nine more at Kent State University. Five days after that disaster, a hundred thousand demonstrators stormed Washington, D.C., and another five days later, state law enforcers fired into crowds during a two-day demonstration at Jackson State College in Mississippi, injuring twelve students and killing two.

President Richard Nixon was plagued with criticisms over the war, strategies, massacres, and peace proposals for years. Almost as if a message were sent from above, on the second-to-last day in October the most devastating monsoon in the past six years would hit Vietnam, almost setting the war at a standstill.

It seemed as if the nation was in need of an anchor. Everything was changing and moving too fast to comprehend.

CHAPTER THREE

Two Different Beginnings Entwined

Claiborne Farm, Paris, KY

From its inception as a Thoroughbred farm in 1915 on its original 1,300 acres, Claiborne Farm's reputation for brilliance in producing champions in the breeding stables was unquestioned. At one point, the establishment's stallions held the Leading Sire title for fourteen years straight, from 1955 to1969, and the farm grew close to 4,500 acres. A scientific approach that breeders adopted over the years, of Thoroughbreds with proven racing blood pedigrees usually bestowing similar traits on their offspring, really held true.

Under the guidance of Bull Hancock, after Arthur Hancock, Sr. suffered a severe stroke in the late 1940s, Claiborne enjoyed fame as one of the world's top Thoroughbred breeding establishments in the country. A passionately intense breeder, Hancock methodically planned meaningful patterns into the pedigrees of the farm's horses.

Many great stallions stood at Claiborne stud, including Sir Galahad III, who was Leading Sire for the early years 1930, 1933, 1934, and 1940. He sired Gallant Fox, the 1930 Triple Crown winner, who, in turn, sired Omaha, the 1935 Triple Crown winner.

In 1950, Hancock imported Nasrullah *chef-de-race* (B), the son of Nearco *chef-de-race* (B/C), undefeated European sire at fourteen runs. He and his associates paid the then-incredible price of $340,000 for Nasrullah and syndicated the stallion into thirty-two shares. The horse was Leading Sire in 1955, 1956, 1960, and 1962, and sired Bold Ruler.

Princequillo stole the Leading Sire title from Nasrullah for the years 1957 and 1958. From a troublesome first couple of seasons at Ellerslie stud in '45 and '46 with a humble $250 stud fee, he sired the champion and Horse of the Year, Hill Prince. Late in '46 Princequillo was moved to Claiborne where his career took off. He was immediately booked full for the following season. Bull Hancock envisioned the stallion's potential, took a chance and never regretted it. In all, Princequillo sired sixty-five stakes winners, most notably the award-winning Horse of the Year, Round Table, whose outstanding multiple championships and monetary awards prompted a majority-interest ownership sale to Travis M. Kerr, which literally rescued the farm from estate taxes of the late A. B. Hancock, Sr.

Pedigree
Sham - 13: 5-5-1
Sigmund Sommer - Bred-Claiborne Farm

Sire:- **Colombo**, (GB) (Champion) 11: 9-1-1
Sire:- **British Empire**, (GB) [B] (Ch. Sire 14 yrs)
Dam:- **Rose of England**, (GB)

Sire:- **Endeavour**, (ARG) 30: 18-0-0

Sire:- **Hunter's Moon**, (GB) (Champion Sire)
Dam:- **Himalaya**, (ARG)
Dam:- **Partenope**, (ARG) Unraced

Sire:- **Pretense**, (USA) [C] (Champion) 31: 13-5-6

Sire:- **Gainsborough**, (GB) [C] (GB T.Crown)
Sire:- **Hyperion**, (GB) [BC] (Champion) 13: 9-1-2
Dam:- **Selene**, (GB) (Blue Hen)(Ch. 3yo)

Dam:- **Imitation**, (GB)

Sire:- **Winalot**, (GB) (Champion)
Dam:- **Flattery**, (GB) Unraced
Dam:- **Fickle**, (GB)

Sham

Sire:- **Rose Prince**, (FR) Unraced
Sire:- **Prince Rose**, (GB) [C] (Champion) 20: 16-0-2
Dam:- **Indolence**, (GB) 5: 1-0-0

Sire:- **Princequillo**, (IRE) [IS] (Champion) 33: 12-5-7

Sire:- **Papyrus**, (IRE) (Champion) 18: 9-4-1
Dam:- **Cosquilla**, (IRE) 27: 7 wins
Dam:- **Quick Thought**, (IRE) 1 win

Dam:- **Sequoia**, (USA) (Blue Hen) 22: 4-2-1

Sire:- **Phalaris**, (GB) [B] (Ch. Spr.) 24: 6-2-1
Sire:- **Sickle**, (GB) (Champion Sire) 10: 3-4-2
Dam:- **Selene**, (GB) (Blue Hen) (Ch. 3yo)

Dam:- **The Squaw II**, (FR) (Blue Hen) 3: 2 wins

Sire:- **Blandford**, (IRE)[C](Ch. Sire) 4: 3-1-0
Dam:- **Minnewaska**, (FR)
Dam:- **Nipisiquit**, (GB)

Sham – Pedigree Chart.

Meadow Stable, Doswell, VA

In a small town named Doswell, The Meadow originally encompassed 2,600 acres when Charles Dabney Morris, an ancestor of Chris Chenery, built it in 1810. Then, after the Civil War, it was lost from the family's ownership.

Born on September 16, 1886 in Richmond, Virginia, Chris Chenery's life had always been a wonderful mixture of knowledge and adventure. Years later his daughter, Penny, the youngest child of three, would remember him as outgoing and "dynamic."[7]

Raised in Ashland, Virginia, Chenery earned a Phi Beta Kappa key and in 1909, graduated from Washington and Lee University with a Bachelor of Engineering degree. During World War I, he served in the United States Army Corps of Engineers. Chenery's career began as a surveyor in Alaska for U.S. Pacific Northwest.

Later, Chenery settled his family in the village of Pelham Manor, Westchester County, New York, for nearly fifty years. He served as president of the Federal Water Service Company and was controlling stockholder through Chenery Corporation. His remarkable success enabled him to pursue his love of horses, and while helping establish the New York Racing Association, Chenery repurchased the Meadow in 1936. He had been warned of serious flooding issues and for years Chenery lovingly rode that land on horseback, constantly overseeing signs of trouble.

Besides his passion for the land, his second great obsession was Thoroughbred livestock. The Meadow grew from fine stallions, most notably Hill Prince—Chenery's first Horse of the Year in 1950. Sun Beau was the 1931–39 holder of the Leading Money Earner title until Seabiscuit's record in 1940. Through years of meticulously researching pedigrees of Thoroughbreds from volumes of the *General Stud Book,* Chenery always took great pride in the production of champions.

* * *

It was interesting that two of the greatest, most respected, well-known breeding establishments became so entangled in breeding strategies and how their resultant competitive forces would dominate the heart of the great world of Thoroughbred racing.

Pedigree
Secretariat - 21: 16-3-1
Penny Chenery - Bred-Meadow Stable

Sire:- **Pharos**, (GB) [I] (Ch.) 30: 14-5-6
Sire:- **Nearco**, (ITY)[BC](Champion Sire) 14: 14-0-0
Dam:- **Nogara**, (ITY) (Ch. Spr.) 18: 14 wins

Sire:- **Nasrullah**, (GB) [B] (Champion Sire) 10: 5-1-2

Sire:- **Blenheim**, (GB) [CS] (Ch.) 10: 5-3-0
Dam:- **Mumtaz Begum**, (FR) 8: 2-0-0
Dam:- **Mumtaz Mahal**, (GB)(B.H.) 10: 7-2-0

Sire:- **Bold Ruler**, (USA) [BI] (Champion) 33: 23-4-2

Sire:- **Display**, (USA) 103: 23 wins
Sire:- **Discovery**, (USA) [S] (Ch.) 63: 27-10-10
Dam:- **Ariadne**, (USA)

Dam:- **Miss Disco**, (USA) (Champion) 54: 10-3-10

Sire:- **Pompey**, (USA)[B](Ch.2yo) 35: 13-7-7
Dam:- **Outdone**, (USA) 21: 2-2-3
Dam:- **Sweep Out**, (USA) 35: 13-6-4

Secretariat

Sire:- **Rose Prince**, (FR) Unraced
Sire:- **Prince Rose**, (GB) [C] (Champion) 20: 16-0-2
Dam:- **Indolence**, (GB) 5: 1-0-0

Sire:- **Princequillo**, (IRE) [IS] (Champion) 33: 12-5-7

Sire:- **Papyrus**, (IRE) (Champion) 18: 9-4-1
Dam:- **Cosquilla**, (IRE) 27: 7 wins
Dam:- **Quick Thought**, (IRE) 1 win

Dam:- **Somethingroyal**, (USA) (Blue Hen) 1: 0-0-0

Sire:- **Polymelian**, (GB)
Sire:- **Caruso**, (USA) 33: 9-5-8
Dam:- **Sweet Music**, (USA) 27: 4 wins

Dam:- **Imperatrice**, (USA) (Blue Hen) 31: 11-7-2

Sire:- **Brown Bud**, (USA) 22: 9 wins
Dam:- **Cinquepace**, (USA) Unraced
Dam:- **Assignation**, (USA) Unraced

Secretariat – Pedigree Chart.

CHAPTER FOUR

The First Months

Sequoia was a loving mother to her newborn, but she wasn't so protective that she would refuse entry to the attendants who occasionally came to muck out the stall, change water buckets, bring fresh hay, and, eventually, handle her foal. Early imprinting with a newborn develops an attitude of trust, familiarity, and respect for human handling while the foal's brain is in the experimental stage of learning. If that horse isn't betrayed by inappropriate treatment later, it will be a lifetime beneficial experience. Just as a foal will learn respect for herd hierarchy when turned out with other horses, so will it learn domestication and yielding to pressure willingly at the hands of human handlers.

"Easy now, girl," the groom crooned in a gentle voice as he slipped into the stall and slid his hand gently up Sequoia's face, effortlessly securing her halter. With the same motion, he ran his hand along the length of her side and casually came to rest on the foal's small forehead. "Easy, young fella. T'day we're startin' you off with yer imprint training, an' in a day 'er so, you'll be jus' as happy to have yer halter on yer face as yer mama is."

While one hand gently ran along Sham's face the other slid lightly along the top line of his back, encircling his rump and giving him the secure feeling of being gently restrained. Feeling the slight pressure from behind, the foal didn't try to back away. Simultaneously, a soft leather halter slipped over the end of Sham's nose and up over his ears. His reaction was to toss his head, trying to rid himself of the foreign object, but the groom never stopped softly stroking his face and neck, making him forget the slight weight of the halter. It gave the foal a feeling of security and knowledge that the groom posed no harm.

With halter in place, the groom reached for the soft linen rub rag in his pocket and gently rubbed it along Sham's body, desensitizing him to the feeling of having his coat stroked. He touched and manipulated each area of Sham's body, including his legs, feet, ears, and mouth with rapid repetitions. It felt reassuring, and Sham no longer responded to his instinctive flight reaction.

Sham's acceptance seemed to indicate that the groom's touch was a welcome thing, like the nuzzling his dam bestowed on him to ease worries and have him yield to her leadership while gently encouraging him to feel his submissive rank to her dominance. Sham's groom deftly slid to the other side and repeated the manipulations there, too.

Being careful not to tire the foal, the groom eased away, giving it more space and watching the reaction to the realization of the halter's weight on its face when all other stimulants were removed. Sham seemed to forget its presence while watching the groom with innocent curiosity.

The groom moved unobtrusively around the stall with the mare and foal, asking them to move over as he worked. He subtly checked their demeanor by every small swish of a tail, ear flick, glance of an eye, and muscle twitch. He continued for another fifteen minutes, gently asserting pressure on their sides when they pressed near him and immediately releasing pressure when they moved away. The groom felt he had succeeded at that day's lesson. Sham was already very accepting of human contact.

"A couple more days' work on the halter, and b'fore ya know it, we'll be leadin' ya both out to the corral fer some daily turnout," he said, gently lifting the halters from their faces before he left the stall.

It was feeding time for the horses, and Sequoia impatiently waited at her feed door as she heard the hay cart's wheels rattling down the aisle toward her. Her beckoning nickers softly filled the air as doors on adjacent stalls swung open on squeaky hinges and hay slid down with a *thump!*

When the mare's door swung open, her eager lips cupped the sprigs of hay that worked loose from the flake as it slid down, easing her anticipation and settling her into a contented state. Her foal sensed her ease. His curious little muzzle lifted to the feeder while his nostrils quivered as he inhaled the sweet smell of rich timothy. Instinctively, he pushed his nose deeper. Not understanding her interest, Sham turned his head to her full udder to nurse.

His hunger appeased, he lay down and rolled onto his side. Breathing a heavy, contented sigh, Sham let his eyelids close and his head and neck settle slowly into the straw. Sequoia turned toward him, munching hay while watching over his sleeping form at her feet.

James appeared at Sequoia's stall to check on them. "My, my. You outdid yourself with this one, old girl. He's a looker."

He gave her a routine examination for ruptures or bruising and checked her udder to make sure all was well. Then he examined the colt.

"Alert and healthy lookin'. Claiborne's done it again. This one looks like he's going places," James mused out loud.

As soon as the groom entered the stall, James asked, "Has the foal passed its meconium, urinated, and been nursing every half-hour or so?" He was alert to the first signs of danger and made sure his staff monitored all new foals carefully.

"Yessir. Shuh has. That young'un's got all the right stuff an' knows what it's for, all right," the groom said proudly. "I've been workin' with him t'day, gettin' him ready for the paddock. Probably take him and Sequoia out in a couple days fer fresh air, if that's okay with you."

"Don't see any reason why not. They both look like they're comin' along just fine. A little fresh air is just what they need. That'll give the colt some space to stretch those long legs and kick up his heels," James replied.

"You got it." The groom went happily about his business and checked on another mare that was due to foal soon.

Feeling satisfied with the groom's replies to his questions and the condition of the mare and foal, James left the stall. He latched the door securely and walked down the aisle toward the farm office. He needed to fill out some paperwork and give the Hancocks the lowdown on the breeding operation for the day. Included in his report would be his observations of Sequoia and her foal. Considering Sham's ease at entering the world, the foal seemed like a strong contender for the rigors of preparing for the racetrack.

Golden rays of sunlight filtered through small cracks in the upper barn door, and after turning millions of fine particles of dust into glitter, the rays found their way to the straw where Sham lay. He was beginning to rouse from his final nighttime nap as the warm beams of light caught him sleeping.

Sham's inborn equine instincts afforded him an almost totally developed state at birth. True to a horse's physical makeup, he was able to do almost everything his dam could within hours. Other than quick, jerking movements with unstable balance and coordination, his only other real difference was his sleep pattern.

Sequoia took an average of a half-hour's nap and between two to three hours' deep sleep each day, while, like all immature animals, Sham spent many more hours lying down in deep sleep than his dam. Other than a ten- to fifteen-minute nap, Sequoia rarely lay down, preferring to get her sleep requirements standing. Equine tendons and ligaments allow forelimb joints and the lowest two hind-limb joints of the legs to lock. This held her upright, but also allowed her to awake in a split second and instantly flee if in peril.

She also had a very sensitive digestive system and lying down too long created gas in her intestines, making it very uncomfortable. In a group, it was common for the herd to take turns lying down to sleep and always have one standing to watch for danger.

Far in the distance a rooster crowed, signaling the start of a new day as the rustle of feedbags began. Scoops dug deep into the oats and poured them into empty pails. The sound of water splashing into buckets heralded another day. Horses nickered and pawed, suddenly impatient for their morning meal. The barn came alive with noises and movement. Barn cats purred while brushing against the employees' legs, hoping for attention while they waited for their food.

While the horses finished their meal, grooms began to enter the stalls, talking gently to the mares and newborn foals as they began their daily routines. Sham was going outside that day. He was introduced to many new experiences since his birth and took each one in stride. Gently, the groom slipped Sequoia's halter onto her face and reached down to secure Sham's. He was already at ease with daily routine and, to his groom's delight, accepted it without much fuss.

"Yeah, little guy, you can't wait to git out there an' see the things in store fer you t'day, can ya?"

The groom clipped a lead shank onto Sequoia's halter and led her from the stall, knowing Sham's survival instincts would compel him to faithfully follow everywhere she went. Sham hesitated at first. He peered through the open stall door at Sequoia and nervously nickered while stubbornly planting his feet in the doorway.

Everything was new. That was the first time he had seen anything except his dam, the stall's interior, and the people who entered to introduce strange objects. Sequoia turned her head as she entered the aisle and gently nickered, beckoning him. Seeing she was comfortable with her new surroundings, he sprang past the open door and into the aisle, almost colliding with her hind legs.

Sham's head was held high, as curious eyes took in everything while ears flicked back and forth in search of danger. As their little procession ambled down the aisle and out of the barn toward the paddocks, the foal's nose moved up and down, left and right, prodding every bucket, brush, broom, and object they passed.

They would be on their own in a paddock alongside the main pasture where the older foals were turned out with their dams. The pair would get accustomed to being with the herd while the fence would protect them from being trapped by an overly aggressive pasturemate establishing pecking order.

Sham's groom led them into the paddock. He unfastened their halters and walked back to hang them on the outside of the gate. Happy to be outside again, Sequoia enthusiastically loped along the fence line, calling to the mares in the pasture. Sham, startled by her quick movements, jumped back and stumbled over awkward legs. Quickly recovering, he bounded behind her, his spindly, uncoordinated legs scrambling to keep up.

The groom chuckled with delight as he watched them for a while, making sure they settled down and were safe. Finally, he turned and headed back to the barn, muttering, "Yeah, jus' as I thought. He was ready. That's fo' shuh."

Back in the barn, he grabbed a pitchfork from the wall, set it in a wheelbarrow, and ambled toward the stall while whistling a tune. He was in a good frame of mind. Expertly, he moved the pitchfork and soiled straw landed in the wheelbarrow. The day's chores had just begun.

The life of a groom is a hard one but has its rewards. Working with and gleaning knowledge from its experts, a groom would usually find Claiborne the perfect place to start in the Kentucky horse industry. It's no secret that accomplished jockeys, trainers and even owners got their start as grooms or hotwalkers before finding their niche. Plenty of beginners remained grooms for one reason or another, but mostly for their love of working so closely with the horses. Spending twelve to fourteen hours daily with the same horse developed a sense of responsibility and pride.

Things were no different at other Thoroughbred establishments across the country. Raised in South Carolina, Meadow Stable's groom, Eddie Sweat, remembered his start. He reminisced about securing a job with a trainer fifteen years prior, which led to work at The Meadow. "Mr. [Lucien] Laurin's farm was just a couple of miles from my parents' place in Holly Hill. When I was about 17, I went over and asked for a job. I've been with him since. I spent a year at the farm learning the business, then I graduated to the track," Sweat explained.[8]

Sweat was one of those grooms who held great pride in caring for the horses entrusted to his care. He treated them like his babies and they seemed to love him for that.

"The first thing I do is make sure he's eaten up his food," said Sweat. "The surest way to tell if a horse is sick is if it hasn't cleaned up its food. He'll more than likely be running a temperature if he hasn't eaten."[9]

At the track, horses eat three daily meals, but routines vary at different stables. As a rule, grooms arrive at 5:00 a.m. to get their quota of horses ready for training around 7:00.

"By the time they [the horses] get back, cleaned up and bandaged, it's 10:30 or 11 and time to feed them," Sweat explained.[10]

"Then around 1:30 in the afternoon," Sweat continued, "I'll go in and pull back the water buckets and see that they've eaten up their food."[11]

Stalls are mucked out, tack is oiled and polished, grooming tools are washed, bandages and blankets are cleaned, folded and put away. Around 4:00 horses are fed again and grooms check on their charges once more around 5:00 or 6:00 to make sure all is well before they quit for the day. Then the night watchman takes over. It's all in a day's work, and a groom seems to get closer to a horse than anyone else. Following instructions from a trainer, a groom establishes a calm environment and routine for the horses.

As the next few days passed, Sham was introduced to the lead rope for short walks in circles around his stall, but only Sequoia was on a shank when it was time for turnout. Sham quickly relaxed, totally at ease with the groom's attentions. He was a quick learner with a wonderfully calm nature, and his early trust and submission would make his future experiences far less intimidating and threatening.

Quickly, the mare and foal graduated from paddock to pasture without mishap. Throughout hot, lazy afternoons in the spring sunshine, the mares grazed in circles around their sleeping foals, watching over them while still totally aware of changes in surroundings. With any indication of danger, the horses would signal to each other with tense bodies, heads high, pricked ears and loud snorts. To protect itself from harm, a foal will instead show extreme submission by drawing the corners of its muzzle up and back. Called *fawning*, the quick smacking motions signal helplessness to other horses.

Becoming more stable on his feet, Sham ran around the pasture, bucking, jumping, and spinning on hind legs, while challenging the other foals. After getting their attention, he turned and chased them in circles back to where he began. Sometimes the mares joined in, cantering in a herd with tails held high. All that was excellent practice for what the future might hold, because the balance required in cantering and galloping makes horses more surefooted and confident.

The foals spent so much time with their dams that their own behavior couldn't help but be shaped by the mares. Even though most emotional behaviors are inbred through family genetics, as they emerge, they are either modified or made more secure by their dams or other pasture mates. Sham, continually testing the abundant flavors the pasture grass offered, became quite happy to spend idyllic hours nibbling alongside his dam.

Spring flowed like liquid into a long, hot summer. When the summer heat began to cool and leaves on the trees burst into colorful shades of crimson red, bright yellow, and rusty orange, autumn heralded the weaning of foals from their dams. That was never a pleasant job for the staff at Claiborne, but it was an annual ritual at any breeding farm that had to be done. The spring-born foals were six months old and the mares had already been bred back to their selected stallions over the summer.

Early one crisp, frosty morning during his morning meal, Sham was haltered and led from the stall. Momentarily distracted by the hay, Sequoia didn't follow. The stall door closed and his terrified squeal instantly alerted his dam. Sequoia's head shot up from the feeder. She gave a questioning nicker while rushing to the door, frantically neighing when she saw him leave the barn. Surrounded by worried foals calling to their dams, the handlers quickly loaded them into a waiting horse van. Once the last foal was inside, the ramp was lifted and the door secured with a finalizing *clang!*

The van's engine roared as it moved the van slowly down the lane to the training facility. While it bumped and whirred along, frightened cries of the foals intensified in the small confinement and pierced the handlers' ears. The worried mares screamed in vain for the rest of the day.

The young foals' new lives had begun. When the van lurched to a halt, the door swung open and the ramp was eased into place. One by one, the foals were led off the trailer toward the pasture behind the training barn. Colts and fillies were separated and stationed in separate barns and pastures. They would be turned out in groups for the rest of the afternoon and brought to new stalls for the night. It would be a very long, lonely night for each and every one of them.

The name Sham certainly didn't suit him, as he was anything but false, an imitation, or counterfeit. His real nature was genuine and courageous, a full-of-life personality with no false pretenses. He simply oozed that aura. It was as if the name Sham had originated from Irish slang meaning *friend* or *buddy*. Or perhaps it came from Marguerite

Henry's 1949 award-winning novel, *King of the Wind.* In that story Sham was the Godolphin Arabian gifted to a French King, eventually becoming the Thoroughbred breed's predecessor.

Most racehorses are given names that have nothing to do with their personality but are mostly fashioned as a lineage brand. As his sire's name was Pretense, Sham's name was intended to imprint the connection with his sire—a precursor to any recognition the colt may achieve in his lifetime as a racehorse.

The trees shed multicolored leaves while the days grew colder. Sham grew a healthy coat of winter woolies to keep him warm. Now independent, he no longer whined for his dam and established a secure pecking order in the group. He comfortably settled into his new stall and daily routine. Every afternoon when he was led in from the pasture, he demanded his evening meal. Sham contentedly devoured all his grain and hay, sometimes looking for more. He grew stronger each day and turnout time with the other colts strengthened his developing muscles, tendons, and bones, preparing him for the rigors of racing.

Throughout the long winter months, the colts were turned out for a portion of each day unless the temperatures were unbearable, or snow and ice conditions too severe. They undoubtedly welcomed their stall even more when they were led in from the pasture on a cold day that consistently turned more miserable as the minutes slowly ticked by.

Sham earned the reputation as an easy colt, one that everyone liked to be around or have on his list. His groundwork and in-hand lessons were coming along perfectly. He was an eager student, always willing to work. Occasionally, his young studdish challenges surfaced as he tested his power over his handlers, but he was never classified unruly or fractious and was always easy to settle down.

A young racehorse's life at Claiborne was truly bliss. The trainers and owners understood the importance of diet in the early years. So many things could go wrong raising a foal, on or off the track. James was well aware of the dangers and maintained a strict semblance of order. The grooms knew what was expected of them and performed or moved on.

At the Meadow, Penny was learning too. Her demanding new position as manager of the Meadow gave her self-doubts. It was difficult to change her life not really knowing what to expect. She had been a housewife and mother for the past two decades. She was an accomplished equestrienne in her own right, "but racing?"[12] She hadn't a clue about the sport—handicap races, maiden races, claiming races, the titles meant nothing to her.

Powerful New York racing professionals seemed to have a lingo all their own—one she knew existed but was totally oblivious to. Just the thought of trying to change her life from country housewife to "Big Apple" Thoroughbred owner boggled her mind. Penny battled with her uncertainties but soon came to a conclusion. Eventually, she saw it as the perfect opportunity to break free from the "supportive role" she settled into for so many years.[13] It was time to satisfy her inner passion for adventure. Ignoring her inner strife, she agreed and headed to New York.

During the transition period in the first few years of commuting between states, Penny struggled to find her course. She, too, knew she needed to perform.

CHAPTER FIVE

The Claiborne Yearlings

The year 1971 marked an important year of change for American Thoroughbred horse racing. Formal racing awards were adopted to honor champions of the sport and would be presented at a special Eclipse Award Ceremony in January, each following year. They were named after the eighteenth-century British champion and sire, Eclipse. The National Thoroughbred Racing Association, *Daily Racing Form* and the National Turf Writers Association would sponsor the awards. These prestigious awards, as well as some additional special awards, would be given to horses, jockeys, trainers, owners and breeders. It was indeed a year to perform.

Claiborne had a reputation to uphold as a producer of fine, young racehorse prospects, and, with any fine establishment, team spirit was very important. A large operation needed cooperation for the establishment to flow smoothly and be productive; Claiborne was just that. Premium foals were only one aspect of the farm's success.

Many champions that weren't foaled at Claiborne ended up there at stud. For twelve years Bold Ruler sired worthy foals, even through the last year after undergoing cobalt treatments for cancer. With twenty-seven of his broodmares in foal for the '71 breeding season, the cancer unfortunately returned, and the great stallion would lose his battle against the malignancy in July.

Reviewer, a son of Bold Ruler, would cover Shenanigans that year with the resultant foal being born at Claiborne on April 17, 1972. That unrelenting, indomitably high-spirited filly was destined for a tragically short but record-breaking career. Over a short span of thirteen months that filly would shatter so many track records that she would earn the title, "Queen of the Fillies." Her name was Ruffian, and decades later her emotional story would continue to bring tears.

A John Schiff-bred success story during 1970, Hoist the Flag, recuperating from a recent leg fracture, would enter early retirement at Claiborne that year.

The Harry Guggenheim-bred champion, Ack Ack, would steal the show at that year's first Awards ceremony by winning three Eclipse

Awards: Horse of the Year, Sprinter and Older Male. That stallion would later retire at Claiborne, too.

Claiborne's multifaceted breeding operation was undeniably impressive.

As quickly as it arrived, the frigid winter melted away and warm spring days gave birth to a lush countryside. There was a feeling of renewed life with every living thing on the farm. Small water droplets formed at the ends of icicles quickly disappearing from the outer edges of the barn roof. Breaking free, they collided with the puddles forming below. They played a musical rhythm, interrupted only by an occasional mass of slush sliding off the barn roof.

Spring would change the main barn staff's chores. The absence of freezing ice and snow would lessen regular maintenance. However, along with warm spring days the yearlings' winter coats became increasingly itchy and uncomfortable. Grooms knew their jobs would become more time-consuming, currying out dead hair and working the winter's accumulated debris from the colts' coats. It was a daily chore to deal with acquired mud packs courtesy of the spring rains' creation of mires in the paddocks. The young colts lavishly enjoyed rolling as they tried to rid themselves of the itch.

Soon, they would be introduced to the unfamiliar and strange sensations that saddle pads, saddles, bridles, and bits would generate. The yearlings' coats must be immaculately free of dirt to prevent chafing of tender skin.

As the days grew warmer it was time for an introduction to a serious bath, the precursor to a daily ritual of hosing down as training progressed. The colts were led to an outdoor wash station in the warm morning sun. Buckets, soap, hoses, badger-haired brushes, and currycombs were neatly arranged out of the yearlings' reach but in full view so natural curiosity would allow them to inspect the objects at a safe distance.

Two at a time, the colts were led out to the gravel pit. While attendants held the lead shanks to keep the colts in hand, a groom slowly ran a sprinkle of water up their legs. Some of them squirmed with apprehension as cool water splashed onto their bodies. Others loved the feel of the water dancing across their backs and swayed until the water hit the right spot. Small clouds of vapor rising from the colts' warm backs dissipated into the air.

As the colts became accustomed to the feel of water flowing down their bodies, sponges were doused in buckets of water and a small amount of mild soap applied. As grooms massaged dead hair and dirt away, the colts relaxed. Most of them enjoyed the new sensation immensely. After the soap was thoroughly rinsed from their backs, shiny aluminum sweat scrapers glinted in the sunlight as grooms expertly squeezed excess water from their coats. Delicate eyes and nostrils were gently cleaned with a soft cloth dipped in warm water.

When the grooms were satisfied with their work, they covered the colts with sweat blankets and handed them off to hotwalkers. They would walk in the sun until a combination of body heat and warm sun dried the remaining moisture in their coats. Moisture on exposed necks made them shimmer while misty clouds of steam shrouded nostrils as they inhaled and exhaled the changing morning air. The yearlings' baby-fine hair dried soft and fluffy very quickly.

Sunlight cut patterns through the vapor clouds, casting reflective prisms of rainbow colors as they billowed and lifted toward the sky. Occasionally the colts' hooves slipped on the damp grass as they pranced along in hand. Sometimes they pulled and jumped back, only to spring up on their hind legs for an instant before shaking their heads as they returned to earth. That set their hotwalkers on edge. The colts were young and felt great to be alive!

When the hotwalkers were satisfied that the yearlings' coats were dry, they returned to the grooms who removed blankets and inspected hooves for unwanted stones or debris. Electric clippers were introduced, first at a distance, then gently touching the horses' sides until they realized there was no danger. Whiskers on muzzles were gently shaved away and a bridle path trimmed at the top of their manes just behind the ears.

As spotlessly clean ears are a necessity for a sleek, refined look, the clippers carefully followed edges, trimming off excess hair, leaving them with a more dramatic, shapely appearance. Tangled tails were picked out by hand. Bushy manes were pulled to keep them at a shorter, uniform length. That way they wouldn't disturb a jockey's vision while racing when blown back by the wind.

Clean, dust-free hair and skin are the foundation of a winning look, and to achieve success, grooming and appearance were of utmost importance. With the final touch of clipping any long hair on the backs of lower legs and fetlocks, the yearlings were instantly transformed into finely pampered works of art. Their coats shone in silvery patterns as they moved in the sun.

Just as the yearlings had to look the part of up-and-coming racehorses, their young bodies had to be prepared for the hard work and stress of racing. At that young age, Sham had to become very alert, agile, and perceptive if he was to excel at this new life of racing. Quickly, his young equine physical stature would become an extraordinary example of a finely tuned engine.

A horse's emotions affect the way its nerve impulses react. To obtain ideal impulses, the horse needs the desire or will to compete. Emotions can cause a horse to freeze up muscles, bind joints, and lose range of motion. Correct training experience develops composure that helps it perform at maximum potential.

Depending on the whole picture of the individual racehorse, most qualities of movement can be maximized through conditioning programs and skill-building exercises. Owners expect trainers to provide results when working with and developing champion hopefuls, so conditioning programs were set for each horse managed.

Sham, doing well at the center, progressed from hand walking to tacking up and accepting the pressure of a rider's weight without a fuss. He was ready for his first ride to the training paddock.

Thoroughly groomed, the bit was gently eased into his mouth with the headpiece of the bridle slipped carefully over his ears and affixed in place with the chin strap and nose band. As he feigned mild interest in the process, his groom moved to his side with the saddle pad, stopping for a moment as he passed to let Sham give it an interested sniff.

As if Sham had approved, the groom continued and gently slid the pad upon his back. Sham remained still. Then the exercise rider came forward carrying the saddle. The groom held Sham's reins, preparing for any form of refusal while the rider eased the saddle onto the pad, and gently slid the girth strap into a comfortable position. Both men eased Sham's anxiety with reassuring praise and gentle pats on the neck and back.

As Sham was led from his stall he called to his stablemates. Some answered his nervous cries but he was quickly ushered outside. The distraction allowed his rider to tighten the girth sufficiently since Sham stopped puffing out his belly to reduce the pressure.

Before the colt could react, in one fluid motion the rider was given a leg-up and had control of the reins. Opening the left rein, he lightly squeezed Sham's right side with his calf, encouraging him to move out with his left foreleg. Sham's nervous energy made him comply and he was sent toward the training paddock a short distance away.

Sham's pace increased in tempo when he approached three other yearlings in the paddock. They were slowly walking in a circle around John Sosby, the facility's lead trainer for yearlings. Raised on the farm, Sosby was a trainer at Claiborne for almost fourteen years since finishing school and proved himself an invaluable asset. He thoroughly enjoyed his job and contentedly settled there to raise his family.

Most of the older colts had been out to the paddock many times before and were complacent with the routine. Other than an occasional squeal, sideways jump, or nervous increase of speed, the lesson was uneventful. Sosby was careful not to overwork the colts with new experiences, so Sham was dismissed after a short twenty-minute session and returned to the barn.

"That colt'll be a very relaxed and eager racehorse if he continues like that," Sosby said. "I can't remember when such a calm yearling entered my training paddock for the first time."

The rest of the riders turned to watch the colt leave the group.

"I'll keep my eye on that one," Sosby continued.

After Sham's tack was removed, his coat was meticulously groomed to a lustrous shine and his hooves carefully picked out. He was led to the turnout corral for some afternoon exercise at liberty, seemingly as a reward for his patience and cooperation throughout the lesson. It was a good experience for him, and his handlers and trainers were pleased.

Sham's daily progress led to the practice track. There, yearlings were encouraged to pick up a controlled trot along the rail and were eased into a rated lope for a short distance while not being allowed to run off or become overly excited. Exercise riders had to be able to deal with and possibly correct any problems with the young horses. They gauged a horse's fitness and relayed wellness issues to Sosby.

Sham was encouraged to use himself correctly, strengthening the correct muscles, and letting his spirit grow with his natural desire for running.

With a furlong being an eighth-of-a-mile, the final 220 yards of the race is crucial. On the track oval, riders used the poles set at half-furlong increments as a measurement—speed per distance. That was a very important tool, called rating, whereby a young horse would learn to control its speed, saving precious energy for the final furlongs.

The rider relayed quiet confidence to Sham through instances of turmoil or confusion. Head tossing, lugging in or out, refusal to switch leads, or leaning on the bit while galloping were corrected quickly, calmly, and intelligently, so they wouldn't become ingrained bad habits. He taught Sham to improve mentally and physically while simultaneously following instructions from Sosby on how far and fast to run.

As Sham progressed, lessons on how to walk calmly into the starting gate, stand, then break alertly and cleanly were repeated.

Sham learned when and how to switch leads on the straight or during turns to maintain balance. Also, to have the courage to break through tight openings crowded by horses and continue increasing speed even with the shock of dirt pelting his face.

Sham quickly proved sufficiently gate-qualified. He could enter and exit the gate without panic that might injure himself and anyone around him. He was started from different post positions and encouraged to run a short distance to get an idea of the width of the track itself. He learned to safely make his way from the outside to the rail while gaining speed.

The colt was introduced to everything and anything to prepare for his first race. He was taken to the track in wind, rain, heat, or cold to become accustomed to running in all types of weather. He was slowly galloped alongside stablemates for short distances just to get the feel of running against another horse while his rider rated him. By the end of that summer, Sosby began clocking Sham at a furlong to see how well he could handle an easy gallop for an eighth-of-a-mile. He didn't push for speed because Sham was still too young.

The training was good practice for exercise riders, too. They would spend years practicing and learning on hundreds of horses before riding in a race. Accidents could easily happen when eager apprentice jockeys began racing at the track without sufficient experience, and these could sometimes prove fatal. An asterisk beside their names on racing programs identified apprentice jockeys. Since it resembled a bug, they were nicknamed *bugboys.*

Training continued through the fall of '71, with the worst of winter earning Sham a lighter schedule. It became an early morning ritual that would continue throughout the colt's racing career.

On the first of January, Sham officially began his two-year-old season. January had long been determined the official birth date recognized for every racehorse to avoid confusion at the track. Racehorses became eligible to compete in races at two. The first season was known as their freshman or juvenile campaign. Depending on Sham's results as a yearling, he would enter either claiming races—where, for the price indicated upon entering the race, he could be purchased—or maiden and allowance races, where the trainer and owner wouldn't have the worry of losing a superior horse by winning.

Sham would start training for maiden races that season. Looking at a strong, beautifully proportioned, sleek horse boasting long, graceful legs, Sosby saw very promising indications of superior ability in that horse.

Owned by The Meadow and named after a black diamond ski run in Colorado, Riva Ridge was preparing for the 1972 Kentucky Derby. He was a lithe, handsome horse. Riva had been on a recent winning streak and attracting plenty of attention for Meadow Stables at the track.

Another young horse from that stable had proven worthy to enter the racing world. He, too, was a strikingly attractive copper-colored colt, and after a year of being known by nicknames alone, the eleventh name submitted to the Jockey Club had been accepted. He was Secretariat—the horse that would become Sham's nemesis.

The Meadow's trainer, Meredith Bailes, knew the young colt had a gift. "If there's any such thing as the perfect horse," he told John Goolrick, a Virginia reporter with *The Free Lance-Star,* "Secretariat was it. I was the first one ever to ride him and he caught on in a hurry. Hell, he'd run out on Route 95 if you'd let him. Now Riva Ridge was different. He was easy to handle but he hated a wet track," he remembered.[14]

After living at The Meadow for the first twenty-two months of his life, Secretariat was shipped to New York to begin his racing career with trainer Lucien Lauren.

A Canadian, born March 18, 1912 in Joliette, Quebec, Lauren started his career at Delormier Park near Montreal as a jockey, at seventeen. After having trouble staying at the required weight through 161 wins, he decided to make a change. One afternoon in '42, he moved to New England where he followed a thirty-year path to success as a trainer. His unmistakable skill and honest nature of intense compassion made him famous, and in his late fifties he retired in Canada.

That retirement was short-lived. In '71, his son, Roger Laurin, suggested to the Chenerys that Lucien replace him as their trainer. Roger had recently accepted employment from Ogden Phipps to train his famed bluebloods. So, Laurin began training for Penny, a decision neither would regret. He was immediately assigned the colts Riva Ridge and Secretariat.

"I was workin' him [Secretariat] but he wouldn't go by a horse, he wouldn't do hardly nothing. So I finally put blinkers on him and you wouldn't believe it. I took him to the gate and with them blinkers on, honest to God, he went five-eighths in fifty-eight-and-three! So I worked him once more with a three-year-old to make sure it wasn't a fluke…and he even beat the three-year-old! So I called Mrs. Tweedy and I says, 'We are ready. We have a horse and I think it can run.'"[15]

Shortly after Secretariat's arrival at Belmont, he was assigned to groom Eddie Sweat. It would prove to be a match of a lifetime. Sweat would later remember, "I was away on holidays when the boy who was rubbing him took sick," Sweat reminisced. "The boy had been wounded in the eye in the Service and it was acting up on him. So when I got back from my vacation Mr. Laurin told me to start with Secretariat."[16]

On May 13, 1972, Riva Ridge won the Kentucky Derby. It was a dream Chris Chenery had waited for all his life. Penny would later remember her presumed incoherent father's response to the announcement on the nightly news. A nurse excitedly shouted to him the fact that his horse was the winner. Penny immediately knew he understood when she looked over at him and noticed tears of joy running down his face. Chris Chenery was crying.

For Penny, it was a time of turmoil. Along with the difficulties of her father's failing health, she was challenged by the stress of her son's struggle to leave behind familiar routine and friends and adapt to his new home.

On top of that, she was having a hard time dealing with Secretariat's untimely fame. At that time Penny held an immense affection for her horse, Riva, and she wanted to concentrate on his stupendous achievement. Later, she would admit to twinges of ill feelings toward Secretariat. No one could understand the personal pressure the horse afforded Penny, but everyone understood the magnitude of that colt's success.

In June, at Belmont's Barn 5, the Meadow's exercise rider quizzed newspaper reporter Bill Nack.

Jimmy Gaffney pointed out Secretariat and asked, "You wanna see the best-lookin' 2-year-old you've ever seen? He's getting' ready. Don't forget the name: Secretariat. He can run. Don't quote me, but this horse will make them all forget Riva Ridge."[17]

Over the summer months of July and August, Secretariat would race twice at Aqueduct and three times at Saratoga before Sham even arrived at a racetrack. Under apprentice jockey Paul Feliciano, they drew all eyes in a debut maiden race at Aqueduct on July 4. Secretariat overcame unbelievable peril and came back fighting for his freedom after being cut off three times in the short five-and-a-half-furlong race. Refusing to be defeated, he swung wide and fiercely accelerated through the final quarter-mile to cross the wire behind a cluster of horses, Herbull, Master Achiever and Fleet'n Royal. That was the only time in his career that he would finish further back than third.

In another maiden race eleven days later, he got revenge on Sigmund Sommer's Master Achiever, beating him handily by six lengths. Nack was watching that race with a Baltimore handicapper, Clem Florio, and when Secretariat crossed the finish line, Clem bellowed, "Secretariat will win the Triple Crown next year."[18]

A New York handicapper, Mannie Kalish, fired back, "Ah, you Maryland guys, you come to New York and see a horse break his maiden and think he's another Citation. We see horses like Secretariat all the time. I bet he don't even run in the Derby."[19]

Sixteen days later Secretariat won an allowance race at Saratoga. He became absolutely notorious for his famous late speed—a *come-from-behind* horse.

Then on the sixteenth of August in his first stakes race at Saratoga, the Sanford, he defeated the previously unbeaten Linda's Chief. The leading two-year-old on the East Coast then, Linda's Chief was the 3-5 favorite in that race, but fate would make it the last time Secretariat wasn't the favorite. Al Scotti, trainer for Linda's Chief, believed his horse invincible with five wins in five starts. Secretariat ended that winning streak, leaving the colt three lengths behind at the wire.

On August 26, in the Hopeful stakes at Saratoga, Secretariat stunned the crowd. Coming from six lengths behind the field, swinging so wide on the final turn he seemed closer to the grandstand than the rail, he blew by stakes winners like they were claimers. He was first at the wire only three-fifths of a second off the track record.

That red horse was unstoppable.

CHAPTER SIX

The Test
August 27, 1972

As the new day wound down, Sham contentedly relaxed in his stall. There was something special in the way the groom had been looking at him all day, assessing his mood, constantly seeking the slightest indication of attitude or, perhaps, readiness.

Readiness for what?

When the groom worked with the horse that evening, the usual routine seemed to have more meaning. The rubber currycomb massaged Sham's silken coat in a more determined circular pattern than before. The soft-bristled brush slid down the horse's legs, searching every inch of bone and tendon for any change or injury, and the rub rag found every miniscule imperfection in Sham's impeccably perfect coat.

The groom knew Sham's senses were sharp as he crooned his verbal communication of sounds and words that the horse only understood by tone and mood. His was a mellow voice, thoroughly encouraging. Through guarded eyes, the groom curiously watched Sham while he worked his dark coat into a shine. The dapples in it resembled a cluster of shimmering Oriental black pearls interspersed with tiger-eye gemstones, under the stall's light.

When Sham's cotton blanket was securely in place to keep his glistening coat free of dust, the groom led him through the barn and into the twilight to a waiting van. Three other colts, already loaded in the small partitions of the van, impatiently tossed their heads, snorted, and pawed. Even though they had trailered before, the groom sensed their frustration and fear.

Sham's equine instincts seemed to scream *panic and run*, but the groom spoke gently to him, soothing him with his familiar voice while stroking his head and neck with a calming touch. The horse walked onto the trailer like a professional. After Sham's halter was snapped to the trailer tie, the divider clicked shut.

Then the door sealed off the exit, which immediately renewed the colts' uncertainty. Their weight shifted and hooves scrambled as the van picked up momentum and turned down the drive toward the highway.

The colts faced a long 700-mile trip. They were on their way to a new life at Belmont Park racetrack in Elmont, New York, where they would stay for the rest of their freshman season. The van would drive through the night, and, if all went well, they'd be at Belmont in fourteen to sixteen hours with a few stops along the way to tend to their comfort.

A humid August breeze left tiny beads of water on the trailer's exterior. Shiny droplets glistened on the trees' leaves and mature summer blades of grass along the highway. While they drove, the sun rose and small beams of light gradually broke through the trailer window slats. The golden rays formed broken lines and patterns, constantly changing whenever deflected by the moving horses' bodies and structure of the dividers. Soon sunlight poured in and the colts blinked as their eyes adjusted.

The afternoon was hot and muggy when the trailer turned off the highway, finally entering Belmont Park. As suddenly as it began, the trailer halted. The colts shuffled in their partitions, pawing eagerly in anticipation of their escape from such narrow confines. One at a time, they were led down the ramp. They seemed relieved to feel solid ground underfoot again.

One colt, feeling exuberant with his newfound freedom, pulled back on his lead. His front legs hopped, lifting slightly off the ground as he prepared to spin on his hind end at the first sign of slack in the shank.

"Easy there, boy," the groom said, trying to soothe the colt before it set off a chain reaction through the group. "Now, settle down there."

The intensely inbred Thoroughbred urge to run coursed through their veins as the young horses were led to the receiving barn. Each one's paperwork was checked before any could enter assigned stalls. Health certificates and Coggins tests had to be current in accordance with state regulations. Infectious equine diseases could quickly become rampant with the quick changeover at a racetrack. Owners and trainers would never chance exposing their conditioned horses to sickness. Not after working so hard to get them fit.

The following day, they were taken to the paddock for tacking up before their races. The races were maiden specials, the first real race for any of them. Claiborne Farm never expected much from a two-year-old's first outing, but it held a special meaning to grooms and riders as it would be the first indication of each one's reaction to the challenge of true competition.

The general consensus among the staff was that the horses would unceremoniously arrive together, run their races, and return to the barn. No one involved in horse racing ever dreamed of having a champion on the threshold of its first race. With so many possible stumbling blocks, it was impossible to tell. Even if a horse was fortunate enough to win its first race, no one could be sure it would win again. Owners, trainers, riders and grooms had to accept fate and realize they were not in control of what the future held.

On August 28 at 2:00 p.m. Eastern Standard Time, it was almost post time for Sham's race. He was up against a field of ten, all carrying 120 pounds in a six-furlong, three-quarter-mile maiden special weight. Claiborne's attending trainer signaled to Sham's groom for prerace preparations.

Sham wasn't lazy or nervous, unlike some horses that dreaded the track and would do anything to avoid going there. Those were the horses that shouldn't be there because they were a constant risk to themselves and everyone around them.

When his coat was touched up with a rub rag, eliminating the dust that settled there while he rested in his stall, the groom coaxed him into the line of horses moving toward the saddling area.

Adrenaline flowed in nervous anticipation. Some of the colts were a bit fractious and constantly tested the patience of their grooms. Their lips flicked up and down their gums, desperately trying to rid themselves of restrictive chains looped through their mouths or over their nose.

Clipped to the crossties, Sham stood still as a brightly colored saddle cloth numbered "4" was placed on his back. Heliodoro Gustines approached as his valet hoisted his saddle onto Sham's back. The trainer cinched up the girth. After the bit was slipped into Sham's mouth and bridle pulled up over his ears, he was released from the saddling stall.

Gustines mounted up, took a firm hold of the reins and headed to the track. Gustines wore Claiborne Farm's legendary golden-orange silks, and the bright sparkle made a striking contrast with the glistening ebony dapples of Sham's finely pampered coat.

Other horses joined the procession and filed onto the racetrack. Even though it was well into race season, there wasn't much of a crowd. The scorching sun and high humidity made it quite uncomfortable in the stands for those fans that did brave the weather. A tractor motor bellowed as it laboriously jockeyed the long trailer line of gates into position, perpendicular to the track.

Even though Sham entered the gates at the training facility's track many times and was fully prepared for what was to come, he seemed different, perhaps apprehensive. Besides Sham, the only other horse in that race for its debut was Angle Light, with Ron Turcotte aboard for the owner, Edwin Whittaker. Master Achiever, another horse in the field, owned by Sigmund Sommer, came into the race off a recent fourth-place finish at Saratoga.

All the horses grew increasingly nervous, perhaps due to some unfortunate experience they encountered before. The young horses fidgeted like rabbits, nervous instincts screaming *Beware!* Jockeys took up slack in the reins, as long legs pranced excitedly. Alert ears flicked back and forth as heads tossed, telltale signs of the colts' uncertainties.

Sham looked uneasy, and, while his tongue played with the metal bit in his mouth, white froth formed at the creases. In the starting gate a slight crosswind gusted in from the backstretch, bringing momentary relief from the humidity.

Suddenly a buzzer screamed, magnets released, gates flew open, and the horses were gone! Angle Light broke alertly and sprinted off like a demon possessed, leading the field by five lengths at the quarter-mile pole. That colt was so eager to be free of the gate and on his way that his time for the first quarter was a sizzling 22 3/5 seconds. Neck and neck, S'thin Else Ag'n and Timeless Moment shot after him with Tell It Like It Is at their flanks.

Sham seemed petrified by the explosion of horses from the gate. By the time Angle Light passed the quarter-mile marker, Sham was ninth—twenty-three lengths off the pace. He struggled with the trailing horses, Tricotaj and Sobre Cut, who appeared to have no intention of increasing their speed for the rest of the race. Gustines felt Sham begin to adopt that same attitude and wanted nothing of it. He dug his heels into Sham's sides, took firm hold of the reins, and urged Sham to oblige. The colt slowly began to pick up speed.

By the half-mile point, they left the stragglers behind and followed six lengths behind the field. They were alone, suspended between the eighth-place horse, Please Don't, and the dawdling tenth, Tricotaj.

Instinctively, Sham's eyes locked on the field ahead when Gustines raised his whip and determinedly urged him forward. With wind whipping through his mane and whistling past his ears, Sham suddenly appeared to understand. He began a furious drive and instantly gained on the horses in front. Gustines swung him wide, heading for the stretch. He soared past Please Don't, Barydown, and Delta's M'n'ytree bunched up along the rail. As his jet-black legs flew, he sailed into fifth place. Then he was at Master Achiever's neck, and vying for third with Tell It Like It Is.

Sham catapulted down the homestretch past Tell It Like It Is. Now only eight lengths off the pace, he hurtled toward the leaders. Timeless Moment, second, began his own final drive in an effort to catch Angle Light, still leading. Those two crossed the wire just three-quarters of a length apart. Sham's momentum carried him over the finish line, seven lengths behind. His first try brought him home third after a bad start that the race chart quoted as "devoid of early speed."[20]

In that first race, Sham turned losing into winning by earning his first purse of $960. With his late drive, he overpowered Sigmund Sommer's colt, Master Achiever, and Sigmund's keen eye for talent noticed. That owner made a mental note to follow Sham's progress carefully as he intently watched the horse preparing to leave the track. Sigmund pondered, *I wonder what that colt would do with a mile?*

Gustines talked with the trainer while removing his saddle from Sham's back. "If we'd had another furlong," Gustines spurt out between pants, "maybe the ending would'a been different. Sham has more to 'im than he shows. I know I had plenty of horse left at the line."

Sham had truly obliged, whittling down the distance between himself and Angle Light by an astounding fifteen lengths in less than 400 yards! He left the track to be hosed down and cooled out. Hosing after a workout is a must for racehorses to remove coat-dulling salts and discourage fungal infections.

Cool water splashed over Sham's sweat-glistened dark coat and small clouds of steam rose above him. He looked like a phantom creature appearing from a cloud of smoke. A hotwalker took up the shank and walked Sham around the shed row until his heart rate returned to normal and his coat was dry. He would return to his stall without the danger of colic caused by stress, overheating, or exertion.

The short trip back to the barn was much more tranquil than the long trip from Claiborne had been. It already felt like home. The staff and horses all shared a mutual feeling of contentment.

Expertly described in the words of professional trainer Noble Threewit, "The racetrack itself kind of gets in your blood. It's a different life on the racetrack. The men that work on the racetrack—like grooms—they come around and do it, and they never seem to be satisfied doing anything else."[21]

Although the colts ran with each other on training tracks before that outing, there was an unmistakable difference to the races at Belmont that day. Unfolding before them was a new life. The distractions of the crowd, a mass of foreign horses breaking from the gates, the loud shriek of the starting buzzer, and the voice beaming over the track from the loudspeakers were all unfamiliar.

Claiborne would continue to race its colts at Belmont, assuming no ill fate, or they would be sold at auction, or perhaps as claimers. At breeding farms and training centers everywhere, people hoped for the greatest accomplishment of all—a champion. Each young horse was there to try and prove its worth in the diverse, exhilarating, ever-changing life of Thoroughbred horse racing while attempting to remain sound throughout an entire career. They were still young, only juveniles.

As Sham settled into his stall with sweet-smelling hay as he'd done at the start of the day, he went full circle through events that would become a ritual. It was a new experience but wouldn't be the last. To break his maiden, Sham needed to win a maiden or allowance race before advancing to stakes or graded races. August twenty-eight proved Sham's career was only in the learning stage.

September 13 proved to be a beautiful Indian-summer day for Sham's second race. It was a seven-furlong race; one furlong farther than his first. An early-morning frost covered the barn with a shimmery dusting of white that glistened like sparkling sequins when the sun rose to melt it away. It was a magnificent example of Mother Nature's beauty coupled with the rich hues of crimson, yellow, and gold interspersed with splashes of green. The East Coast, famous for its breathtaking display of fall colors, once again made the populace proud of its heritage.

Fourteen horses were entered in the third race that day, but only thirteen went to post. Knightly Dawn, another young horse that had never raced before, was entered but for some reason was scratched. He was a newly acquired prospect of Sigmund Sommer's that would someday have his life entwined with Sham's. Of the thirteen horses that reached the starting gates, all were unproven, and Scotch Rumor, Lord Victor, and Royal Key West were making their debut.

Sham's eyes appeared to take in every detail of his surroundings as his head spun from side to side while he fussed in the enclosure of gate one. Gustines firmly held on to the reins, knowing Sham's nerves were on edge from the almost imperceptible spasms making the colt's skin crawl. If Gustines were unprepared, he would be left behind in the dirt. However, Sham's distress wasn't the starters' main concern.

Down the line, Royal Key West was rank. The horse was delaying the race by refusing to enter position nine. Sensing fear, surrounding horses already loaded skittishly banged around in their gates. The colt reared, spun and bucked while its wild-eyed head snaked back and forth, frantically searching for a way to escape the enclosure in front of him. Assistants' bodies flew left and right as they tugged and pushed at the horse while it thrashed around.

Momentarily distracted by the starters, Royal Key West plunged forward into the gate. An assistant grabbed and lifted the horse's tail clear as another swung the door closed with a *bang!* Instantly the colt reared and, suspended in a crouched position on hind legs, protested its capture. The jockey, Angel Cordero, Jr., buried his head in the colt's mane, desperately trying to avoid injury. Royal Key West seemed even more crazed and frantic to be free than before entering the enclosure.

Starters on both sides of the gate grabbed the bridle simultaneously as Angel Cordero, Jr. pulled down on the reins. The frightened colt settled to the ground, hind legs braced and ready to bolt. It was like watching a cowboy preparing to leave the chute on a frustrated bronc determined to lose the weight on its back. The colt held all four feet on the ground for an instant before the bell shrieked. Off they went, with Royal Key West breaking last.

Sham, lucky to be on the rail away from the fractious colt, effortlessly gained second position to Br'dway Playboy in first, as Please Don't and Dicks Boots stayed close to Sham's flanks. While the horses flew down the backstretch toward the quarter-mile post, a disaster unfolded.

Royal Key West pitched forward into the hind hooves of Lord Victor, momentarily making that colt stumble. Angel Cordero, Jr. was thrown over the neck of his somersaulting mount, circling through the air before hitting the dirt. As the jockey rolled, his horror-stricken eyes saw a massive twelve hundred pounds of horseflesh closing in on him.

He instinctively threw his body weight to the right, changing direction just in time as his mount whizzed past, then stopped, legs arching in a final path through the air and crashing to the ground where Angel Cordero, Jr had been.

Other than Lord Victor, who immediately recovered from the collision, none of the other horses or jockeys were hindered and they sped on. Lord Victor struggled to remain with the field but fell farther behind.

The announcer's shocked voice bellowed, "Royal Key West has broken down!"

An ambulance raced up the track. Angel Cordero, Jr. was amazingly on his feet, shaken and hovering over his mount, which was thrashing in agony on the track where it landed.

Not totally oblivious to the turmoil behind, Sham overtook Br'dway Playboy and was first by a length-and-a-half at the half-mile post. The ambulance distracted him as his peripheral vision enveloped much more than just Br'dway Playboy closing in along the rail. Rounding the turn, Gustines tried to keep Sham focused ahead.

Laffit Pincay, Jr. unleashed his whip and aggressively pushed Br'dway Playboy toward the finish line. With the whip repetitively striking the horse's flanks, that colt shot forward with renewed determination and flew past Sham's left side.

There was something about Pincay that baffled other jockeys. "Laffit was a very aggressive rider early in a race and he always had a forward position," jockey Kent Desormeaux once said, "and you would always think, well you know, he's used that horse up. But when you hooked into Laffit, you'd better have some horse, and you'd better come full head of steam, because he always had something left."[22]

Gustines urged Sham on in a final attempt to gain control, but it was too late. Sham weakened in his drive to the wire while Pincay soared across the finish line two-and-a-half lengths ahead. Sham finished second, a half-length in front of Dicks Boots, with Bid to Win another head back in fourth.

Sham earned $1,760 for placing. It was a nerve-wracking race for the colt but he didn't get the worst of it. Royal Key West might never race again, and poor Lord Victor was so shaken, he remained in last place throughout the race, finishing nine lengths behind the field.

The next race was ten days later, the twenty-third of September, and favorable weather brought the promise of a fast track. In a field of eight all attempting to break their maiden, the young horses would run one full mile, eight furlongs. Sham was up against Dicks Boots again.

After breaking in the middle of the field at the start, Sham burst free of the cluster and raced up to take the lead from Dicks Boots at the three-quarter-mile pole. He gamely held on to first place through the final turn but was distracted by the crowd in the stretch and failed to rally with his opponent in the drive to the finish line. Braulio Baeza, Dicks Boots' jockey, furiously drove his mount alongside Sham in a late, fast-closing rush.

It was close, but Sham relinquished the race to Dicks Boots by a head. Once again, Sham earned a second-place purse of $1,760 but had yet to learn the satisfaction of winning. Perhaps the colt didn't understand where the race ended, and why reaching that spot first was paramount. The horse needed to find a little bit of aggression, like Great Prospector, who turned on his opponent during the Tremont Stakes. That horse savagely bit Golden Derby on the neck, motivated by a rapt desire to win—at all costs.

Sometimes Sham lost ground when he broke to the outside, not focused on a straight line ahead. Or, coming from behind to challenge the leader, he was easily distracted and refused to stave off all comers through the final stretch. The colt was definitely still learning. He had proved one thing, though: He was ready and able to sprint to the lead in the first or second quarter if asked. It appeared he needed something he wasn't currently getting. He was definitely lacking somewhere and was inconsistent. It wasn't quite right. Something was missing.

Over the last month of summer and first month of fall that year, Sham raced without success. However, his three races had certainly proved his potential.

Seven days earlier, in the September 16 Futurity race at Belmont, Secretariat again proved his worth by coming in one-and-a-half lengths ahead of the field. As his stablemate, Riva Ridge, battled with Autobiography, Key to the Mint and Canonero II for the 1972 Eclipse Award, Secretariat took the juveniles by storm.

In two-week intervals, he amassed stakes races one after another. Stop the Music, Step Nicely and stablemate Angle Light became aggressive competitors, but he continuously beat every one of them through the Futurity, Champagne, Laurel Futurity and Garden State races. The only way any could best him was by a foul in the Champagne Stakes, where it was claimed he interfered. The stewards disqualified his win and turned it over to Stop the Music, who finished second.

PART TWO

CHAPTER SEVEN

Hancock Dispersal Sale, Elmont, NY
November 20, 1972

After the sudden passing of Bull Hancock on September fourteen, his son, Seth, took over the Claiborne dynasty. Bull had preferred racing his yearlings while still holding a percentage ownership in them, rather than being a commercial breeder as his father, Arthur, had been. However, recognizing growing economic concerns, Bull's last will and testament specified that Claiborne would return to the marketplace for a while.

Upon taking control of the farm, Seth put many of the yearlings and two-year-olds up for auction. As Sham had lost all three of his races, he became part of the Hancock Dispersal Sale that November. An impressive advertisement in *The Thoroughbred Record* filled two full pages side-by-side, heralding the upcoming event with headlines boasting, "The Greatest Concentration of Blood Leading Sires Ever Offered in a Single Consignment."[23]

The estate of A. B. Hancock, Jr. consigned fifteen yearlings and twenty horses of racing age that were jointly owned with William Haggin Perry. Fasig-Tipton Co., Inc. would auction them off at Belmont Park on Monday, November 20, at 9:30 a.m. Large, bold print on the pages of the magazine touted famous sires, such as Bold Ruler, Buckpasser, Round Table, Damascus, Sir Gaylord, Pretense, and Dr. Fager. It was an event that was certain to attract the most discerning group of Thoroughbred racehorse owners.

Sigmund and Viola Sommer, hearing the widely advertised news of the upcoming dispersal sale, instantly planned to attend. Sigmund, a well-known New York real-estate development magnate, followed in his father's footsteps. Real estate was a family business since 1885, and even his son, Jack Sommer, after studying business at Boston University, joined the family's construction firm.

Sigmund, always an ardent fan of Thoroughbred racing, was also a sponsor of the New York Racing Association, Inc. for many years. The Thoroughbreds so interested him that his passion for racing quickly drew the attention of his wife, Viola, making her a lifelong participant too. Together, they built a small Thoroughbred racing empire of their own and enlisted the expertise of Frank "Pancho" Martin in '65, as their trainer. Sigmund was the leading United States Money-Winning Thoroughbred Owner for '71, grossing a world-record $1,523,508 in prize money, and he broke his own record the following year with a total of $1,605,896.

Frank Martin was born in Havana, Cuba, on December 10, 1925 and began his career as a hotwalker. He purchased his first horse, My Goodness, from a trainer for $150 and struggled to work his way up to trainer by age sixteen. After working in Cuba until '47, he moved to Ohio with a prospect named Constant Aim. He was nicknamed Pancho by his acquaintances due to his Spanish heritage.

In 1949, he was the leading trainer at Sunshine Park, now known as Tampa Bay Downs, while also being named one of the Leading Trainers for '50 and '51 in New England. Then he moved to New York, where he met the Sommers and began training for them while their horses were stabled at Belmont. He enjoyed huge success in his career while being honored by the New York Turf Writers Association and presented with the Outstanding Trainer award for '71.

Pancho was a suave, well-groomed man with a determined, no-nonsense demeanor. The thunderous tone of his voice, mixed with a Latin fervor, immediately implied a sense of command. Stubborn, when he set his sights on anything he was certain to follow through. His current achievements also included New York's Champion Trainer award for '71. His fame as a well-respected New York trainer preceded him wherever he went, and he beamed with enthusiasm.

As the Claiborne horse trailers finally turned off Cross Island Parkway and through Belmont's gates at the 430-acre park, a new day dawned. A blast of winter chill cast a heavy white frost everywhere. Small puddles that froze into icy geometric patterns during the night crunched as the trailer wheels rolled through.

The yearlings' trip from Claiborne in Paris, Kentucky, was thankfully uneventful. They drove through the night in roomy box stalls that gave the young horses extra space. A couple of stops to check on them meant a few hours' delay, but the staff was well experienced and expertly tended their needs. Sunlight sifted through fluffy clouds gliding across the Mediterranean-blue sky and was still trying to warm the autumn air as the vans pulled into the parking lot.

The Belmont barns were surrounded by billowing white canvas tents carefully secured in place for the auction. Rows of chairs would accommodate the crowd of prospective buyers that had been arriving since early morning. Everyone wanted to get a good look at the horses before the sale.

Numbered hip tags assigned to each horse established an orderly lineup for the auction block. In a large adjoining paddock, Claiborne staff tended the yearlings while the crowd mingled and inspected every detail and pedigree. Hooves, teeth, toplines, muscle and bone, as well as shoulder and hip, angle and length, were taken into consideration and studied carefully. Each equine expert formulated an opinion while jotting down assumptions on sale programs.

Sham and the other two-year-olds were led from their stalls to join the procession of yearlings being prepared for sale. Finally, at 9:30 a.m. the horses were led single-file to form a lineup outside the tent while people took their seats inside. The sale was about to begin.

With a stud chain pinching tender gums, a nervous yearling colt by Sir Gaylord, wearing *Hip No. 1*, was led in to the crowd's noisy drone. It took one look at the people and shied, pulling away, which caused even more discomfort as the chain tightened.

Patiently, the groom worked to settle the young horse. The handler remained cool and quickly the colt gave him its head without further protest. Instantly, the sharp pressure from the chain subsided and the colt clung to its handler submissively, obeying the order to move on. The din of the crowd suddenly vanished as the auctioneer's rambling voice echoed over the loudspeakers.

One after another, horses were led into and out of the tent. Sham appeared to watch intently from position thirty in the lineup. As he was moved closer and closer to the front, horses continued to disappear into the tent. From his vantage point, there was no way to see that they were exiting unharmed through the other side.

The auctioneer's voice rang loud and clear as the next yearling colt, tagged with *Hip No. 8,* entered the tent. The young horse was a big, gangly yearling with hindquarters towering over its withers, which gave it a *downhill stance*—a good sign of speed. Its pedigree was impeccable, having been sired by Round Table.

"This colt is as yet unnamed," the auctioneer said. "Sired by Round Table, this year's current leading U.S. sire, who has been one of the top-ten leading sires for six of the last seven seasons. The first foal of Gamely, a champion three-year-old filly and champion handicap mare at four and five years old…."

The man's voice rambled on, increasing in tempo as he asked for an opening bid, and immediately got $100,000. His sales fervor took over. In minutes, the hammer struck the podium, signifying the final bid. It would be the top price of the day at $240,000, set by Johnathan Irwin representing British Bloodstock Agency, Ltd., of Ireland. It would also prove to be the highest U.S. auction price paid that year for a yearling.

A yearling filly wearing *Hip No. 12* entered the tent, and, as the auctioneer rattled off her lineage, Penny Chenery conferred with trainer Lucien Laurin. The unnamed filly was the product of the second-leading U.S. sire, Buckpasser, out of Rose Bower (by Princequillo), who was a stakes-winning mare of $141,034. As the hammer fell, Penny bought the filly for $120,000.

Sham was next. He had been standing patiently at the front of the line while bidding inside the tent continued. As his groom motioned him to proceed, pent-up nervousness gave him an instant surge of energy,

The Hancock Dispersal Sale of 1972 at Belmont Park with Sham at the auction block. Courtesy of California Thoroughbred Breeders Association.

and his feet danced as he snorted. When he shook his head, foam flew from his mouth and floated through the air to land on his chest and legs.

Sham reached the podium and came to an abrupt stop. With his head held high and inquisitive ears pricked, satiny ripples danced across the beautiful dapples in his shiny dark coat. He was a regal picture of equine perfection and his observant eyes scanned the surroundings while he solidly stood his ground. The bidding started.

Mrs. Cloyce (Liz) Tippett had her eye on Sham for Llangollen Farm. She owned his sire, Pretense. Liz raised her hand, signaling the auctioneer. The bidding continued.

"I have one hundred and ninety-five thousand dollars now. Do I hear two? Anyone for two?" He scanned the audience and his eyes met Sigmund's. Sigmund nodded.

"And it's two, now. I have two hundred thousand dollars. Anybody for two-ten? Do I hear two-ten? Give me two-ten, two-ten for anyone? Two-hundred-five. Give me two-five now? Anyone?" Once again he scanned the crowd but there were no takers.

"I have two hundred thousand dollars. Going once, going twice, sold, for two hundred thousand dollars!" The hammer struck the podium, and Sham's sale was complete.

The drop of the hammer was final. There would not be any changes to the sale after that. As Sham left off the auction block, another finely groomed two-year-old filly proceeded to the platform and the auctioneer's voice began the familiar fast-paced pitch once again.

Sigmund's eyes widened with satisfaction and a smug grin encompassed his face. He wanted Sham from the moment he first saw him standing in the paddock before the lineup began. He remembered seeing the colt run at the track—a magnificent animal that captivated onlookers. When the bidding was over, Sham's $200,000 sales tag was the highest paid in the racing-age group, and second-highest price that day!

The sale was a huge success. Claiborne netted a total of $2,580,000 with an average price of $73,714. Sales were scheduled to continue for two more days, and Fasig-Tipton would auction off another eighty-five horses of other consignments from different stables.

Sham was led out under the massive oak trees onto the sun-dappled grass of the paddock. Sigmund and Viola followed close behind, talking with Pancho about their new purchase. Even though Sham had placed three times for Claiborne, he hadn't broken his maiden. That was the main topic of discussion, but when Pancho first saw him, he knew he wouldn't have any trouble achieving that goal.

He liked Sham's looks. The colt's movement, conformation, and breeding were superior. He was sure that with the right training and opportunities, Sham would become a great racehorse. Pancho's eyes glistened in the sun as he stared toward the paddock, while Sham's fine physique and near-ebony coat reflected in their depths. *This horse is special,* Pancho thought, watching Sham rear, spin, and run the paddock fenceline. His glossy coat shimmered as his mane and tail flew. The horse appeared incredibly elated to be at liberty again, totally unaware of its new fate.

Belmont was home to all of Sigmund and Viola's racehorses since the mid-1960s. Hitchcock, Never Bow, and Rube the Great were just a few of their 1970s winners. They unmistakably had a good summer with their four-year-old racehorse, Autobiography. A robust colt with bloodlines tracing back to Bold Ruler, Man o' War, and Nearco, he was an excellent handicapper and could easily carry top weight. By '72 he had earned $366,045, placing first in twelve of thirty-one starts, second in ten, and third in three. He even defeated champions Riva Ridge and Key to the Mint in an outstanding performance in the Jockey Club Gold Cup.

Mike Casale summed it up in the article he wrote for *The Thoroughbred Record:*

> Sigmund Sommer's Autobiography won the classic
> Jockey Club Gold Cup by the incredible margin of 15
> lengths at rain swept Aqueduct on October 28.[24]

Everyone was thoroughly amazed of that achievement. It became even better. The horse went on to win the Eclipse Award for its achievements that year as Champion Older Male. Pancho's training was superb, and the Sommers knew it. Throughout the years, the three of them proved a worthy trio. Casale's article continued:

> The Sommer-Martin combination, one of the most
> successful in the business, purchased Autobiography at
> private terms last summer from Ogden Phipps, and the
> colt later won the 1971 Discovery Handicap.[25]

The rest of the Sommer-Martin team was its backbone—always there for them no matter what—and Pancho kept it that way. Lalo

Linares was his longtime assistant trainer, right-hand man, and trusted confidante, with a quiet nature that helped withstand Pancho's intensity over the years. His loyalty was steadfast.

Isadore, Pancho's brother, was another key player who stood at his brother's side, helping things come together. Pedeo Cachola, the exercise rider, was an expert at following Pancho's instructions and kept the horses at their physical peak between races.

Then there was Pancho's faithful groom, Secundino Gato, born in Cuba on January 7, 1943, who developed a passion for horses at a young age. He dreamed of being a jockey, but, as he matured, height and weight foiled that plan. When he passed the five-foot mark and approached six, he decided that a groom's position suited him just fine. He loved the horses entrusted to his care, and his expert handling and grooming techniques kept all the Sommers' horses pampered and satisfied.

Together, they formed a tight-knit operation. Pancho set up the play, and they all worked together. No one questioned that group because they were on top with record winnings, earnings, and awards.

Sham became familiar with his new handlers in a short time and was soon deeply involved in Pancho's training regimen. The trainer was extremely pleased with Sham's attitude and demeanor, as well as the obvious training he received at Claiborne. His immediate concern was Sham's race record—three losses. Pancho wondered why.

As training progressed, Pancho noticed some repetitions. The horse had a tendency to bore out badly at the start. Sham also seemed content to maintain the same speed of surrounding horses, not wanting to break away or pass.

Pancho knew that many young horses just beginning to race bore out badly at the start or in the straight. Also, many come-from-behind horses that were capable of giving more seemed content to stay with the stragglers—never feeling the desire to show their full potential and challenge the speed horses until asked.

Pancho applied a full-cup blinker to narrow Sham's view, making him concentrate on the finish line—not on what was happening around him. That would also encourage Sham to lift his head, channel his binocular line of vision on the situation two strides ahead, and block out any peripheral vision of horses beside or behind him. That should increase his speed and enable him to take the lead from any horse in front.

Clad in blinkers, Sham was breezed a few times with some stablemates. Pancho began to notice a difference in Sham's performance. Soon the horse improved. With that brief two weeks since the dispersal sale, Pancho felt confident the colt was ready to perform and he excitedly approached the Sommers.

Sigmund answered the phone on the third ring. "Hello?"

"Hi, Sigmund. It's Pancho," he said matter-of-factly. "That new colt, Sham, is as ready as he'll ever be. I want to enter him in a maiden special at Aqueduct this week." He felt quite confident. "That's good news, Pancho. Viola and I trust your decisions, and you know you don't need to ask. Just give us a call with particulars, and we'll see you there. We wouldn't want to miss his first race in our silks," Sigmund replied.

"I'll do that. Be talking to you. 'Bye." Pancho hung up.

While Sham prepared for his debut, another year was coming to a close. It had been an intriguing year fueled by the continuing space race with the Soviet Union—perhaps a diversion from bad publicity over Vietnam. At the start of the year, President Nixon had ordered the implementation of a space shuttle program, and on February 4, *Mariner 9* filmed Mars. The Soviet Union quickly rallied with their launch of spaceship *Luna 20*, which returned to earth with Moon rock samples just twenty days later.

Not to be outdone, America then sent its *Pioneer 10* satellite into space on the second of March. With a satellite orbiting the earth, New York was successful with the first cellular phone call on April 3 and a glimpse into the future.

However, not everything was upbeat. A seed of political deception had begun to grow. After two failed attempts, the first Watergate break-in occurred on May 28, which led to the arrest of five White House personnel. In June, President Nixon and Chief of Staff H. R. Haldeman were taped pitting the CIA against the FBI's investigations into the Watergate Scandal.

It was an election year, and, hoping for an end to the war, Democrats nominated Senator George McGovern for President, while Republicans renominated Nixon for a second term. Even though America seemed desperate for a change in leadership, it proved to be the poorest turnout in the past twenty-four years with little more than half the electorate voting. On November 7, Nixon defeated McGovern in a landslide election.

All indications were that the Vietnam War was finally coming to an end. By the twelfth of August, Nixon withdrew the remainder of American ground troops. Then, after a visit to South Vietnam, Henry Kissinger voiced his thoughts that peace was imminent. As if laughter could help the country recover from the war's devastation, the comedy series *M*A*S*H* began its televised debut the following month.

Television continued to boost its stronghold as an all-important part of the American dream, already providing nearly two decades of worldwide broadcasting. The 1970s only strengthened that invention's popularity with the introduction of color.

Newly discovered arthroscopic surgery, a revolutionary procedure allowing surgeons to visualize damaged joints through tiny incisions, became prevalent for horses. Magnification through an arthroscope helped veterinarians diagnose and repair otherwise fatal equine injuries.

After years of research and experimentation, scientists discovered a breakthrough in DNA that would change the future of biological science. At the turn of the century, DNA testing would be implemented by The Jockey Club to assure accurate breeding verification for Thoroughbreds.

Life was moving fast and definitely changing.

CHAPTER EIGHT

Aqueduct Racetrack, Jamaica, NY
December 9, 1972

The weather was foul with a soggy, thin layer of snow on the ground, leaving a dank, chilled-to-the-bone feeling in every creature at Belmont. The regular routine of chores was dutifully carried out, but there was a more solemn approach to everything people did that morning.

Pancho went through the barn like a storm, unable to hide his ire over the solid-gray cover of East Coast winter and promise of more bad weather to come. All he could hope was by lunchtime the wet snow would stop falling and the track would turn up, at worst, muddy. What a day for Sham's first race! Sigmund and Viola were lucky their plans had changed and they wouldn't be able to attend.

Pancho shook his head in disbelief again and mumbled a string of incoherent Spanish as he turned from Sham's stall. He stomped off to the tack room to see if the proper equipment was being prepared and loaded into the waiting trailer.

He was also taking Projective, another of the Sommers' horses, to Aqueduct that day. Projective was a three-year-old that hadn't shown any real promise so far and had been entered in a mile claiming race with a $7,200 winning purse. If Projective won that race, Pancho hoped he would be claimed for the $30,000 claiming price, as he couldn't account for any more precious time being invested in that horse if he wasn't going to perform. It was far too costly to keep horses that weren't about to amount to anything, and Pancho had a terrific sense of judgment for such assessments. In the colt's last race at Aqueduct on November 23, Projective had once again come in fourth. The horse would have to perform or be out.

Sham, however, had never raced at Aqueduct before. The trainer would be running two different horses in two totally different spectrums.

A New York jockey, Jorge Velasquez, would ride Projective in the fourth race. Jorge was also riding Sham in the second race, a mile maiden special, and a horse named Just de Duc, owned by Mrs. A. Fitzgerald, in the third.

With many expenses to cover, jockeys were expected to stay fit on starvation diets. Every day they rode as many horses as they could, just to survive. Malnutrition and anorexia plagued them as they starved themselves to maintain the nearly impossible male weight requirement of 110 to 115 pounds. Often they became bulimic, overeating then immediately throwing up. It was such an acceptable ritual that they even had their own lingo for it—*flipping*.

Jockeys became very competitive with each other; a lot of stress and tension led to arguments and fistfights. Stress also turned many to diuretics and laxative or alcohol abuse—because if they didn't make weight, they didn't ride. Losing strength and composure meant losing control of the horse. It was a hindrance factor in communication between man and beast.

With an overzealous agent, if they could even afford one, they could be carded for several races a day. Sometimes six or seven. If they managed to finish the day in one piece, they returned to the track the next. It was quite a feat to earn a living if they didn't win, but it was even worse if they couldn't book enough mounts. With the demands and pressures of the profession, it didn't help knowing it was the "only sport" where an "ambulance followed the action."[26] Whenever the topic surfaced, everyone had an opinion.

"I'll be honest with you, I think they are underpaid," said veteran trainer Bobby Frankel, "because any time you get yourself on a horse and you go in that starting gate, it's a real dangerous job."[27]

"To do what we do," explained jockey Alex Solis, "you truly have to love it because dying tomorrow is in the back of your mind every day."[28]

The risk factor was immense with permanent debilitating injuries or death, pushing insurance premiums to among the highest of all professional sports. Some would come back and ride in pain with injuries not yet healed, and never complain.

Award winning trainer Wayne Lucas once said, "They go through one of those and they climb back on board....You really wonder why a guy, even if he loves the sport and has a passion for it, is going to get back on after one like that."[29]

Jockeys were programmed to win, and every day they risked their lives, whether in actual races or workouts.

"There's a saying and it goes like, it's not how you win, but how you play the game. But it's not that in horseracing," Pincay said, shaking his head to reinforce his statement, "In horseracing it's how you *win* the race. How you win."[30]

By late morning, the temperature climbed to forty-five degrees and the snow tapered off to a fine, misty drizzle. A trailer at the front of the barn was meticulously loaded with the necessary racing equipment and awaited the horses' arrival.

Sham and Projective were groomed and blanketed, their legs wrapped in cotton pads and track bandages for the short trip from Belmont Park to Aqueduct Racetrack. Unlike their human counterparts, the two horses felt a surge of exuberance at being led from their stalls on such a chilly morning and danced their way to the van. Eagerly, they followed handlers up the ramp and settled into partitions without mishap.

At 12:40 p.m. Eastern Standard Time, the call for the second race echoed across Aqueduct. Velasquez mounted up and guided Sham through the saddling ring toward the track. The weather turned to showers on-and-off with a cold wind. The track was definitely muddy.

Sham's new green satin blinkers with the stable's golden S in the middle of his face were already streaked with water lines where cold raindrops landed. He shook his head, no doubt in an attempt to remove the wet garment, but it was firmly secured.

Velasquez ushered him down the track, warming him in a slow canter to the backstretch prior to entering the gate. He could sense that Sham was distracted—so completely distracted, the horse hadn't noticed they were already loaded. The twelve other horses quietly joined them. Sham continued to shake his head, definitely not focused on his task.

Velasquez lifted the goggles from around his neck and fitted them securely over his eyes. He gripped the reins snugly and twisted a lock of Sham's mane through his fingers and over the reins.

"They're off!" the announcer shouted. His voice sounded muffled through the heavy mist but the sound of the buzzer was loud and clear. Sham's startled jump thrust him clear of the starting gate in shocked disbelief. He landed forcefully on his front hooves while his hindquarters gathered and shot into the slop, spraying mud onto his belly. As the long line of horses clawed at the ground for secure footing, they left the post as one. It was 12:50, and the race had begun.

Anono, Water Wheel, and Radnor managed to get their feet under them first and shot off in that order, with Sham, Dulan, and Dr. Penny in their wake. Mud flew into the air, pelting their faces as the lead horses' hooves dug at the ground in front of them.

While Velasquez tore a layer of mud-spattered goggles from the remaining ones over his eyes, the rest of the field strained and grappled for a clear position out of the line of fire from slinging mud. He knew Sham could hear the slapping and plunging noises close behind, but would have his peripheral vision cut off by the blinkers.

The stress of not knowing the proximity of the impending field appeared to drive Sham into an early sizzling sprint. Anono couldn't take the pace and stopped badly, throwing the race. That colt drastically fell back to ninth place as Sham overtook him in a mad rush.

Velasquez kept Sham out of the deep mud on the rail and they flew past Water Wheel, then Radnor. His colt sprinted to the quarter-mile marker in 22 3/5, distancing him by an amazingly early four-length lead!

Radnor fought desperately to stay with them and keep his hold on second place. Trying to match Sham's early burst of speed, Dulan battled head-to-head with Water Wheel further back. By the half-mile post the intense effort burned Dulan out. He faltered, giving way to Water Wheel. Dr. Penny was gunning for them on the rail, but deep mud forcefully pulled on the colt's shoes and he also succumbed to fatigue and faded back.

Commanding the front, Sham's sleek, dark form glistened in the cold rain. The colt sped on while Velasquez became mesmerized by the sound of hooves smacking the mud and the squeak of his fine leather boots rubbing against the saddle. They were rolling.

Sham battled Mother Nature and reached the three-quarter pole in 1:10 4/5! There was no challenge from the rest of the field so Velasquez let the colt run on his own courage, the whip all but forgotten. As they rounded the final turn for home, the wind picked up and the rain mercilessly bit their faces. Sham eased off a little.

Out of nowhere, Radnor rounded the turn like a charging bull. That horse earnestly started to drive for the finish line with an all-out effort, closing the gap until it was just three lengths behind. Water Wheel rallied in a flat-out gallop fighting for second place, a mere half-length off Radnor's flank.

Velasquez heard the intensified slapping sound but concentrated on Sham's slight hesitation. He quickly raised his right arm into the air and unmercifully thrust it back. The whip struck Sham's wet flank, leaving a searing pain. Instantly, Sham lugged in as he tried to move away, while Velasquez, who anticipated Sham's reaction, changed hands and countered with a stinging smack on the left. Startled, Sham took off in a renewed burst of speed.

Water Wheel gamely overtook Radnor, and then charged after Sham. The colt groaned with the extreme effort against wind and pelting mud.

Velasquez looked back and realized that Sham's increased speed was carrying them faster than Water Wheel's drive, so he steadied Sham in a hand-ride down the final seventy yards. His colt continued to pull away on his own urging and crossed the finish line six lengths ahead of Water Wheel.

"At the wire it's Sham! He wins the mile by six lengths in one thirty-seven. Water Wheel is second by one-and-a-half, Radnor, then Rib Roast trailing by a head." The announcer's voice crackled through the loudspeakers.

Sham had won through the snow, wind, rain, and mire, breaking his maiden in his first outing for the Sommers. Velasquez pulled him up and headed back to where Pancho and Gato waited. After quickly inspecting his horse, Pancho positioned Sham for the track photographer and blatantly smiled at the camera. He knew Sham could do it—and the horse had! It was Sham's first visit to the winner's circle and the horse strutted as cameras clicked and people fussed.

In the words of the late jockey George "Iceman" Woolf, "You don't have to tell good horses when they win or lose. They know. I guess they come by it kinda natural."[31]

After posing for photos, Velasquez quickly dismounted and pulled his saddle from Sham's back. He immediately went to the scale to verify weight requirements. With the weather still foul, Gato quickly led Sham from the track to the spit barn for his tests. He wanted to get Sham cooled out, dried off, and back to the stall for a well-deserved rest.

Pancho was proud of Sham, and himself, as his training expertise brought the colt to the winner's circle his first time out. Too bad Sigmund and Viola missed it. Celebrations would be in order when they received first-place winnings of $4,800. They would certainly be impressed with their horse.

Pancho had to hurry back to the barn. His thrill of winning was cut short as he needed to focus on preparing Projective for the fourth race in less than an hour.

Velasquez seemed to be on a roll as he brought Just de Duc home first in the third race, too. However, as Pancho predicted, Projective didn't fare anywhere near the likes of Sham in his race. He came in fourth, again, six lengths behind the winner, Flying Crimson. Pancho didn't try to conceal his ire. Everyone kept their distance.

Sham immediately landed in a peak-conditioning program to get him in the best shape imaginable before his three-year-old campaign. Pancho wouldn't race him again for the rest of December. He had a hunch about Sham entering the most prestigious race a horse could win, the Kentucky Derby. After watching Sham break his maiden in that one-mile race, Pancho believed the colt had a chance. He was determined to gradually bring Sham to a peak before the Derby, believing that more desirable than constant stiff work. Overwork might ultimately sour him, or worse, debilitate him.

One well-known example of that happened in the mid-1930s with a Wheatley Stable colt named Seabiscuit. Under James E. (Mr. Fitz) Fitzsimmons, a well-respected trainer of such champions as Gallant Fox, Omaha, Nashua and Bold Ruler, Seabiscuit ran an unbelievable thirty-five times as a two-year-old. The horse lost most of those races and became unruly. Mr. Fitz believed the horse would never improve; in fact, *everyone* doubted it. A lot depended on the horse's athleticism and will, but final decisions were usually the trainer's.

With a change of ownership and tactics, Seabiscuit became a champion and Horse of the Year in 1938. Through an incredible career of eighty-nine starts, he had thirty-three wins, fifteen seconds, and thirteen thirds, with total career earnings of $437,730.

By the end of '72, Secretariat was a racing hero. His whole team seemed to set records everywhere they went, including the November Garden State stakes. Paired with Angle Light, it was the first time an entry finished first and second giving the trainer, Lucien Laurin, 10 percent of the combined winnings of $238,932. It was also the first time brothers finished the top two in a race: Ron on Secretariat and his younger brother, Rudy, on Angle Light.

In his first nine races, Secretariat lost only one and was disqualified from one other. The colt was so determined to win that Turcotte seldom had to ask for anything.

Secretariat was to be rewarded for his incredible efforts. At the Eclipse Award Ceremony scheduled for January, he would receive two awards: the Eclipse Award for Champion Two-Year-Old Colt, and, the highest American Thoroughbred horse racing honor given, Horse of the Year—a triumph achieved only twice before by a two-year-old, Native Dancer in '52 and Moccasin in '65.

He topped all champion horses including his stablemate, Riva Ridge, who won that year's Kentucky Derby and Belmont Stakes. La Prevoyante, the unbeaten Canadian Sovereign Award Horse of the Year and U.S. Eclipse Award winner for Champion Two-year-old Filly, and Autobiography, winner of the Eclipse Award for Older Male, also had to bow to Secretariat's superiority.

Arnold Kirkpatrick of the *Thoroughbred Record* would later write:

> *It seems that every time a really good horse comes along, the pundits find it imperative to compare him with Man o' War. Secretariat has reached that plateau, not only through his race record thus far, but from his way of going, his physical appearance and—as some of the older racing writers tell me—even his color.*[32]

Pancho was well aware of the stories but stubbornly believed Secretariat could be beaten. He had tested the copper colt with a couple of the Sommers' horses, and Master Achiever already bested the colt once. Unperturbed, Pancho decided to start Sham's quest for the Triple Crown.

New York was preparing for snow and closing its tracks for winter, so Sham was shipped to Arcadia, California to prepare for his upcoming sophomore campaign. Secretariat was sent to Hialeah, Florida for his. Both Sham and Secretariat would train without weather complications and closed racetracks as the winter became increasingly severe.

Pancho started out west with Linares, Gato, Isadore, Sham and Knightly Dawn. It was early morning rush hour on a business day when they headed into the city. Traffic was snarled, and, after entering the freeway, the van inched along at a snail's pace in bumper-to-bumper traffic. It was a frustrating trip to the airport on Long Island.

To ward off boredom, Sham and Knightly Dawn could pull at the small portion of hay suspended in the net between their partitions. The horses weren't allowed to drink for two hours before boarding the plane, as male equines can't urinate in a small enclosure, which could possibly cause bladder damage.

John F. Kennedy International Airport loomed in the near distance. Airport security personnel stopped every other vehicle headed to the gates for routine inspections. The horses curiously peered through the window bar slats. This would be the colts' first plane trip, and both seemed to sense something very different was at hand.

The horses' paperwork was in order, so the guard waved them on and the van proceeded to the loading dock. The plane being prepared for the flight had already been fueled. It was thirty minutes before takeoff, and shipping containers were secured into place with tie-downs to the aircraft pallet. The floors of the containers were lined with aromatic pine shavings.

As the huge turboprop engines whined, massive silver blades spun inside them. Sham and Knightly Dawn would be loaded into a double stall container with attendant access at both front and rear for Gato to tend their needs. The horses hadn't been tranquilized for fear of adverse affects during the flight and were terrified by the sight of the wide-body freighter that bellowed and roared. Every slight movement made them spook and shy, which caused chains to tighten, bruising gums and drawing blood.

"Here now! Get up!"

"C'mon! This way."

The handlers grew impatient and shouted commands, in an effort to be heard over the roar of the engines. The horses were surrounded by chaos. Whenever one was brought under control the other seemed to panic, which hurtled both back into a state of terror. Finally, the attendant slipped a blindfold over Knightly Dawn's eyes, securing it to the halter at his cheeks. Within seconds, he became submissive and dutifully followed his handler into his stall.

The sight of Knightly Dawn disappearing into the container compelled Sham to follow. After he entered, his halter was immediately secured by the safety-tie. Sham's hooves scrambled as he tried to attain a foothold in the shavings, while his sides bumped the padded walls. The protective chest bar swung closed and was secured just below his neck at the shoulder.

Knightly Dawn's blindfold was removed and his feet drummed a rhythm on the floor. Damp patches of moisture formed on his cotton blanket while his eyes rolled as he struggled.

Quickly, Gato appeared at the bars on the stall doors and soothed both horses with his familiar touch whispering, "Easy, boys, easy."

The loading ramp rumbled and clanked as it rose to seal the rear opening of the aircraft. Once the ramp was secured, the plane moved away from the gate toward the taxi strip. Trains of open-sided baggage cars with tiny rubber tires that seemed too small to bear weight circled the craft. Exhaust fans blowing fumes away from the loading dock spun on shafts like pinwheels in the wind.

The freighter taxied to the runway, turned right, straightened, and paused as the engines' roar intensified in preparation for takeoff. With a sudden jolt, a burst of speed thrust the aircraft forward. It bounced and jumped over imperfections in the pavement, increasing momentum, until the front wheel lifted off the runway, tipping the plane toward the sky.

The freighter climbed higher and higher. The horses scrambled to stay balanced as it banked over the Atlantic Ocean. It continued gaining altitude and made a sweeping 360-degree turn, dipping and tilting its right wing as it circled over the water before heading back inland.

The horses persevered while the aircraft continued to climb and air pressure adjusted. Violent turbulence shook the freighter up and down, back and forth, taking them on a roller-coaster ride into the sky. Cloud mist split apart as massive wings sliced through. As brilliant sunlight embraced the aircraft emerging from the dispersing mist, it reflected off the plane's silver wings as vapor formed almost imperceptible white lines flowing from the engines.

They were on their way. There was no turning back. As if in a trance, the horses were calmed by the whine of the engines as they soared thousands of feet into the sky, disappearing on a path across the country they'd never taken before.

With a safe landing at Los Angeles International Airport, Gato and Linares loaded the horses into a van and were in motion once again. After the myriad of highways out of Los Angeles, they arrived at Huntington Drive in Arcadia. The noise and commotion of the city instantly vanished when they entered the elaborate gates of Santa Anita Park. As the van idled in the drive, Sham neighed, then stood quietly in anticipation of an answer. An inquisitive reply came from a distant shed row and then there was silence.

Sham and Knightly Dawn were taken to the receiving barn. Pancho ran his hands up and down the colts' legs to ensure that the shipping bandages hadn't slipped and the horses didn't sustain any unseen injuries on the trip. After confirming paperwork, he helped Linares and Gato stable the two horses.

Santa Anita Park was beautiful. Warm, humid breezes drifted over the racetrack from the Pacific Ocean, leaving the grounds lush and tropical. When the sun rose above the magnificent San Gabriel Mountains, that racetrack was transformed into a gardener's paradise. The renovated '64 design was inspired by Granada's breathtaking Alhambra gardens. Thousands of blooming bushes and exotic flowers lined the roadway and park entrance amid towering rows of Washingtonia robusta palm trees that gracefully swayed in the breeze.

The solidly built brick-and-stucco entrance gates welcomed visitors to a vivid display of fertile green lawns and colorful rose gardens sprawling out from a spectacular double-tiered water fountain. Intoxicating fragrances from the roses mingled with the pungent aroma of the ocean, creating an enticing scent that subliminally beckoned.

Spanish architectural design and exquisite ornamental sculptures throughout the park enhanced the grounds. A massive bronze statue of Seabiscuit proudly gazed out over the manicured box hedges at the base of the stairs that cascaded down from the Clubhouse Restaurant.

Melodic sounds from bands entertaining race fans filled the air. People mingled around statues and strolled past gardens of fiery red-and-orange bird of paradise that cast shadows over pastel cosmos and pansies blanketing the earth.

Sham stood with his head poking over his stall door, looking out over the meticulously landscaped paddock gardens surrounding the saddling barn and walking ring. Birds swooped through trees, singing musical songs. With tall, gracefully swaying palm trees piercing the cerulean sky, and millions of exotic tropical flowers in perpetual bloom, the grounds held a whimsical feeling of timelessness—a mysterious kind of Shangri-La.

CHAPTER NINE

Santa Anita Park, CA
December 1972

Santa Anita was a busy racetrack when it opened each December, boasting 320 acres, 61 barns, and enough stables to accommodate over 2,000 horses. The mild winter weather was a bonus to keeping a young, upcoming racehorse in peak condition.

Sham and Knightly Dawn settled comfortably into their new surroundings. Sigmund had purchased Knightly Dawn at the '71 Saratoga Yearling Sale for $57,000. Bred in Kentucky by Arno D. Schefler, his sire, Sir Gaylord out of Somethingroyal, gave him Nearco and Princequillo bloodlines. Knightly Dawn began racing as a two-year-old in July. With a bad start in his first three months, he finally broke his maiden on October 14 at Belmont Park by a convincing eight lengths.

He had a few more disappointing losses in New York, including the Garden State Stakes where he finished fifth to Secretariat but was credited with fourth by default. However, the Sommers and Pancho had other plans.

A contributor to *The Thoroughbred Record* later wrote:

> *His connections had their eyes on another objective—the $100,000-added California Juvenile Stakes at Bay Meadows on December 15....*[33]

That time, Knightly Dawn didn't let them down. On the final turn approaching the homestretch, he grabbed the lead and won the race by three lengths.

Sham already seemed to thoroughly understand what racing was about, and the blinkers Pancho assigned kept him focused on the path ahead and cured his problem of boring out at the post. It was also clear that shown the whip, he understood it as a cue for increased speed and his enthusiasm for running full out moved him into second gear.

It was obvious to Pancho that Sham would be ready for stakes races early in the coming year, so he decided to enter Sham in a few allowance races to begin his sophomore campaign. He entered Sham in a New Year's Day allowance race for three-year-olds that had never won anything but a maiden or claiming race.

Now that he'd found the perfect horse, he needed the perfect rider, and he immediately looked for—and found—the right jockey.

He was a young jockey named Laffit Alejandro Pincay, Jr., who had earned a fabulous reputation on the East Coast, and was even more famous in the years following his move out West. Born on December 29, 1946, in Panama City, Panama, he was raised in a small downtown apartment along with his sister and two stepbrothers. Cherished childhood memories included fishing with his grandfather and attending Sunday mass with the family.

In the early years, Pincay's idol was Mickey Mantle, so he dreamed of becoming a professional baseball player. He excelled on the Central American Championship team as an all-star second baseman for Panama's Little League. As he grew, everyone began telling him he would be too small to be a major leaguer so he quickly changed his plans and headed to the racetrack. With his mind on the future, Pincay started working as a hotwalker, eager to move up the ladder of success.

"The first thing I had to learn was not to be afraid of horses. I had a lot of fear at first, and the horses are more wild over there in Panama. They get scared very easily and try to throw you off," he later told writer Lenny Shulman during an interview.[34] "Then galloping was difficult because over there we had to learn bareback, no saddle. And breezing them bareback, it's very, very difficult. Once I learned that, I started putting a saddle on the horses and that's when I started to create my own style. I watched other riders and did my own things to create a style," Pincay said.[35]

Laffit would forever remember the arguments he got into with his mother, Rosario, and her concern over his fasting. "I started right away watching my weight. I didn't want to eat. I remember my mother being very worried because I was fifteen years old at the time…and I didn't want to eat."[36]

Nevertheless, Pincay persisted and told everyone, "Well, if I cannot be a baseball player, I'll be a jockey."[37]

His father, Laffit Pincay, Sr., was a jockey. However, the son never learned from his father as his parents divorced shortly after he was born. Headstrong, Laffit was determined to follow his new aspiration but wasn't enthusiastically received there either. He remembered the dissuading remarks.

"Oh, you're the son of a jockey," Laffit continued his story. "They start telling me that I was going to be too big to be a jockey and it bothers me, really bothers me, so I thought—I'll show them...."[38] At seventeen, with the mystery of destiny beckoning, he acquired his jockey license.

By nineteen, his fierce effort at Presidente Ramon racetrack quickly earned him a reputation as the leading rider in Panama. He earned a very good living and had everything going for him. Confidence emboldened him with a hot temper and tough riding style. As he fought his way to the top he earned the nickname, *The Pirate,* which explained the skull-and-crossbones tattoo on his arm.

Pincay admitted, "There was no field patrol over in Panama and you could get away with a lot of rough riding."[39]

The gutsy jock quickly captured Fred Hooper's interest. Hooper was a Thoroughbred horse owner well known for discovering and importing young contract jockeys from Panama, including the well-known Braulio Baeza.

Arriving at Arlington Park, Chicago, on July 1, 1966, he signed on with Hooper for a five-hundred-dollar-a-month, three-year contract and rode Teacher's Art to victory that day. He worked under Hooper's trainer, Cotton Tinsley, and agent, Camilo Marin. Not knowing a word of English and feeling alienated, he dismally pined for his home country. For the first two years, Camilo translated Tinsley's instructions. Feeling uncomfortable with his situation, Pincay resolved to keep to himself and guard his emotions.

An inch over five feet tall and nothing but muscle and bone, he diligently fought to keep his weight around 114 pounds on a meager diet of 700 calories a day.

"I've had to fight weight since I started. I tried to do everything. I went in the sweatbox, I took diet pills, I took water pills. I heaved my food," he said.[40]

Like all jockeys, he tried everything, but the basis of his success was his inexorable mind control. Every bite of food he put in his mouth was deliberately chewed nearly fifty times, and desserts were enjoyed by sight alone.

Fellow jockeys described his conduct with one word: *disciplined.* Pincay was destined to make it even though he was overwhelmed with life's chaotic pace and the speed of American racetracks.

"I should have listened to my mother," Laffit would later say, "I should have gone to school, because I'm going to kill myself over here."[41]

"And Cotton, if he had been a tough guy, I probably would've gone back," he added.[42]

Laffit soon met and fell in love with a beautiful woman, Linda Radkovich, whose father was a Las Vegas construction magnate and Thoroughbred owner. They married in 1967, and three years later had an adorable baby daughter they named Lisa. Linda became so enthralled with her husband's success, that she never missed a race while chronicling his victories. Even his daughter, Lisa, loved the horses and constantly begged through infantile whimpers to accompany him.

With a religious background, Pincay was constantly saying prayers and giving thanks for small miracles. He was extremely superstitious and many times believed his winning was due to some peculiar incident, thus, that event became ritualistic. Always stressed over the pressure of race day, he made a personal rule to be last leaving the jockey's room, and went to great lengths upholding that promise.

He fondly remembered something Rosario once asked of him, "My mother said to me, 'Do me a favor and I want you to wear your underwear inside out.' And I say, 'Well, why?' And she say, 'Well because, for people that have bad wishes, well, it won't work.' So ever since, I wear my underwear inside out."[43]

When Laffit's contract with Hooper ended, he moved to the West Coast and settled in nicely at Santa Anita Park racetrack, amassing wins one after the other and earning many titles and awards—Leading Money-Winning Jockey in '70 and '71, the George Woolf Memorial award in '70, Leading Jockey in Races Won for '71, and the prestigious Eclipse Award for Outstanding Jockey of '71.

Pincay quickly gained popularity in California and settled his family there. He became best friends with jockey Willie "Shoe" Shoemaker, who had recently surpassed Johnny Longden's record for most racing wins. Shoe was always there for Pincay, and they developed a special bond. For years they would get together after a day's races and boast about their winnings while laughing at defeats, only to return to competition the following day.

"I would like to be like Shoemaker and keep riding a long, long time," Pincay said,[44] and he would see it through.

Competitors grew to hold great respect for Pincay. "They don't make words to describe what he's brought to the game," fellow jockey Pat Day later said.[45]

Chris McCarron added, "He's from another planet,"[46] while Jerry Bailey called him "an anomaly," and Eddie Delahoussaye anointed him "the ultimate race-rider."[47]

Pincay earned the respect of trainers, too. It almost seemed to help that he understood the English language better than he spoke it.

Trainer Joe Pierce, Jr. couldn't find a single fault with him and years later praised him by saying, "Every jock should be like Pincay. He'd listen attentively, and never talk back, never ask questions, or argue or debate instructions. He'd just nod—then go out there and do the job just like you told him to."[48]

Laffit Pincay, Jr. at the weigh scale, Santa Anita Park, Arcadia, California. Copyright © Bill Mochon Photography. Used by permission.

Pincay was at the top of the list when Pancho scouted for an accomplished rider for Sham, and the Pirate signed on with Pancho, agreeing to ride Sham on the first of January at Santa Anita Park. That would be the longest race Sham had ever run, a distance of one-and-one-sixteenth miles.

"I like your style, Pincay," Pancho said matter-of-factly. "Just go out there and bring him across the finish line first. Then we'll see where we go from there." That was his only instruction to the jockey. He wanted to watch horse and jockey become one on the track.

Pincay nodded as he looked down at Pancho from Sham's back, still struggling with his English and finding it easier to respond through body language. He felt confident on his new mount, as he had breezed and galloped Sham in a few workouts to get the feel of him and establish a riding style according to Sham's individual way of going.

Pincay mentally planned his strategy in the race as he rode away from the trainer and approached the starting gate. He had every intention of winning. He knew his starting position of number seven was a definite advantage. His favorite *was* number seven.

Pancho watched them go, then hurried to the grandstand box seats to watch the race with Sigmund and Viola, who had recently arrived from New York. It was a sultry afternoon and the track was labeled fast.

Sham seemed distracted and Pincay worked the reins to steady him in the gate as the assistant starter tried to keep the horse's head up by tugging on the bridle.

Buzzzz! Pincay was caught off guard when Sham's head flew up giving slack to the reins as he sprang forward to clear the gate. The jockey's hand automatically grabbed up mane, halting his backward motion as he gathered the slack and expertly stabilized his seat.

Sham struggled to regain balance and Pincay gave him time to collect his stride. Hovering low over Sham's withers, the jockey urged the colt on. Sham recovered, but his brief hesitation cost them precious time.

"It's Fran's Dancer with Quantum Jump in second, Prove It Mike third, Double Variety, Untangle, Native Reel in that order, and Sham last at the break," the announcer droned.

Pancho watched through binoculars from the stands as a sinking feeling engulfed him. *Why was Sham off the pace? What was Pincay doing out there?* He turned to Sigmund, and, with a sullen look of helplessness, shrugged, not knowing what to say.

However, as the field flew past the quarter-mile post, Sham moved up along the rail, deftly overtaking Untangle and Native Reel as he moved into fifth place. Pincay felt the untapped power beneath him come alive. His horse was begging to run but held in check by the pressure he exerted on the thin piece of steel bridging its tongue. Focusing on Double Variety in front, Pincay eased Sham off the rail and the colt surged forward. At the half-mile point, he settled Sham at Double Variety's side, rating him and assessing his reserve while studying the field.

"Prove It Mike in first since the quarter-mile pole and holding at the half, with Fran's Dancer a close second. Quantum Jump is third by a half-length, and it's Double Variety leading Sham by a head in fourth. Then it's ten lengths back to Untangle and Native Reel."

Pincay noticed Fernando Toro was sustaining the lead on Prove It Mike but he knew the colt's stamina was fading after expending most of its energy early. As he glanced over at Double Variety, he could see that colt was weakening. He figured the two trailing colts wouldn't be a threat as Donald Pierce and Wayne Harris had let their horses lose too much ground by the half. That left just two horses in contention, Fran's Dancer and Quantum Jump.

"Now Quantum Jump is making his move, approaching the three-quarter mark, easily passing Fran's Dancer and is now on the heels of Prove It Mike." The announcer's voice increased in tempo as the field moved to the final furlongs.

Pincay saw an opening on the rail as Double Variety began to falter, and turned his horse toward it. Instantly Sham flew to the rail. In microseconds, they sped four lengths past Double Variety and were a half-length from Fran's Dancer. Pincay's arms seemed to be an extension of his horse's front legs as his vision locked on Prove It Mike and Quantum Jump battling for first on the turn. Pincay swung his mount wide coming into the stretch, raised his crop high, and brought it down on Sham's side with a resounding *smack!*

Like a bolt of lightning, Sham's hind legs speared the dirt. Undulating muscles tossed his weight onto fully extended front legs. Moving like a hurricane, Sham punished the ground with his sharp hooves as he shot past Fran's Dancer, Prove It Mike, and Quantum Jump. He ate up the earth as he soared into first place and blazed his way down the homestretch.

"Sham's made an unbelievable move to first place," the announcer screamed. "Easily passing horses out of the turn and into the stretch, he's ten lengths in front of the field! Quantum Jump is second, then

Prove It Mike third by a head. Fran's Dancer is a half-length back in fourth, with Double Variety, Untangle, and Native Reel trailing."

Driving to the wire in the final furlong, Sham is all alone—fifteen lengths ahead of the field in his first race at Santa Anita Park, January 1, 1973. Used by permission, courtesy of Santa Anita Park.

Pincay was going to prove his ability to bring his horse home first. He could taste victory and tapped Sham's right flank again to hold the colt's momentum. Sham's reaction was intense. He sped off even faster, distancing himself from the rest of the field as he approached the finish line. His body became a blur as he flew down the track in that final six seconds.

"Sham is still gaining ground and charging to the wire at an incredible pace! He's outdistancing the field by thirteen—now fourteen lengths and driving!"

The crowd surged to its feet, screaming and shouting encouragement as horse and rider flew past the grandstand. People cheered as they waved their fists in the air. Many had wagered bets on Sham because they knew the odds were in their favor with Pincay aboard.

Pancho, unable to conceal his pride, ran down to the mezzanine floor just above the winner's circle to watch his horse approach, out in front and entirely alone.

Pincay heard the crowd's rising clamor and, worrying that there might be a challenger vying for the lead, quickly checked under his right arm. To his surprise, the competition had practically vanished from sight!

Sham's nose crossed the finish line and Pincay shot up in the stirrups, his arm raised high into the sky as an exultant sign of victory. A huge smile parted his lips. He had certainly done his job! Pancho would be impressed.

"And Sham takes it by fifteen lengths! Double Variety is second, a head in front of Quantum Jump, another head back to Untangle in fourth, then Prove It Mike, Native Reel, and Fran's Dancer...." The announcer's voice was all but drowned out by the raucous screams of the crowd.

Sham's victorious fifteen-length triumph at the finish line, Santa Anita Park, January 1, 1973. George Andrus, photographer. Used by permission, courtesy of Bill Mochon Photography.

Proud owner Sigmund Sommer turns to look at his colt Sham in the winner's circle at Santa Anita Park, while the rest of his entourage look on. George Andrus, photographer. Used by permission, courtesy of Bill Mochon Photography.

Pincay looked for Linda and quickly found her joining the victory ceremony with Sigmund and Viola. Gato had already jogged onto the track to catch hold of Sham's bridle and guide him into the circle.

It wasn't very often that an allowance race was won by such a large margin, and the Sommer team knew they had something special with that horse. He was a true diamond in the rough. Pincay brought him home just 1 3/5 seconds off the track record of 1:40 2/5, winning by fifteen lengths! When Sham passed his postrace test, the horsemen's bookkeeper would add $4,950 to the Sommers' account.

Pancho distractedly posed for photographs as he envisioned his horse's potential. The trainer just witnessed an incredible demonstration of speed and skill, but wasn't about to cancel his plan to enter Sham in the February second allowance. It was another one-and-one-sixteenth-mile race, and that would prove Sham's ability to move up to stakes races. Then he would know beyond a doubt.

Sham's workouts continued to improve. Pancho was impressed with the colt's ability to handle the longer distance. It showed that the horse had plenty of stamina. In a short time Sham had developed his own racing style; he knew his job and how to accomplish it. He now appeared confident leaving the rest of the field behind as he sprinted home.

Pincay made sure of that. When he sensed Sham was ready to ease off and relax in the stretch, he immediately reminded the colt to stay focused on the finish line. The pair would not rest until the wire was breached. Pincay's determined, aggressive style seemed to hit it off with Sham's easygoing nature and big heart. The jockey knew Sham would give all he had.

It was the awaited second of February, and Gato led Sham from the stall down the long path toward the saddling ring. Pancho followed close behind. His mind was on the field that Sham would compete against that day, and he glanced at his program again. Four horses out of six entered in the race had come off a win. Sham was one of those. The only horse of the three that Sham already defeated was Untangle. However, Untangle was obviously improving, too.

Sham's starting position was second from the rail, with one of the other winners, Black Moss, first. Table Run was assigned gate four, a good spot as long as none of the other horses lugged in or out at the start. Untangle, the remaining winner, had a definite advantage with the outside position, gate six. Pancho knew Sham had to break fast to be up close with the leaders and avoid being crowded into the rail.

After the steward's call, Pincay arrived at the saddling ring resplendent in the Sommer green-and-gold silks. Pancho briefed Pincay, then watched as Black Moss, Table Run, and Untangle entered the saddling area around them. Looking for telltale signs of uneasiness, he found none. The rest of the horses in the eighth race that day were fit and sound. Barring mishap, it would be a fair race.

Pancho checked the saddle girth, gave Pincay a leg up, and walked with them through the tunnel to the track where the lead pony waited. He glanced at the clear, sunny sky, and then watched Pincay and Sham for a moment before he turned and left for the grandstand. So far, the day was in their favor.

Sham's head bobbed over the neck of the lead pony as he tried to scan his surroundings past the limited field of vision his blinkers afforded. He seemed to know it was a race day.

Pincay was eager to warm his horse up, so the pony rider released their reins and they cantered off to the starting gates. Black Moss was already in gate one and Pincay steadied Sham in gate two as the rest filed into place.

Muscular calves quickly gripped Sham's upper ribcage, gunning him from the gate at the start. Sham exploded forward in a spray of dirt like pellets from a double-barreled shotgun, recoiled, and immediately fired off again, breaking first. To his right, Sassoon and Table Run broke second and third while on his left, Black Moss broke slowly in fourth.

Instantly, a wall of horses flowed from the gates like a tidal wave and Sham seemed caught in the middle! Donald Pierce, Table Run's jockey, piloted his colt out of the tangle and into the lead, leaving Sham engulfed by the surge. Indefatigable and Black Moss squeezed Sham back to fourth.

Table Run continued sprinting to the quarter-mile pole with Indefatigable trailing by one-and-a-half as they eased toward the rail. Sham was losing ground, and, sensing his colt's intimidation after the break, Pincay worked fervently to settle him. It had cost them the lead, and they lost five lengths.

By the half-mile, Indefatigable and Black Moss earnestly began to challenge Table Run for first as Sham followed three-and-a-half lengths back. Pincay sent Sham to the outside as they gained momentum. Driven by Pincay's intensity, Sham stretched his neck on cue with the push of his rider's arms. In two strides, he left the rail and was at Black Moss' flank. In two more, he distanced that colt by a half-length.

Black Moss stubbornly hooked into Sham and they quickly distanced themselves from Untangle and Sassoon by six lengths. That challenge only served to goad Sham on. His stride became rhythmic and his body entranced in a fluid state of ecstasy, lifting and carrying him effortlessly over the track.

Pincay heard Black Moss' labored breathing and knew the colt couldn't hold the pace as they swung wide coming out of the turn. They were only three lengths behind Indefatigable and Table Run turning for home.

Overtaking Indefatigable, they tackled Table Run. Hooves shook the ground, tendons sprang, muscles tensed, and heads bobbed. Sham's neck snaked out past Table Run's as he valiantly gained first place.

They battled together down the final yards, distancing themselves by five from the rest of the straining horses. Breaths came in distinct pants as the horses rallied. The jockeys became intense as they physically pushed their mounts to breaking point while their eyes darted back and forth, looking for some indication of the other's weakness, but Pincay and Sham weren't backing down.

Gripping the stirrups with the balls of his feet Pincay leaned forward and pushed harder, expertly driving his mount as if the animal were a finely engineered Lamborghini. Sham's half-length lead became two, then three, four, and five, as he broke away and led Table Run to the wire.

Determined, Table Run fought in vain while distancing the rest of the field by another six lengths. Though he tried, he couldn't catch the leader and his tired muscles cramped while he fought for more.

Pincay and Sham flew across the finish line as one, six lengths before Table Run, and another six ahead of Untangle. They were a blaze of unequivocal teamwork, standing separate and apart from the rest in their conquest of the race. They did it again, and very impressively in 1:41 2/5—missing a track record by one second! It was a fantastic display of courage, desire, and triumph.

Jockey Laffit Pincay, Jr. and Sham's groom, Secundino Gato, are all smiles as they pose for photographs in the winner's circle, February 2, 1973. George Andrus, photographer. Used by permission, courtesy of Bill Mochon Photography.

Pancho subconsciously tallied the purse of $6,600 with a proud, knowing smile. He had raced Sham three times and won all three. The Sommers would be elated when he called that evening, but that was only the beginning. He had much larger plans for Sham if things kept going so well. *Much* larger.

That night as Sham dozed in his stall, Pancho diligently worked. He had found something in that horse. There was no question about it. Sham seemed to benefit from the extra distance of the last two races and proved his ability to handle it without tiring.

As a bulb burned hot in the lamp over the papers on the desk, Pancho carefully laid out his plan. All he needed was approval from the Sommers. Pancho's intent was crystal clear. Sham was undoubtedly at the threshold of his first stakes race.

The scene at Meadow Stables was anything but jovial. Chris Chenery's chances for survival were now critical. Sanctioned in '72 by his own bloodstock, Riva Ridge, son of First Landing, he had achieved his lifelong quest. It was his reward for pressing on with his breeding beliefs. A fitting justice for Chenery after the unfortunate accident his '62 Derby favorite, Sir Gaylord, had suffered. That horse sustained a bone chip just days before the derby that ended his racing career.

Chenery passed away on January 3 without realizing his young colt, Secretariat, was there to try and pick up where Riva left off.

Unintentionally, Chenery left steep estate taxes for his children to manage, but fortuitously, Secretariat's recent Horse of the Year title seemed to inspire a way to raise funds. Penny and her brother quickly contacted Seth Hancock at Claiborne to establish a plan.

It was meant to be. Seth took on the task of beginning Secretariat's private syndication. One stipulation of syndication would be that the horse enter stud after his three-year-old season, which meant this would be Secretariat's final year of racing.

While that was being settled, everyone expected that Lucien would start the horse in Florida's traditional Derby prep races, but time proved a factor. Training for Secretariat was delayed pending syndication. Frustrated, Lucien could only work the colt enough to keep him in shape. It was impossible to plan for upcoming races until negotiations were finalized.

CHAPTER TEN

The Santa Catalina Stakes, Santa Anita, Arcadia, CA
February 12, 1973

Dark clouds hung drearily overhead while Sham stood tacked up in racing gear. It had been raining the past few days, and with the foul weather, the track was muddy. Pincay was no stranger to racing in bad weather, so the call didn't bother him one bit. The previous year, he won this race by a head on a lesser horse and fast track, but he wagered his chances were better on a good horse in the mud.

Pancho was more than a little concerned. The trainer had also entered Master Achiever in the mile-and-one-sixteenth race, but scratched him due to footing. He relayed his fears to the jockey as he explained his strategy.

When Pancho spoke it appeared he was shouting orders while Pincay dutifully listened. The trainer knew deep, heavy bog on the rail would prove to be a trap. Taking a horse into that would be suicidal. Pancho didn't want his horse hampered and told Pincay to stay wide at all costs.

Sham approached post three as Out of the East entered gate one and River Lad took second without mishap. Perhaps Sham had a fleeting sense of dread because he hesitated, staring intently at the steel box ahead. Pincay felt his mount's uncertainty and firmly urged him forward just as a scuffle broke out between two of the horses.

Sham's eyes instinctively searched for the perceived danger, but blinkers hampered his vision and instinct shot him forward. Pincay expertly held the horse straight and they sprang into position three. The colt's tense body came to a halt inside the gate and a gatekeeper quickly swung the door closed. Portentous and Scantling were brought under control and settled into posts four and five.

Alvaro Pineda, a good friend of Pincay's, who in just two years would meet with a tragic end from a crushed skull in that same starting gate, was riding Out of the East for JBJ Stable. The two jockeys exchanged amicable nods for luck, both silently knowing friendships would not interfere with their quest to win. In the brief moment of silence that followed, the jockeys braced themselves.

At the buzzer, River Lad bore out and slammed into Sham, almost knocking him over. Simultaneously, Out of the East seized first, Portentous, second, River Lad, third, and Sham struggling for a firm hold in the mud, was fourth, with Scantling last. Pincay quickly collected Sham's head and sent him wide in keeping with Pancho's instructions. Mud bombarded them as they angled behind the group in front. Sham's ears were tightly pinned in an effort to avoid the muddy clods while Pincay hovered low to his neck.

River Lad was first on the turn giving Scantling a clear run to second with Sham, wide, in third. Out of the East and Portentous were shuffled back and crowded into the rail. The heavy mud pulled them deeper with every stride, tiring them and rendering them last at the quarter-mile pole.

Rounding the turn, Pincay stayed clear of the rail and turned Sham loose. The quarter fractions were relatively quick for the muddy track, showing 23 4/5, and 47 2/5 at the half.

Pineda pulled Out of the East off the rail to escape the mire and quickly moved to the leaders. Suddenly, Scantling, River Lad, Out of the East and Portentous created a blockade foiling Sham's intended drive for second, knocking him back to last. The time flashed 1:12 4/5 at the three-quarter mark. Sham courageously struggled as Pincay took back to avoid clipping heels. Frustrated at being stopped, Pincay's sharp eyes keenly scanned the bottleneck approaching the turn.

Through mud-splattered goggles, he saw what seemed to be an opening forming on the rail. An impulsive urge tortured his resolve as Pancho's words resurfaced, *"Keep the horse wide at all costs."* He remembered the intensity of the orders and dreaded the resultant outburst if he failed. Feeling Sham's confined power as he held him back yet knowing the peril, he instantly decided to risk it. There was no other way out!

In a frenzied attempt to break through, Pincay roused Sham into second gear and they veered toward the rail. Sham's muscles rippled, then stretched taut, as he sprang into the narrow opening. Instantly, Sham's hooves sunk deep and Pincay's boot met the rail. While Sham plunged forward, the jockey's foot burned as it skimmed along, pinned between the horse and rail. Pincay grimaced in pain as he hung on.

Tearing through the gap like a tornado, the duo managed to pass Portentous and River Lad. Rebounding, Pincay drew his whip coming out of the turn as they burst into the homestretch, overtaking Out of the East. Then they swallowed up five lengths, annihilating Scantling. Instantly they were in the clear and bounding away.

The passionate roar of the crowd instantly confirmed the jockey's split-second decision and the colt's courageous charge.

Gaining momentum, Sham's hooves pulled from the muck with fast slapping sounds, grabbing and firing it into the air as he drove to the wire. Pineda gunned Out of the East as he struggled to catch Pincay, now two lengths ahead. His colt shot past Scantling but couldn't match Sham's blazing pace.

"Sham gets it by two-and-a-half lengths with Out of the East second! Scantling in third, four lengths ahead of Portentous, with River Lad trailing the field." The announcer's voice rang out across the soggy racetrack.

Pincay's heart pounded with nervous agitation as he brought Sham to an easy canter. Pineda quickly caught up with them.

"That was amazing! I can't believe you pulled that off!" he shouted.

Smiling, Pincay reached out and tapped hands with his friend as they momentarily moved together, then turned and loped to the winner's circle.

Laughing, Sigmund and Pancho led Viola through the sloppy footing toward the approaching mud-streaked horse and rider. Pincay pulled the goggles from his mud-speckled face as a boyish grin once again tipped the corners of his mouth. They all knew Sham could win his first stakes race and the horse did, impressively!

It wasn't just the horse. Even Pancho would sarcastically admit that later. It was the jockey's gutsy last-minute decision. Through unbelievable opposition, Pincay *made* the horse break free of the field and conquer the sloppy track.

Pancho proudly held the victory trophy plate. He knew the race instantly affirmed that Sham's lackluster juvenile season was truly behind him, and he was on the threshold of a prosperous three-year-old campaign. Sham had yet to lose a race for Pancho, and now added another purse of $19,800. Believing it was Sham's first stakes victory of many to come, they felt there was good reason to celebrate.

That night was Sigmund and Viola's last in California as they had an early morning flight to New York the following day. Undoubtedly, it was a wonderful chance for the group to meet for dinner and celebrate the day's highlights as well as discuss upcoming events. All night long, they toasted their good fortune and exchanged best wishes for its continuation into the future.

The Derby, a popular restaurant on Huntington Drive close to the track, had always been a perfect setting for race fans to rejoice.

Sham pulling away on a sloppy track coming to the finish line in the Santa Catalina Stakes, with Out of the East second and Scantling in third. George Andrus, photographer. Used by permission, courtesy of Bill Mochon Photography.

On his way to victory, Sham leads Out of the East by two-and-a-half lengths at Santa Anita Park in the February 12, 1973 Santa Catalina Stakes. Courtesy of California Thoroughbred Breeders Association.

Santa Anita Park winner's circle—Santa Catalina Stakes—Laffit Pincay, Jr. up, with Frank "Pancho" Martin and entourage looking on. George Andrus, photographer. Used by permission, courtesy of Bill Mochon Photography.

Trainer Frank Martin and jockey Laffit Pincay, Jr. accepting the trophy in the winner's circle for the February 12, 1973 Santa Catalina Stakes race at Santa Anita Park. George Andrus, photographer. Used by permission, courtesy of Bill Mochon Photography.

Founded in 1922 and purchased sixteen years later by George Woolf, there couldn't be a better haven for Thoroughbred enthusiasts.

The new owner, Charles "Chip" Sturniolo, swore the Iceman's spirit roamed the building. "I swear George Woolf's ghost lives here. Woolf lived above the restaurant, you know. Sometimes, looking through old scrapbooks or walking around, you can almost feel him there with you," he relayed to sportswriter William Reed years later.[49]

Though the Iceman was renowned for his sportsmanship and stakes-winning fame, perhaps he felt incomplete never having won the Kentucky Derby in nine attempts. It had bothered him and he often admitted, "I guess I jinxed myself when I named my place The Derby. Maybe I'll just have to settle for a Derby in Arcadia instead of one in Louisville."[50]

On January 3, 1946, riding W.W. "Tiny" Naylor's horse, Please Me, the Iceman toppled to the ground, landing on his head. No one ever understood the accident. Some said he clipped heels with the horse in front, or his horse took a bad step, while others presumed he fainted as a result of his bad diet and diabetic condition. Nonetheless, the thirty-five-year-old went into a coma, never regained consciousness, and died the next morning.

Perhaps the most intriguing memento in the restaurant was Phar Lap's saddle, given to Woolf by his jockey friend, Billy Elliott, only weeks after the horse's mysterious death. Through hundreds of races, it became the Iceman's "lucky saddle," and, oddly enough, he didn't use it in that fateful race. That day he rode in a borrowed saddle.

With graceful oil paintings of jockeys and champion Thoroughbreds adorning the walls and overlooking tables, track talk was commonplace. Glass cases of memorabilia collected from historical eras greeted patrons who entered the cherrywood doors. Over the years, various silks, Johnny Longden's riding crop, framed photographs of Derbies past, Derby mint julep glasses, trophies, tack, newspaper clippings and track programs have entertained guests prior to being seated. It has historically been the truly perfect place to formulate plans for a victorious season.

Sham was training wonderfully, clocking out faster and faster in his workouts as he quickly became accustomed to racing at Santa Anita. Pancho kept him on a regimented fitness plan, and Sham's stamina and confidence blossomed.

Pancho seemed to wonder how Sham would fare if subjected to a weight impost. Even though three-year-olds may also enter, by the age of four, most big races open to Thoroughbreds are the handicap races. In a handicap race, each horse's ability is estimated by the track handicapper who assigns weights according to his estimation of that horse's chances of victory. Two pounds of weight can cost a horse one length, about a fifth of a second, so a horse's advantage over a ten-pound weighted horse can give him a head start of five lengths. Pancho wanted to try Sham in a handicap.

"Sigmund?"

"Hey, Pancho," Sigmund replied over the phone.

"Yeah, it's me. I wan'a run an idea past you and see what you think," he told Sigmund, who was in New York City. "I was considerin' runnin' Sham in a handicap race comin' up here at Santa Anita the middle of March. He's been showin' a lot of confidence in his pace, and I want to see what he'll do with some weight at the mile-and-a-sixteenth. Test his staying power.

"They'll probably give him a pretty hefty impost since he won those allowances and that stakes race so easily. The clockers 'ave been keepin' an eye on him in his workouts, but I think he's ready, and there's no better time to check it out," Pancho said.

"He's proved to me twice he's a mudder. It'll help me see where he's at with some weight. He'll be runnin' against some graded winners bein' primed for the Kentucky Derby—Linda's Chief, Gold Bag, Ancient Title, and Groshawk. It'll be a good test to see if he's really where I think he is. What's your feeling on this?" Pancho waited for Sigmund's reply.

"Well, Pancho, it seems like you've got your racing strategy all planned out, and I don't see anything wrong with trying a handicap right now. After all, he's early into his sophomore campaign, and it'll help us see just what we're working with. What did you have in mind?"

"The San Felipe Handicap on March seventeenth. Weights are assigned on March twelfth. Closing time for entries is the seventh. Race value's double what Santa Catalina was, topping out at $69,700 with $42,700 to the winner. If he's ready, and I think he is, it could be a good move career-wise, too. If he does as well as I think, I've got a racing schedule set leadin' him to the Kentucky Derby, by way of the Santa Anita Derby on March thirty-first, and the Wood Memorial on April twenty-first. The cross-country trip will be tough, but I'm sure I'll get him back to peak in twenty-one days. What do you think?"

"Like I always said, if you feel he's ready, what are we waiting for? Go ahead and follow-up on his nomination for the San Felipe. Viola and I won't be able to make it for the seventeenth. We've got too much business to take care of that week, so good luck. We wouldn't want to miss the Santa Anita Derby, though. We'll let you know when we're coming to town for the end of March."

"Right. I'll let you know if anything changes. 'Bye." Pancho hung up. It was set. He hurried out of the office toward the stables to check a few things with his staff before he went to the track office.

On the afternoon of March 17, the San Felipe Handicap stakes was about to begin. Gate time was exactly 4:40 p.m. Pacific Standard Time.

In a curling motion, gathering energy and preparing for that first powerful thrust, Ancient Title blew out of gate one, commanding the first position. Aljamin, Mug Punter, Linda's Chief, Gold Bag, and Out of the East followed in that order.

Where was Sham? Pancho wondered.

Sham struggled from gate three almost last, only slightly ahead of Groshawk and Indefatigable, who sauntered from their gates as if not realizing they were in a race against time. Sham had been given a 123-pound impost in the race, the only larger being 126 given to Linda's Chief.

Could the weight impost be the problem? No, that was ridiculous, Pancho speculated. His heart sank when the race commentator's voice echoed over the track announcing Sham's late start and that he was still losing ground to Groshawk. He had placed himself second-to-last to Indefatigable, who, with a mere 110-pound impost, would do no better than last throughout the race.

Ancient Title, carrying 120 pounds, set a burning pace with fractions of 22 4/5, 46, and 1:10 seconds to the three-quarter-mile, with Mug Punter and Gold Bag both carrying 114, in his wake. As Aljamin and Out of the East fell back from the blazing early fractions, Sham struggled to keep his hold on sixth place.

Pancho watched helplessly as the shocking scene played out through his binoculars. *What was going wrong?*

After a pitifully slow start, Sham seemed to settle along the rail on the first turn. Lacking room to increase speed there, Pincay took him to the outside where Groshawk and Out of the East were trying to move up with the leaders. Passing the three-quarter-mile pole rounding the turn, Pincay once again saw an opening forming on the inside and drove Sham back to the rail, staying clear of the tiring horses ahead.

As Groshawk, Aljamin, and Gold Bag faltered and fell behind, Sham prepared to break through. He moved like lightning on the heels of Out of the East, who rocketed from eighth place to fourth around the final turn. However, Sham was not as lucky as that horse and the small opening closed as quickly as Out of the East passed through, leaving Sham cut off. Linda's Chief flew across the finish line in 1:41 4/5, just 1 2/5 seconds off the track record. Ancient Title earned second and Out of the East, third.

Pancho watched, visibly unnerved by the loss. Even though Sham's burst of speed at the head of the stretch carried him from sixth place to finish fourth at the wire, it wasn't good enough. The horse still finished fourth, earning $4,500, but that wasn't Pancho's plan. Sham's recent winning streak of four in a row was now marred by this untimely loss.

Pancho continued to watch through his binoculars while the horses slowed as jockeys pulled them up. His mind spun and his stomach twisted into a knot. Sham had just two more races to prove himself before the Kentucky Derby, along with a grueling cross-country trip from California to New York in between. Suddenly, things looked uncertain.

Pancho quickly approached the rail. He spoke to Pincay while he inspected his horse, his voice full of displeasure. "What's going on? What happened out there? I cringe when I see it again in my mind."

Pincay's eyes sheepishly lifted to meet Pancho's red-hot glare. "We're cheated. Sham cut off...couldn't break out."

"That's what ya 'spect me to tell the Sommers? Come on, man! That won't fly!"

"Couldn't get 'im out trouble. He's good. Jus' luck bad. You see. Next time we win." With a shrug, Pincay turned. He had nothing left to say. Neither did Pancho.

Then, tragedy struck the Sommer barn. It was their champion four-year-old, Autobiography. His life was quickly cut short at Santa Anita Park when he broke a leg so severely he had to be destroyed. Pancho, already stressed over having to relay Sham's inexplicable loss in the San Felipe, couldn't believe things were getting worse.

The old adage, *The great life can't go on forever,* seemed to ring true as he fretted over Autobiography's loss. *Hadn't they already had their share of heart-breaking accidents by losing Dust the Plate, a promising two-year-old, from a broken leg, and Hitchcock to a heart attack? Or what about the loss of Never Bow, to a broken neck in an unbelievable accident of falling from a loading dock while boarding a plane? What did the cards have in store for them in the upcoming Santa Anita Derby? A race Pancho had been counting on but suddenly felt doubtful and insecure over? Was it a sign to beware of things to come?*

Laffit Pincay, Jr. weighing out after the race.   Copyright © Bill Mochon Photography.   Used by permission.

Across the country at the Sommers' New York residence, things weren't much better. Viola had been through an onslaught of medical tests and was scheduled for surgery the week of the Santa Anita Derby.

Linda's Chief, winner of the San Felipe Handicap, March 17, 1973. Copyright © Bill Mochon Photography. Used by permission.

While Sigmund was quietly reading the newspaper and relaxing with Viola, who was also trying to unwind from a hectic day, he said, "Pancho and I were discussing Sham's future plans a while ago, and he feels Sham has a good chance at the Kentucky Derby this year."

"What? Sigmund, you know how I feel about that! It's so risky, too big a chance of injury, not to mention the pressure. I can't believe you two would consider that with Sham when we only just bought him! I'm not even over Autobiography yet, and you're considering Sham? How could you even ask?" She was very upset.

Sigmund looked at her over the top of his newspaper. He saw her face, strained and agitated, in the glow of the living room lamp. "I know you're still on edge from that, but Pancho says Sham's the one. He feels we have a great horse, and sure, Autobiography's loss was devastating, but that was a freak accident. It doesn't mean you should panic and think of holding all our horses back. They're racehorses.

We're going to race them. One race is as much a risk as another.

"Besides, we've never had the opportunity to enter the Derby before. Sham has shown a huge amount of potential in a short time, and Pancho thinks he's a shoo-in. After all, Sham will only have this one chance. This spring is his sophomore season, and you know the Triple Crown races are only for three-year-olds." Frustrated, he threw the newspaper down onto the sofa.

Viola looked at him with deep concern in her face, her eyes filling with tears as she remembered their recent loss of a horse so soon after being proclaimed a champion in his own right. "I can't discuss it further tonight. I've had a very trying day." Forcing back tears of frustration, she quickly left the room and went to bed.

Meanwhile, the start of '73 brought changes for Secretariat, too. Seth announced in February that a newly formed syndicate had purchased Secretariat. Each of the thirty-two syndicate owners paid $190,000 for breeding rights to Secretariat with their chosen mares. No other stallion had been syndicated for such an incredible price—a record $6.08 million. That was to be his first world record.

For Seth, just twenty-four, it was a risky decision and his first major deal. Secretariat could destroy him through failure, or enhance his reputation forever if the horse proved a champion.

Now Lucien had to scramble for a plan. The Florida prep races would begin that month and he wasn't ready. After much deliberation, he opted for the New York prep instead, which would give him until March to bring his colt back to peak condition. Immediately, Secretariat was shipped to New York and put to work on a rigorous fitness plan.

At home in Huntington, New York, sportswriter Bill Nack read the news and shouted, "Hot damn! Secretariat is coming to New York!"[51]

The first race Secretariat entered was the Bay Shore at Aqueduct on March 17, and the horse arrived seven days prior. Soon, Nack's green Toyota arrived and he hurried to stall 7, Secretariat's new home. That became habitual while the reporter logged the copper colt's progress. Penny's red Mercedes, sporting a bumper sticker that read, "Secretariat for President," also became a familiar sight in the parking lot.

When the seventeenth arrived, the weather in New York was wicked. Coming down the homestretch in the Bay Shore, Secretariat was cut off by a sea of mudslinging horses. Neither of those hindrances stopped him as he found his path through a tight squeeze. Turcotte and Secretariat conquered the field and ran to victory, winning by four-

and-a-half lengths. No doubt Big Red, as his adoring fans nicknamed him, proved he was a mudder, too.

"He's too much horse! They can't stop him," Laurin's son, Roger, screamed from the stands, victoriously shaking his fists as Secretariat stormed the finish line. His excitement electrified the crowd as he continued his broadcast, "They can't even stop him with a wall of horses!"[52]

In a short time, Secretariat reigned over the rest of the East Coast three-year-olds and it seemed that no one could name a comparable challenger. The horse had just two more races at Aqueduct before the Derby—the Gotham on April 7 and the Wood Memorial on April 21. However, unlike Sham, he was already on Long Island, not 2,800 miles away.

Across the nation, events seemed to be shifting into top gear. After President Nixon's inauguration for his second term in the White House on January 20, the Vietnam war was coming to an end with the signing of the Paris peace accord seven days later. On the eleventh of February the first American POWs were released. Then on March 29, the remaining soldiers came home.

With the country focused on the soldiers' return, a letter to Judge John Sirica concerning Watergate allegations that named Attorney General John Mitchell operations chief momentarily seemed to go unnoticed. Then, scandal over Watergate's Saturday Night Massacre later brought calls for Nixon's impeachment.

On April 4, the New York populace swelled with pride as the World Trade Center officially opened, with the North Tower being the tallest and the South Tower the second-tallest buildings in the world at 1,368 and 1,362 feet, respectively. However, in less than one month, Chicago would claim the North Tower's short-lived fame with the completion of the Sears Tower, topping out at 1,450 feet.

In keeping with the Women's Liberation Movement of the 1970s, the televised tennis "Battle of the Sexes" ended at the Astrodome in Texas with Billie Jean King's brilliant defeat of Bobby Riggs. It was as unexpected as George Foreman's end to Joe Frazier's undefeated heavyweight boxing championship reign earlier that season.

America continued the space race by launching *Pioneer 11* on April 6, and the Soviets rallied with their *Mars 5* launch on July 25.

All around, it would indeed prove to be a very competitive year.

CHAPTER ELEVEN

The Santa Anita Derby, Santa Anita, Arcadia, CA
March 31, 1973

Pancho had already been at the barn for hours when the staff began preparing the horses' morning meal. He was up all night wondering if there was any reason to feel such stabbing doubt concerning the race. Sham's workouts that week were less than impressive. The horse had only once finished six furlongs with a speedy 1:10 3/5. Pancho knew he shouldn't dwell on a single loss and a few poor workouts, but some subconscious inkling refused to leave him alone. After all, this was the Santa Anita Derby, a $124,400-gross, nine-furlong, prestigious Grade 1 test of the fittest sophomores. It rivaled the Santa Anita Handicap, nicknamed the *Big 'Cap,* which became famous as the nation's first $100,000 race with its inaugural running. That race grew in popularity when Seabiscuit finally won it in 1940 after two previous attempts.

The trainer knew he shouldn't be unduly concerned because he had the best horse, and the best jockey. Pincay won the Derby on Solar Salute in a blazing 1:47 3/5 the year before, so he was primed. Pancho knew his luck was holding out when that jockey, who was also asked to ride Linda's Chief, opted for Sham. Pincay had a point to prove with Sham that kept the bettors' preferences divided on those two colts. Feeling Sham had "a rough trip," Pincay told *The Thoroughbred Record* that "he rode the son of Pretense wrong" in the San Felipe weeks earlier.[53] In fact, both Pancho and Pincay were determined to prove Sham the superior horse and set the record straight.

Leon Rasmussen, a writer for *The Thoroughbred Record*, wrote:

> *And the rivals' trainers, Bobby Frankel for Linda's Chief, and Frank "Pancho" Martin for Sham, expressing rather bitter, positive views in the press, left little doubt they would be honored to be the other's pallbearer.*[54]

Sham's number one California competitor, Linda's Chief. Copyright © Bill Mochon Photography. Used by permission

Ancient Title, winner of numerous stakes races, and second in the March 17, 1973 San Felipe Handicap at Santa Anita Park. Copyright © Bill Mochon Photography. Used by permission.

Besides Linda's Chief, Sham would meet Ancient Title and Out of the East again and they had been turning in good workouts, too. Pancho made it a point to clock them himself a couple of times to know what he was up against. Linda's Chief was particularly good and wagering held him the favorite at 3-5.

Pancho had been drilling Sham with Knightly Dawn, who proved to possess great sprinter qualities. That colt could break from the gate quickly and cleanly and loved to command the front position with early speed. Together, they wagered at 19-10.

Ancient Title set a searing pace in the San Felipe, and Pancho intended to challenge him for the early lead this time with Knightly Dawn. That returned to the issue at hand—would Sham pick up speed quickly enough to overtake them in the backstretch, or would he fall too far back at the start, putting him in danger of facing another blockade of horses?

Pancho resolved to tell Pincay to keep close to the lead horses from the start. When he headed out of the barn office, his mind was at ease.

The rest of the morning proved uneventful, giving Pancho a chance to thoroughly unwind. By early afternoon he was calm and confident when Sigmund came to the barn to talk and see his horses before the race. Viola wasn't able to attend because of her surgery, and Sigmund promised to call her as soon as the race was over.

Pancho and Sigmund excitedly discussed their chances of winning the race. They waited at the saddling ring for their riders to arrive from the jockey's room. The steward's call, "Go to your horses," echoed from the loudspeakers in preparation for the eighth race of the day. When the two appeared, Sigmund gave a last few words of good luck. He turned and walked toward the sprawling concrete staircase leading up to the pastel cream-and-green striped awnings of the clubhouse. Pancho began going over last-minute details with Pincay on Sham and Milo Valenzuela on Knightly Dawn.

There was an incredible crowd that day of 49,564 people, filling all 26,000 seats including the elite box seating of the Clubhouse and the grandstand boxes and seats. The overflow of people crowded the spacious mezzanine overlooking the homestretch, while thousands more crowded the picnic areas on the carefully manicured grounds of the infield. The California sun refused to shine but the air was warm and the immense crowd certainly proved that clouds wouldn't spoil the day.

Sham, No. 1, with Laffit Pincay, Jr. up, and Knightly Dawn, No. 1A, with Milo Valenzuela up, lead the post parade for the 1973 running of the Santa Anita Derby. Copyright © Bill Mochon Photography. Used by permission.

Located close to Hollywood, the racetrack was a popular spot for movie stars and business magnates, who usually filled the expensive private boxes. Santa Anita's popularity among celebrities was a tradition going all the way back to 1934 when the track opened. Race programs detailing the competing horses were read and reread as race fans returned to place bets at the cashiers' windows throughout the day. When the call for the eighth race sounded, people scrambled to purchase last-minute tickets.

As the horses filed out of the paddock alongside their pony horses, the crowd's anticipation built with cascading shouts and cheers as favorite horses came into view. Upon seeing the crowd surrounding the track, Sham grew nervous. It was the first time he encountered such an enormous crowd and the sounds and movement set him a little on edge.

Out of the East, No. 2, with Jerry Lambert up, and Groshawk, No. 3, with Willie Shoemaker up, in the post parade for the 1973 Santa Anita Derby. Copyright © Bill Mochon Photography. Used by permission.

Then the horses flushed from the gates like a herd of deer startled by an unseen intruder.

Knightly Dawn veered in sharply just as Ancient Title broke outward, sandwiching a dazed Linda's Chief between them. As Baeza struggled to regain hold of Linda's Chief, Valenzuela and Toro gunned their horses, pulling away. Baeza expertly settled Linda's Chief into third place after the break, with Sham, Groshawk and Out of the East following.

A horse's instinctive flight system can take it from zero to thirty miles per hour in seconds, and this race was proof. Knightly Dawn and Ancient Title clocked 23 seconds in a quarter-mile! The two speed horses appeared to take flight as they aggressively sprinted on. By the half-mile Ancient Title got a head in front and those two set another 23-second clip while fiercely fighting for first!

Knightly Dawn takes the lead at the start of the 1973 Santa Anita Derby with Out of the East second in the center, Sham obscured in third on the rail, Linda's Chief a close fourth on the outside, and Groshawk in fifth place on the rail. Copyright © Bill Mochon Photography. Used by permission.

Feeling his mount was holding the pace while racing on his own courage, Pincay kept Sham on the rail a safe three lengths behind. Flying sand stung their faces as they hugged the rail, but that didn't deter their resolve. The sun momentarily broke from the clouds, casting a beam of light on them like a spotlight on a dark stage as the jockey's colorful silks glistened.

Pincay eased Sham to the outside as he saw Knightly Dawn begin to tire and lose ground in front. He wouldn't be trapped again, and he realized by the rhythmic breathing of his mount that Sham had horsepower to spare. While Ancient Title rolled on first, Sham's speed increased. He easily passed Knightly Dawn then locked on to Ancient Title's bobbing hindquarters.

The race fractions were sizzling—23, 46, and 1:09 4/5 seconds at the three-quarter-mile pole. As Knightly Dawn fell back to sixth, Sham bulldozed his way to second a mere length-and-a-half from Ancient Title as they rounded the final turn. In two short bounds, Sham overpowered Ancient Title.

Thundering down the stretch to the finish line, the horses thrilled the crowd as they stampeded past. Pincay felt Sham begin to pull up, so he cocked his whip. As he fervently urged Sham on, he heard the unmistakable thunder of horses gaining on them. With a quick glance under his arm, he saw Linda's Chief with Out of the East at his side making their all-out bids and closing—only two lengths behind!

Baeza's whip whizzed through the air, punishing Linda's Chief's rising flanks with a stinging blow. He pushed his mount forward in a desperate attempt to overtake Sham.

Pincay wasted no time. He aggressively took hold of Sham, applied the whip to his heaving side and scrubbed the colt's neck. Instantly, Sham stretched out and reached through the air like a black panther springing for the kill. He pulled away from Linda's Chief as that horse, in turn, sped up and distanced himself from Out of the East. They were matched stride for stride only two lengths apart, both jockeys reaching and pushing in rhythm.

Sham coming down the homestretch in the March 31, 1973 Santa Anita Derby with Linda's Chief second, Ancient Title and Out of the East battling for third. Courtesy of California Thoroughbred Breeders Association.

Sham's famous March 31, 1973 Santa Anita Derby victory—at the wire. Copyright © Bill Mochon Photography. Used by permission.

Sham's speed increased again as the finish line loomed ahead. The horse skimmed over the dirt in a blur, each footfall driving him faster as he quickly surpassed Linda's Chief by another half-length. Pincay froze immobile for Sham's final thrust across the wire.

"And it's Sham! First, in a burning drive, he wins it by two-and-a-half lengths equaling the stakes record of 1:47! Linda's Chief second, another two-and-a-half lengths in front of Out of the East, with Ancient Title fourth. Groshawk and Knightly Dawn are fifth and sixth," the announcer screamed above the pandemonium of the crowd.

The crowd poured from the Clubhouse across the mezzanine and crammed the space surrounding the winner's circle. Pincay's wife, Linda, her heart soaring, leaped down the stairs, two at a time, as fast as she could run. Gato held Sham while an assistant removed the horse's blinkers. A race official hoisted an intoxicating garland of exotic flowers over the horse's withers as Gato led him into the circle.

Sigmund, Pancho, Linda and Isadore were elated as they gathered around. Major Hayden Lockhart, a former POW, and Lynn Stone, the president of Churchill Downs, were all smiles as they presented the gold cup to Sigmund. Sham's purse was $79,400 in prize money. What a race! Sham equaled Lucky Debonair's 1965 stakes record with Shoemaker aboard, a feat that would only be duplicated once in 1998 by Indian Charlie with Gary Stevens up, but never surpassed by the turn of the century. Lucky Debonair had gone on to win the Kentucky Derby.

Sigmund handed the cup to Pancho, who immediately thrust it high above his head as the crowd cheered and cameras clicked. Newspaper reporters with microphones in hand tried to get as close to the winners as possible. Liz Tippett, Pretense's owner, joined in the winning celebration. She regarded Sham with envious eyes while pondering memories of underbidding Sigmund at the dispersal sale. As Pincay sat on Sham's back, he tipped his hat to the crowd while cameras clicked around them. Excited fans fought for every inch of space, all wanting to be part of the ceremony while they cheered and applauded.

Sham must have been proud of himself, too. With arched neck and head tucked up to his chest, he let Gato steady him while Pincay dismounted. Sham had already entered the winner's circle four times that year, but it was a new experience as the already suffocating crowd grew larger and louder as seconds passed.

Suddenly, a hush went out across the grounds, quickly followed by an array of angry shouts and boos when a signal flashed on the tote board indicating a foul in the race. Braulio Baeza, who rode Linda's Chief, claimed a foul against Knightly Dawn for the start of the race.

Stunned, Sham's team stared at the board.

"What's this?" Pancho demanded. "What's happening? Sham won that race fair and square!"

Time dragged on for the winning team whose mood instantly went from elation to despair. The race stewards were deliberating on a possible disqualification. The crowd waited in shocked silence. Then almost as quickly as it appeared, the light disappeared, and the original race placement returned, indicating that the race stewards had disallowed the claim.

It was later learned that Baeza claimed the foul on Knightly Dawn for lugging inward and crowding Linda's Chief at the break. If Knightly Dawn had been found guilty of causing a foul while running paired with Sham, the race would be declared unfair and Sham would relinquish his victory to Linda's Chief who finished second.

The stewards considered ordering the top five horses to the testing box as a precautionary measure while they deliberated. However, their decision was quick and they ruled the complaint out, noting that it was actually Ancient Title who improperly broke outward as Knightly Dawn headed to the rail, thereby closing off Linda's Chief. They firmly disallowed the claim as it wasn't interference on Knightly Dawn's part. Sham's team was relieved.

Once again, cheers went up from the crowd as the numbers on the board remained unchanged. With renewed smiles in the winner's circle, congratulations were again in order. Sigmund's gaze slowly turned to Pancho and Pincay, then back to catch a last glimpse of Sham as he disappeared out of sight, headed for the spit box.

Hellman and Frankel were furious, ensconced in the belief that Linda's Chief had been fouled. When the press confronted Pancho with those allegations, the trainer publicly announced his agreement to a nine-furlong match race "for any amount of money at any time and any place."[55]

After winning what was considered the most important West Coast prep race on the road to the Kentucky Derby, Sham's recognition and fame blossomed. He had definitely matured through the winter, and the spring races certified that. Sham became one of America's most accredited Derby hopefuls and was now titled *Best Horse on the West Coast*. Newspaper headlines praised Sham's competence in that race, boasting, "Sham Makes a Shambles of the Field," while the official race chart touted "Sham's Big Moment," under a photo of him crossing the wire.

Neil Hellman began to wonder about sending his horse to the Kentucky Derby and decided to hold off. He would run Linda's Chief in the April $100,000 California Derby instead and wait to see how Sham would fare in the Wood Memorial against Secretariat. For Sham, Hellman's decision was a monumental conquest in itself.

Sham's team was exonerated by the win. They were ready to challenge Big Red on the East Coast and couldn't wait for the chance. Only Viola had not yet come to grips with the thought of the Kentucky Derby and pressures of the Triple Crown.

That night in his hotel room, Sigmund stared at the telephone on the dark mahogany desk. He had to call Viola, but didn't know how to present the news, especially since she was resting in bed after surgery. Finally, he picked up the phone and hesitantly dialed.

"Hello?" she answered on the second ring.

"Hi, Hon. It's me." He managed to sound relaxed, masking his mixed emotions.

"Sigmund! I knew it would be you! Tell me everything!" She was very excited.

Her mood was contagious and Sigmund perked up as he recounted the events at the track. In his haste, he blurted out the fact that he and Pancho had decided to enter Sham in the Derby.

"Sigmund, I think you should reconsider. I know you and Pancho have your hearts set on that race, but it's such a risk! There're too many unqualified horses attempting it, and no real favorites since Secretariat's been picking them off one by one. Sham could get injured. I don't think I could take that," she pleaded.

His eyes warmed as he heard her plea and his face softened. He didn't want to upset her further yet didn't know how to ease her fears. They'd been through the argument many times. His hand slid down the phone cord as if gently caressing her arm, then he grasped the receiver again with a gentle squeeze.

After changing the subject, he ended up saying nothing further about the upcoming race.

Meanwhile, Sham and Knightly Dawn were sent out East together to prepare for the Triple Crown. Pancho took his staff with him again as he needed their help on the long journey and Gato would personally tend the horses, ensuring their safety.

After much fuss and preparation, the horse van left Santa Anita Park, pulled onto Huntington Drive and headed toward Highway 210 for Los Angeles International Airport. Certainly the horses had no idea what was in store as they fretted in the crossties, trying to peer through the barred windows above the partitions. An ocean fog had settled in before dawn that morning and seemed to get thicker as time passed. In no time at all, they would be in New York once again.

On the final leg of the trip from John F. Kennedy International Airport on Long Island to Belmont Park, the horse trailer turned off Laurelton Belt Parkway onto Hempstead Turnpike and headed to Barn 5. Ironically, the Sommers' horses were stabled in the same barn as, but at the opposite end from, Secretariat's stall.

Pancho didn't care. His mind was settled. He was confident and ready to meet the ultimate challenger. In fact, it had turned into a personal quest because he really believed he had the superior horse.

Reporters swarmed to the barn to get the first scoop on Sham's incredible journey across the country. They thronged Pancho and his entourage, completely dumbfounded by Pancho's move to run Sham in the Wood at Aqueduct after his long trip from the West Coast. Everyone knew the horse would need to be shipped off again on another 700-mile journey to Kentucky. The Preakness, in Maryland, would be another journey of 800 miles, then back 200 miles to New York for the grand finale of the Belmont. It was *not* the traditional West Coast Triple Crown preparation, as most trainers would have shipped directly to Kentucky.

Questions flowed one into another.

"Why'd you enter Sham in the Wood Memorial?"

"What made you think you needed to enter the Wood before the Derby?"

"Was it merely to test your luck against the media's favorite, and create an upset before the Triple Crown?"

"Why didn't you settle Sham directly in Kentucky and enter a prep race there? Isn't that more traditional?"

Pancho's confidence couldn't be undermined. "We want to get a true line on our colt, and the best way to do that is to run against Secretariat."[56] He steadfastly summed it up by firmly stating, "The Wood's the way I wanted to go, and that's all,"[57] and, that was that.

Pincay, temporarily obligated to remain in California with family and racing commitments, was being hammered with the same questions from West Coast reporters.

Ever since childhood, Pincay had this dream. "I heard of the Kentucky Derby when I was a little kid growing up in Panama," thoughts he held inside for years quickly surfaced, "so I grew up thinking, gosh, what would it be like to win that race? And that's what I wanted. I wanted the experience to win. The feeling of winning that race."[58]

Like every jockey, he envisioned the prowess of winning the Kentucky Derby and imagined the feeling of that achievement. It wasn't "just another race" to a jockey, it was the ultimate conquest. This would be his second attempt after finishing fifth aboard Unconscious with his first try in '71.

"I remember Don Brumfield winning on Kauai King when I was just starting out, and that made a big impression on me because he said something to the effect that coming down the stretch God helped him to get there," Pincay later told journalists. "You didn't just need ability or talent or luck, but help from Above to win this race because you want it so bad," he said.[59]

That night, at Santa Anita Park, in an interview with reporters who were desperately trying to build up the hype leading to Derby Day, which had already built to grandiose proportions, all questions centered on Pincay and Sham.

His determination already solidified, Pincay simply replied, "This is my Derby horse."[60]

April 7 arrived, and Sham's picture appeared on the cover of *The Thoroughbred Record* magazine, headlined "Sham—Winner of the Santa Anita Derby."

As Sham acclimatized from his long journey to New York, Secretariat proved his worth in the Gotham at Aqueduct, with ease. He equaled the track record of 1:33 2/5 seconds for the mile with an uncharacteristic tactic. On the pace from the start carrying 126 pounds, he held off Champagne Charlie at 117, who came on with a strong challenge at the three-sixteenths pole.

Champagne Charlie's courageous burst of speed couldn't match Secretariat's, though, and he came in second, three lengths behind the copper colt. However, the determined challenger's final drive was so intense that he distanced third-place Flush by an amazing ten lengths!

As Turcotte pulled Secretariat up, some clockers timed him at 1:59 2/5 for the extra quarter-mile, an unbelievable time that would have broken other hard-earned records.

"This sucker breaks records pulling up. He might be the best racehorse I ever saw. Better than Man o' War," Charles Hatton, a writer for the *Daily Racing Form*, exclaimed.[61]

As Sham had emerged victorious from the West, Secretariat still triumphed over the East.

Pincay all smiles after victory in 1973 Santa Anita Derby on Sham, winning the one-and-an-eighth-mile 1973 Santa Anita Derby in 1:47. Copyright © Bill Mochon Photography. Used by permission.

Sham, Laffit Pincay, Jr. and Secundino Gato head to the winner's circle after the race stewards disallow foul claim and Sham receives the victory blanket of flowers over his withers. Courtesy of California Thoroughbred Breeders Association.

Frank Martin and Isadore Martin join Sham, Gato and Pincay in the winner's circle as the concerned crowd looks on following the stewards' disallowance of a foul claim. Copyright © Bill Mochon Photography. Used by permission.

Sham in the winner's circle for the Santa Anita Derby, Pincay up, while Lynn Stone, President of Churchill Downs, and Major Hayden Lockhart, former P.O.W., present trophy to Sigmund Sommer and Frank Martin. Courtesy of California Thoroughbred Breeders Association..

Sham's owner, Sigmund Sommer, trainer Frank Martin, jockey Laffit Pincay, Jr., Linda Pincay, and Isadore Martin in the winner's circle at Santa Anita Park. Copyright © Bill Mochon Photography. Used by permission.

CHAPTER TWELVE

The Wood Memorial, Aqueduct, Jamaica, NY
April 21, 1973

The Wood was always a very important Grade 1 stakes race and a major prep for the Derby. Named in honor of Eugene D. Wood, past president and a founder of the Jamaica Racetrack, it was originally one mile and seventy yards from the mid-1920s to 1930s. From the 1940s to 1950s, it was changed to a mile-and-a-sixteenth, then to a mile-and-an-eighth.

By 1973, three of its winners, Gallant Fox, Count Fleet and Assault had continued on to win the Derby and capture the Triple Crown. The late Mr. Fitz was the winningest trainer with seven horses, four of them in succession from 1936 through 1939. Eddie Arcaro was the winningest jockey with nine, including Hill Prince and Bold Ruler. It was aboard Bold Ruler in 1957 that Arcaro set the stakes record of 1:48 4/5.

Public interest in horse racing had been tapering off, many believing that the Triple Crown would never be achieved again. However, since Big Red's appearance in the East, Thoroughbred racing had become a hotspot of activity. Fans just wanted to *see* the big red colt. His mere name garnered interest from men, women and children around the world. He was a superstar, and although he was only a racehorse he quite often overshadowed popular human idols. Everyone expected his performance to be phenomenal.

Sham, full of life, was up for the challenge of the Wood, even after his disquieting trip. His Belmont workouts were hot—one mile in 1:37 2/5 at the latest clocking. Sham was at his peak after having conquered the Santa Anita Derby and was drilling some of his fastest workouts. The clockers watched him like hawks.

Pancho entered three of his horses in the race: Sham, Knightly Dawn and Beautiful Music. Laurin entered two: Secretariat and Angle Light. John P. Campo also entered two: Flush and Expropriate. As a matter of fact, there were only three horses that were not part of a paired entry. A race card like that quickly spread rumors that spiraled out of control.

Sports headlines insinuated that Sigmund and Pancho were entering so many horses to "bother" Secretariat. Journalists began taking jibes at the men every chance they had. They implied that Knightly Dawn's disallowed foul in the Santa Anita Derby had been planned all along to beat Linda's Chief. At first, the pair just laughed it off, inferring that notion was "simply ridiculous!" During that race, Sham hadn't needed any help. He won on his own and very impressively, too. In fact, very few trainers who were there that day felt the disallowed foul had anything to do with Sham's victory.

The week leading up to the race seemed to intensify the accusations, criticism, intimidation, and ill will. Pancho offered to run Sham as a single entry if Laurin ran Secretariat and scratched Angle Light, but, because Laurin was the trainer for both horses with separate owners, it wasn't up to him. He had no choice in the matter. Angle Light would run in the Wood Memorial.

As far as Pancho was concerned, he should be able to run more than one horse, too. He felt Knightly Dawn was a perfect entry for the race, and also believed in Beautiful Music. That horse had an impressive pedigree, the son of Northern Dancer, and although started in only one race before the Wood, the colt won it so well Pancho and Sigmund believed him promising. The horse wasn't as experienced as the others but was willing and capable.

Laurin innocently told reporters he didn't want Secretariat to be hurt, or for there to be a possibility for Sham to steal the race. With that comment, the media began touting Pancho as a possible thief, and that infuriated Laurin because reporters had changed the meaning of his statement.

Pancho refused to speak to Laurin, which set up a mutual feeling of distaste as they continued working in close quarters.

Hatton's columns in *The Daily Racing Form* didn't help by suggesting there would be nothing but fouls. His columns were quoted by *The Blood Horse* as stating:

> The Wood is supposed to decide who has the most horse, not the most horses....We can't think he [Martin] wants to run three or even two.[62]

And...

> Another [Angle Light] was leading the Louisiana Derby field by three entering the stretch and stopped with his mouth wide open.[63]

That made Sham's team furious, and Edwin Whittaker, the owner of Angle Light, was prepared to fight. He never had so many people trying to ruin his horse's reputation before, not to mention his own!

When race time finally approached, things were going wrong everywhere.

Pancho had been under severe scrutiny by the media playing up on Hatton's columns all week. One column publicly implied Hatton's belief that Laurin was right—interference, or, stealing the race by sending one horse to the lead at a slow pace and saving energy to challenge down the stretch—was a possibility.

Hatton wrote:

> We shall not be surprised if the Tote board lights up
> with foul claims like Times Square on Saturday night.[64]

Pancho, furious with the implications, snapped. He acted hastily and made a decision he would later regret. He kept telling himself it was the coach's job to set up the play for the team. It was a good plan to see how all his horses fared against the group of Derby hopefuls, but he knew it wasn't going to happen. Besides, Viola had always hated running doubles or paired entries, and she earnestly wanted to scratch two of the horses.

"Mrs. Sommer," Pancho told reporters, "she don't like to run entries. In California, every time we ran an entry, she did not like it. If I do it, I run everything. I run four horses."[65] Pancho spat, "After the story in the paper, what you going to do? We scratch 'em."[66]

She would get her way. Pancho would eliminate both Knightly Dawn and Beautiful Music. In a cloud of temper, he stormed off to the steward's office to make it official.

His mind kept torturing him. He mulled over the matter endlessly and returned to the barn angrier than ever.

Everyone knows Knightly Dawn and Beautiful Music are excellent sprinters, he thought. *Why accuse me of having them set a slow pace or gang up on another horse? Knightly Dawn set a blistering pace at the Santa Anita Derby, challenging the other speed horses. There was no fault in that.*

Angle Light, Secretariat's stablemate, is a speed horse, too, and he'll be sent out with the same instructions—to take the lead. My intentions were never to create foul play! Sham would have to overcome Angle Light the same as Secretariat would have to overtake Knightly Dawn or Beautiful Music. Why try to imply that Sham needs foul play? What nonsense!

Then, at the last minute, Pancho learned that Pincay wouldn't be able to make it to the East Coast to ride Sham in the race. Luckily, he had two jockeys lined up for his scratched horses and quickly signed Jorge Velasquez, the New York-based jockey who rode Sham in his first race for the Sommers and won.

Pancho had faith in Velasquez. He was a highly capable, well-known jockey. However, Pincay had been riding Sham in his recent races, and after he won the Santa Anita Derby so impressively, Pancho felt Pincay understood Sham and knew instinctively what to do. He wouldn't need any instructions. Pancho had been counting on Pincay.

Life wasn't going well for Secretariat's crew, either. Secretariat's workouts were poor. He was unfocused and slow without reason. Even Angle Light had bested him in some. Everyone saw it, especially the trainer.

In Lucien's own words, he said, "Angle Light is a free-running colt who sometimes opens long leads when the pace is slow. The jockey has been told that he is to try to conserve his horse so he will have something left in the stretch…I wouldn't be surprised to see Angle Light right there at the finish of the Wood, especially if the track is fast."[67] Words he would later regret.

Secretariat was the one the public would be coming to see, not Angle Light. Secretariat's mere name had gone national, worldwide, literally off the charts. The entire world regarded him as America's hero. That worried his whole team, especially Penny. Under so much pressure, she added a lot of doubt to Laurin's mind, who took out all his frustrations on Turcotte.

After receiving the news of his father's untimely death that week, Laurin wasn't himself. He punished Turcotte for not following instructions in Secretariat's workouts, harshly scolding him for riding 4 2/5 seconds slower than he instructed in his final breeze over the track.

Turcotte was also weighed down with problems. He had his own pressures—trying to be bodyguard to a six-million-dollar horse in a workout on a chaotic track with young, green horses! Turcotte repeatedly quizzed himself, *How would Laurin have handled the stress of rating such a prized possession on a track knowing there was a loose runaway out there with him?* Mental anguish tortured him while his reasons for the slow time dissipated like vapor.

Nerves couldn't have been more frayed.

The time had come. Circumstances being what they were, there was no way to change fate. What would be, would be. Sham went to the post as the second favorite with odds of 5-2 without his two stablemates. If Sham won, he would pay $5 for every $2 wagered, as the tote board quoted the odds indicating the amount of winnings one received on a bet.

Secretariat was the favorite and paired with Angle Light, at odds of 3-10. If one bet on either horse in that entry, he would win on either wager.

The starting gate had been positioned in front of the grandstand. When the horses shot from their positions, Angle Light went straight to the lead from the outside post. Sham broke cleanly on the rail and blazed after him with Champagne Charlie two lengths back in third. Leo's Pisces, Step Nicely, Expropriate, Secretariat, and Flush chased the three leaders but none were trying hard to catch up. True to form, Secretariat moved along behind the field seemingly unhurried as he gathered his momentum.

Jacinto Vasquez, Angle Light's jockey, felt his colt was going at a far-too-easy clip and couldn't understand why Velasquez wasn't trying to take him with Sham. Bewildered, he set Angle Light on the rail and took his time, constantly checking under his right arm for the shining green satin blinkers with the glinting golden "S."

Velasquez nervously held Sham two lengths behind in second, and the two leaders moved through the backstretch with the rest of the field far behind. Sham's jockey was very concerned. *Why weren't the others trying to rally with them for the lead? What was going on? Where was Secretariat?* He had bad thoughts of his own while he periodically watched the field behind.

The jockey had strategically set up his horse to overtake the leader, but knew Secretariat was still behind and hadn't yet made his move. He didn't want to send his horse too soon. His instructions were to be prepared for Secretariat's burst of speed and to rally in the stretch. Unchallenged, he felt Sham's hold on first place was guaranteed, so he settled at an unhurried pace into the stretch to wait. He didn't realize the six furlongs had been run at a ridiculously slow 1:12 1/5!

Coming into the turn at the head of the stretch, Turcotte moved Secretariat to the outside and began racing past horses while going wide. He thought the big red colt was in a perfect position to commence his charge to the wire, so he tightened up on the reins. Secretariat immediately tossed his head as if trying to tell Turcotte something. He lugged in slightly, coming off the turn.

Puzzled, Turcotte thought, *What's this? There's no response! He's
refusing to challenge the lead horses!* Every time the jockey asked for
speed, Secretariat fought him, tossing his muscular neck and head,
trying to get relief from the pressure of the bit. Turcotte and Secretariat
began a game of tug of war. Turcotte went to the whip.

Velasquez had waited long enough—maybe too long—and was
relieved when he finally saw the copper colt swing wide. Panic-stricken
when he realized they were already into the final furlong, he grabbed
the reins in his right hand with a viselike hold while his whip came down
on Sham's left side.

Sham's response was instantaneous. His head leveled, ears
flattened, and nostrils flared red as he released the most powerful
propulsion imaginable in one forward stride. In two furious bounds
he was only a length off Angle Light's flank and driving for the wire.
Velasquez lowered his body, streamlining it against the sudden rush of
wind.

Sham was flying! His energy exploded toward the wire and came
on so strong he was at Angle Light's neck, only feet from the finish line,
grabbing at the earth with ravenous limbs.

Angle Light mustered a final burst of energy and gamely fought
to hold the lead as he struggled to ward off his rival. Sham was still
gaining, his hooves tearing into the track in perfect succession with a
pendulous swing. The two horses were alone for that last moment of
flight, four lengths ahead of Secretariat.

As their hooves hit the dirt at the wire, Angle Light won by a nose, with
Sham still driving hard, gaining ground but narrowly missing his mark.
With his next footfall he pulled ahead by a nose, but he was too late.
He lost by a microsecond, the shortest interval of time imaginable.

The crowd was stunned and booed Angle Light and Secretariat off
the track. They were furious. No one had imagined such an outcome.
Sham, the newcomer, beat Secretariat by four lengths and almost upset
Angle Light, too. Secretariat finished third, a bare half-length ahead of
Step Nicely in fourth, with Champagne Charlie, Flush, Leo's Pisces,
and Expropriate slowly crossing the wire behind them.

To the fans, the most frustrating aspect of it was losing a race that
was supposed to be won by their superhorse. He hadn't even tried to
drive for the wire and seemingly refused. *What went wrong?*

Pancho knew Sham had conquered his adversary and had he run
Knightly Dawn, Sham would have won. Sham bounded to the rail with
a proud bearing, totally oblivious to the unmistakable rumors that he,

Secretariat and Angle Light sent through the grapevine. The same fans that cheered and screamed encouragement to Secretariat on his way to the post, now punished him with chants and boos as he hurried to his assigned position at the rail. He was hastily attended to and quickly disappeared from sight.

Unfortunately for Angle Light, a dark cloud of doubt rose above the winner's circle as he stepped into it with assistant trainer Henry Hoeffner. Poor Lucien couldn't bear to face the crowd and sheepishly asked Penny which horse won, because he couldn't watch the finish. Penny quickly quipped, "You won it, your horse was first."[68]

Edwin Whittaker accepted the trophy from Robert J. Kleberg, Jr. as Jacinto Vasquez looked on. Their weak smiles for the cameras timidly held back the joy they felt at winning the race. They both wished it had been under different circumstances. Angle Light's share would be $68,940 out of the total winnings of $114,900.

All afternoon, reporters crowded around Sham's barn, trying to get a hint of what Pancho thought happened. Pancho tried to satisfy them. He was proud of Sham and felt he ran a good race. He knew Sham should have won it.

What a fitting turn of events it was for Sham's team. After almost being accused outright of conspiracy, Secretariat's own stablemate unintentionally did the one thing Hatton accused Knightly Dawn of being sent out to do. His Latin vehemence started bubbling over as he spit out loathsome remarks about "cheap people" and "cheap stories."[69] His favorite horse had proven he was a real threat to Secretariat and now he *knew* he had a fabulous chance for the Derby.

This colt's the one, Pancho thought. *What could stop such a fit and gamely horse other than bad racing luck?*

He told sportswriters for *The Blood Horse* and *The Thoroughbred Record*, "I stated before the Wood that I thought my colt had a good chance of beating the champion and Sham beat him fairly and squarely, as I expected. Had I run Knightly Dawn or Beautiful Music to assure a real pace, Sham would have won easily."[70]

Sarcastically, Pancho added, "I don't like to run against cry babies. They were crying before the race."[71] His final words to reporters when he left the track that day were, "When I go to Kentucky, take two."[72]

"What happened to Secretariat?" That seemed to be the question of the day.

"It must've been the abscess in his mouth," Lucien said, searching for an answer.

He dismissed the press with a shrug. He had been asked all the questions he could possibly endure. The quiet little trainer was still in shock from the day's turn of events. As the crowd of reporters slowly dispersed, Ron's questioning look pierced Lucien's eyes.

"Why wasn't I told about that?" Ron demanded.

In a weary voice laced with his French-Canadian accent, Lucien said, "I didn't think it was much to be alarmed about. It didn't seem to be botherin' him. He was only slightly irritated by it. Dr. Gilman examined him before the race and thought there was no need to alarm anybody. It just didn't seem crucial at the time. I didn't know he had a slight blood infection 'till the tests came back.

"Had I known about the abscess before hand, I would have loose reined him all the way instead of trying to ride him on a tight rein as I had been doing ever since I started riding him," Turcotte later stated in a letter to fans. "I am absolutely sure that, had I loose reined him, he would have won but because it hurt him so much when the reins were tight, he kept throwing his head up in the air."[73]

"Don't beat yourself up over it, Ronnie. You ran the race the way you've always run him. There's no way you could've known. Let it go." Dismayed and frazzled, Lucien turned and exhaustedly trudged back to Secretariat's stall to check on him.

Ron went in the opposite direction, not feeling very good about himself, or anything, at that moment. He wished he knew of the abscess under Secretariat's upper lip earlier. He thought he had hindered his colt's chances to win by fighting the head tossing.

Ron didn't sleep well that night, nor did Lucien. Neither wanted to believe their colt wasn't perfect after watching him at Aqueduct, winning the Bay Shore on a sloppy track—then equaling the track record in the Gotham. Each great man felt less of himself that night.

Could there really be truth in the theory that Secretariat's problem is in Bold Ruler's not passing on the stamina needed for distance racing?

That seemed to be the general consensus of the media at the Chenery stables that day, as well as with loyal fans and the general public. Bold Ruler was notorious for having trouble holding his searing pace past the mile marker. The Derby was another furlong longer than the Wood. Should people worry? Was the abscess just an excuse?

Nobody wanted to see any of Secretariat's team expelled that way. Nevertheless, there was doubt. Lucien and Penny were so concerned about their chances in the Kentucky Derby that they confronted Ron with the ultimate question, *"Can your horse win?"* If he didn't believe Big Red could do it, they wouldn't enter him.

After a heated argument that lasted through the evening and into early morning, the doubts provoked by the unremittingly accusative media, public, and syndicate were quelled. A new form of hope and trust began to surface that seemed to draw the team closer together, into a tight bond.

The argument was over. Ron assured them his horse could do it. The only doubt Ron ever had in his horse was during the Wood and that was immediately explained when he heard about the abscess.

He knew his horse well, how he broke last and slowly gathered his unbelievable stride into a perfectly flowing rhythm while his powerful limbs reached out and determinedly struck the track. Ron reveled in the way that Secretariat loved to swing wide on turns, increasing speed as he looped around the field. He knew the horse lost ground by distancing himself from the rail, but then the colt would unleash his devastating drive coming out of the final turn and charge down the homestretch for the simple pleasure it afforded him. Almost effortlessly. Ron had no doubts.

"I was confident that he could outrun a horse going a mile," Turcotte later said, "any horse going a mile. And all I had to do was gallop him the first quarter of a mile, and you know, let him take his time. So they told me, they said, 'Well, you're the rider and if you think you can win the race, we'll run him.'"[74]

It was settled. The next day, Secretariat and Angle Light would be loaded into a horse van en route to the airport. They were going to Louisville for the Kentucky Derby.

Sham and Knightly Dawn had already left the airport, safely arrived at Churchill Downs, and were headed toward Barn 42. Sham proudly carried a silky, satin blanket of hunter green and royal gold that rippled in the warm breeze and shimmered in the sunlight. He looked admiringly noble. His finely tuned body was the fittest it could be. His muscles undulated with the fluid movements of his prancing legs. The sun cast satiny lines of silver in motion, rippling out across the finely pampered raven-dark hair of his proudly arched neck. He was breathtaking, ready for any challenge.

The ever-present media was waiting for him when he entered the barn. Just as the New York reporters couldn't get enough at Aqueduct, the Kentucky reporters felt the same. Pancho was again subjected to the media's incessant presence along with every other form of curious onlooker. This time, he relished the chance to tout Sham's abilities and confidently acquiesced.

Sham, oblivious to the commotion, loved any attention he could get. His dark head curiously snaked out over his stall door, inspecting everything around him. Gato kept busy overseeing Sham's physical and mental welfare. He made sure his colt's feed, grooming and exercise schedules were strictly enforced according to Pancho's instructions.

Trying to maintain the best care for his horses while ensuring peace of mind for the Sommers kept Pancho at wit's end. Good help wasn't cheap and expenses could quickly multiply without a good trainer pulling it all together. He counted on his staff—Linares, Isadore, Cachola, and Gato—to be there for him. They were the only ones who really understood his intense, hot-blooded nature.

Sham was Pancho's best chance of winning and he took every precaution to ensure his horse remained at peak fitness and well-being. He fussed over him and Sham blossomed. The colt was a glowing beacon, a picture of health, and his inspiring workouts gained immense attention and caused quite a stir with the media and fans nationwide. Crowds appeared whenever Sham worked out, and many felt he was a serious threat to Secretariat.

Pancho became increasingly confident as Sham kept proving himself. He had Pincay for the next race and knew his team would, once again, be a tower of strength. His horse was unstoppable.

As the clock ticked, race day quickly approached.

CHAPTER THIRTEEN

Derby Week, KY
May 1973

The Kentucky Derby has long been considered the best two minutes in the history of American sports and the most prestigious race in the country. Not only is it an unmistakable honor to win that race, but it still remains the primary race of the Triple Crown, racing's greatest honor, and it holds the conqueror immortal. Hundreds of horses have tried to achieve the Triple Crown, and, by 1973, only eight had walked away with the honor, the last being Citation in 1948.

To win the Triple Crown, a horse has five weeks to run three different races—the Kentucky Derby, the Preakness Stakes, and the Belmont Stakes; in three different states—Kentucky, Maryland, and New York; on three different tracks—Churchill Downs, Pimlico Race Course, and Belmont Park; and at different distances—one-and-a-quarter miles, one-and-three-sixteenths miles, and one-and-a-half miles. All the while, the entrants must remain sound and ward off any injury or illness. Would 1973 be the year the abstinence would be broken?

Tempers flared and nerves were strung taut at Barn 42 as Derby week wore on. The twenty-eight syndicate members who spent over six million dollars on Secretariat became very nervous after his loss in the Wood and wondered if they had made a terrible financial blunder.

Angle Light's owner, Edwin Whittaker, quickly tried to firm up a syndicate deal of his own for one-and-a-half million dollars on Angle Light. He had no intention of running Angle Light in the Derby, preferring to get out of it all and cash in on his colt's fame and fortune. As time passed, the sale fell through, foiling his plans.

After the pressure of the winner's circle at the Wood, Whittaker wanted out. Feeling the need to apologize in some way, he told Penny, "I do not think my horse will be going to the Derby."[75]

His emotions were mutinous. Deep down inside, he was elated to be the owner of a horse who had just beaten Secretariat—it was truly unbelievable! Wouldn't any owner feel that way? Outside, he felt like the spoiled brat who had just ruined his best friend's birthday party. He could barely face her.

Penny was shocked. How could he back out now? It would only drive the knife deeper into the wound. How could he and Laurin embarrass and demoralize her so, and in public? She had an understood duty to keep America's treasure safe and unspoiled. How was she going to explain *this* to everyone? The more she stewed about it, the angrier she got. Her head snapped around as her frantic eyes found and burned into Whittaker's like a branding iron, "Ed, I think you should go."[76]

In the end, he was almost pushed into entering his horse in the race because he could never live down the fact that his horse had stolen the Wood. No one would let him forget it, either.

He wasn't the only one tormented by the upset. Lucien was so distraught he told Whittaker he was making a request to the Kentucky State Racing Commission for separate entries. He wasn't going to run the two horses as paired entries again if he could help it. He told reporters, "If they don't, he [Whittaker] will have to get a new trainer."[77]

Later, after the request was denied, Lucien, frustrated, threw up his hands, saying, "They will just have to run as an entry."[78]

When one of the many reporters who'd been pestering Pancho all week asked what the mood in Barn 42 was, he tersely replied, "Tense." When asked if Sham could win, Pancho started all over again, "If Pincay had been on the horse in the Wood, he'd have been in front at the half-mile pole...I don't know why the rider ran the race like he did; only he knows that. He said the colt was trying to lug in. He never lugged in before, he use to lug out."[79] With a sour look of disgust, Pancho repeated, "Lugged in." He was still upset with Velasquez.

Sham and Secretariat were only eight stalls apart—too close. It was unnerving to do or say anything without the fear of it appearing in a newspaper or magazine, and the meaning in print always seemed skewed. It was almost impossible to carry on with daily routines, everyone watching their backs.

As the Derby drew near, Knightly Dawn seemed to gain unparalleled media attention again. Pancho was training both horses for the Derby and both gave some fast workouts, but he was hesitant to race Knightly Dawn lest that open another difficult situation. He knew if he did, he would meet resistance again. The press found no end of pointedly accusing questions. If indeed possible, Pancho became even more infuriated and impatient. His loud manner made that perfectly clear.

"I said we'd beat Secretariat in the Wood and we did," Pancho told a writer for *The Blood Horse,* "and we'll beat him again Saturday. I don't know how Secretariat is doing, but I can tell you my horse is ready and can run all day. I think I've got as good a shot as Secretariat to win the Triple Crown."

He was so sure of Sham's abilities, he even "offered to put up $5,000 head and head, for the Derby between the two horses," if they were the two trainers' sole entries.[80] He was unmistakably confident that Sham was completely capable of running the race alone and thought it only fair that Secretariat do the same. As race day neared, gossip spread.

Arnold Kirkpatrick wrote in *The Thoroughbred Record:*

> *Great Copy. The Press was ecstatic. It was the high-society trainer against the Cuban immigrant; the upstarts against the establishment. Only rarely, if ever, did it occur to anyone, that Mr. Laurin is a Canadian immigrant and that anyone training the likes of Sham…for a gentleman of the caliber of Sigmund Sommer…is not precisely going to have trouble paying the feed bill.*[81]

With Secretariat's weak performance in the Wood, all other trainers who had previously made up their minds to stay clear of him suddenly felt their horses deserved a chance at the Derby, too. The last ten days before the race would be the deciding factor. The pre-Derby preps would make or break each trainer and owner's final decision on whether or not they would pay the $4,100 entry fee.

Linda's Chief had barely held on to win the California Derby when his tongue slipped up over the bit at the start of the race, giving him unbearable pain through the whole event. His new trainer, Bobby Frankel, indicated that Linda's Chief ran the race under very adverse conditions, just as he met bad luck in the Santa Anita Derby, but he came out of both races perfectly sound. However, Frankel and owner, Neil Hellman, made up their minds to forgo the Derby against Secretariat. Linda's Chief would stay in California and race at Hollywood Park.

Another promising colt up for Derby nominations, Mr. Prospector, owned by A. I. Savin and trained by Jimmy Croll, had only been beaten in one previous race. He was entered in the Derby Trial run on the first of May. However, after he broke poorly, recovered, and then rushed to the lead, he tired in the final sixteenth and lost to Settecento by one-and-a-quarter lengths.

Savin and Croll ran his stablemate, Royal and Regal, in the Florida Derby, where he beat Forego and Restless Jet by six lengths. But then in the Blue Grass Stakes on April 26, he lost badly, finishing seventh out of nine. They were still uncertain which horse, if any, they'd run in the Derby.

Forego, who ran as the favorite in the Blue Grass Stakes over My Gallant, Our Native, Warbucks and Impecunious, finished fifth behind all of them. He was also favored over Royal and Regal and Restless Jet in the Florida Derby but didn't win that one, either, coming in second. Trainer Sherrill Ward and co-owner Mrs. E. H. Gerry felt their horse was extremely talented but maturing slowly, and they remained unsure about running him in the Derby.

My Gallant, who won the Blue Grass Stakes over all the other Derby hopefuls, would definitely run in the Derby, according to owner Arthur Appleton. Trainer Lou Goldfine favored running him over his stablemate, Shecky Greene, because he was better at distances.

Shecky Greene won the April 28 Stepping Stone prep just one-fifth of a second off the track record, leaving Restless Jet and Knightly Dawn in his wake. His owner, Joseph Kellman, had every intention of entering his horse as long as the track was fast, though Goldfine tried to talk him out of it. Goldfine believed that Shecky Greene was an incredible sprinter—not a distance horse.

"If it were an ordinary horse," Goldfine told the media," I might say to go ahead and run, but this is a good horse, and I would hate to see him get knocked out."[82] He worried that such a great horse could endanger his future career trying to keep up his breakneck pace through one-and-a-quarter miles. Eight days before the Derby, Shecky Greene was still unconfirmed, though Goldfine predicted that if he were entered, he would set the pace.

Our Native, co-owned and trained by Bill Resseguet, Jr., was in. Resseguet confirmed the colt was perfectly sound and had been the most consistent candidate as he won or placed in all but two of his nine races as a three-year-old. "Our Native's 100 per cent, man, and he's just like a cannon—he fires every time. Whoever wins this race is going to have to beat him," he said.[83]

The other two co-owners, Mrs. M. J. Pritchard and Dr. E. W. Thomas, wholeheartedly agreed, knowing their tough colt was a fighter and could stay with the best.

Warbucks and Impecunious were definite entries, and while their chances of winning against the stalwarts in the field were doubtful to almost everyone, their owners and trainers were more than satisfied with their chances.

Restless Jet's trainer, Carter Thornton, vowed he would continue preparing the colt for the Derby after his courageous rally against Shecky Greene bringing him home an impressive second. He felt his colt had as good a chance as any.

However, Jimmy Jones, whose wife was a co-owner of the colt, had other feelings. He thought it was a mistake to enter him, too risky. It would be hard on the colt, and if he were injured, he could be sidelined for the rest of the summer. "I kept hearing 'go on, it won't hurt him to run in the Derby.' I said, 'Hurt him? It'll probably kill him.' They forget there are bills to pay, and a race like that might knock him out for the rest of the summer."[84] To Jones, it wouldn't have been his choice of races.

Twice a Prince and Pvt. Smiles both ran poorly in the Stepping Stone, leaving owners and trainers facing the ultimate question of whether their horse could win.

Another nominee, Gold Bag, owned by Randy Sechrest and Dr. Milton Gottdank, was changeable for the Derby after having won the Coronado Stakes in California and shipped out East for the Derby Trial. This decision could only be one more stress on Lucien's mind, as Sechrest recently purchased Gold Bag from the colt's breeder— *Mrs. Lucien Laurin!* How would Lucien feel if Gold Bag repeated Angle Light's performance in the Wood?

Wanting nothing to cast a shadow over Sham's performance, Pancho did nothing to encourage that. After Knightly Dawn's poor performance in the Stepping Stone, he decided the colt would run in the Twin Spires Purse on Derby day, instead. With that decided, he sat smugly in his folding chair outside Sham's stall and thought, *Wait till Sham shows them what he's made of.* He smiled to himself. *He'll tell the media his own story.*

In the dark hours of early morning on Kentucky Derby day, Laurin fretted outside Secretariat's stall, dreading what the new day would bring.

For the past two weeks, reporters had converged on him everywhere he went. They even waited for him at the barn or at his hotel. Being a formidably friendly trainer and not wanting to sound gruff or rude, he did his best to answer the mobs of reporters' questions on everything from Secretariat's health to his pedigree.

"Is he lame?"

"Does he have arthritis or just weak knees?"

"Will you scratch him from the race?"

"Can he go more than a mile, or is he like his sire, Bold Ruler?"

"Why'd he lose to Angle Light in the Wood when he beat him by three-and-a-half lengths at the Garden State, and sixteen in the Laurel Futurity?"

"What makes you think Angle Light won't beat him again?"

One reporter in particular, Bill Nack, was torn between believing in Secretariat and not. He heard that Jimmy [the Greek] Snyder reported that Secretariat's knee was being iced. Nack wasn't buying that. He knew the horse's closest contact with ice "was in a glass of tea."[85]

"Naturally there was a lot of guessing during the week," Lucien related to Arnold Kirkpatrick for *The Thoroughbred Record*, "quite a lot of pressure—more pressure than I've ever had in my life."[86]

Throughout all the accusations, Laurin slowly began to doubt his confidence in his colt and himself. Was Secretariat really ready?

It was a slightly different situation for Pancho outside Sham's stall that morning. He wasn't being harassed as harshly as Laurin, but condemning questions kept surfacing.

"If Sham overtakes Secretariat, will he be able to take the lead before the wire?"

"What strategy will you use?"

"Will Pincay be instructed to take him to the front from the start, or wait for Secretariat to make his move?"

"Did Velasquez wait too long to make his move in the Wood?"

"Who'll be Sham's hardest rival to beat, Secretariat, Angle Light, or another rival?"

"There are some names getting a lot of attention like Forego and Shecky Greene. What do you think of them as threats?"

The press was tireless. The reporters had the privilege of freedom of speech and the right to inform the public of whatever information they could glean. That was their job. Pancho remained obliging, certain of Sham, and spoke nothing but praise for his horse.

He had confidence in him and felt secure in his race strategy. Pincay would go for the lead without waiting for Secretariat. That last race cost him one of his four chances to prove Sham's superiority and he wasn't about to give up another.

The trainer wouldn't let the hype get to him. The more talk he heard, the more determined he became. He knew there was one other great colt in the 1970s crop—his name was Sham.

He was ready.

CHAPTER FOURTEEN

The Kentucky Derby, Churchill Downs, Louisville, KY
May 5, 1973

Kentucky Derby day in Louisville has traditionally been the first Saturday in May. A record crowd of 134,476 fans filled the stands between the famous Twin Spires that gave the Derby its landmark, while thousands more spilled out across the abundant infield lawns of Churchill Downs. Spring was in bloom, and early crocus, tulips, daffodils, forsythia bushes, and crabapple trees were everywhere. The air held an unmistakable fresh scent, carrying the intoxicating blossom fragrances of red roses, hyacinths and lilacs, along with the pungent scents of magnolia trees. It was a beautiful day, the perfect setting for such a prestigious race. The weather couldn't have been better, and the track was rated *fast*.

The Derby, considered the race of races, is known as the Run for the Roses, and it attracts people from all walks of life. Immense crowds flock to the track annually just to be part of the event. Every form of attire can be seen there. It's not uncommon to see men in silk suits with pampered women in chiffon cocktail dresses, designer hats and gloves, diamonds, pearls, and high heels, trying to avoid an unfortunate encounter with horse manure in the stables or paddocks. That was the glamorous part of the crowd, the celebrities.

Then there were the hippies sporting a fashion that was all their own for the '70s: torn jeans with leather patches, tie-dyed T-shirts, peasant tops, miniskirts, beaded hiphugger belts, go-go boots, braids, long hairdos and muttonchops. They were the *in* part of the multitude, lying on blankets across the luxuriant infield grass, picnic lunches beside them. They were the peace-seeking side of the crowd, proclaiming their "make love, not war" and "flower power" mottos throughout the Vietnam era.

A vast array of food scents drifted through the air, from garlic-sautéed lobster tail emanating from the posh restaurants, to flame-broiled hamburgers basted in barbecue sauce over outdoor grills. No matter the lifestyle, all found their niche and enjoyed their time at the track that day.

Only hours prior to post time, Nack stood in the jockeys' room with Turcotte discussing his chances in the Derby after the fiasco of the Wood. Nack's newspaper already knew his pick for the Derby, and he gave Turcotte his honest opinion, "I don't think you'll win, I picked My Gallant and Sham one-two, and you third."[87]

Turcotte confidently looked him in the eye and replied, "I'll tell you something, he'll beat these horses if he runs his race. I don't believe the Wood. I'm telling you. Something was wrong. But he's [Secretariat] O.K. now. That's all I can tell you."[88]

Looking at Turcotte with concern, Nack gave him his best wishes and headed off to the press box.

As music played and people hummed or sang along to *My Old Kentucky Home,* the horses began their post parade, making their way past the excited crowd. All eyes were on the 3-2 favorite, Meadow Stable's Secretariat. Wearing number 1A, he quietly would be in post 10 of the thirteen-horse field. He remained calm under Turcotte's steady hand. Shecky Greene, the third favorite at 6-1, would be on his right and Forego in the number 9 gate to his left.

Wearing number 5 and sent off as the second favorite at 5-2, Sham eagerly trotted into his assigned gate, number 4, beside Warbucks, in number 3. Navajo was about to enter gate 5 when he suddenly hesitated at the last second, tossing his jockey, Weston Soirez, forward in the saddle. The horse balked, trying to avoid the commotion Twice a Prince was causing as gatekeepers tried to snare him in gate 6.

As the other horses stirred, Soirez circled Navajo to try again after the gatekeepers finally captured Twice a Prince. Navajo settled into gate 5 and Our Native entered position 7.

Twice a Prince was washy. His eyes rolled from side to side as he worked himself into a nervous sweat. Angel Santiago, his jockey, frantically tried to keep all four of the horse's restless hooves planted firmly on the ground as the gatekeeper grabbed his bridle.

Suddenly, Twice a Prince rocketed into the air, rearing and almost slamming Santiago's head into the cold steel above while unbalancing the gatekeeper on his precarious perch beside them. The frightened colt's front legs became hung on the gates. He frantically grappled on two legs while struggling to free himself from the solid steel bars. Tiny barbed flaws on the steel cut his legs, increasing his fear. Sharp aluminum shoes on his trapped feet flailed in the air dangerously close to Our Native, ensnared in the gate beside him.

The brief minutes that assistants worked to free Twice a Prince seemed like hours to Don Brumfield, Our Native's jockey, who desperately tried to stay out of harm's way, cornered like a mouse by a cat.

All of the horses were now on edge. Finally Twice a Prince was untangled and the remaining horses ushered into their gates. In the confusion, it seemed that the moment the colt's trapped legs were freed, the buzzer pierced the air. That only sent a new terror through his panic-stricken mind and his tense body jettisoned out of the gate straight up into the air.

To his immediate left, Navajo caught the scent of fear and instantly jolted away from the offensive colt just as Sham sprang into action to clear his gate. Sham's right blinker shielded him from peril for a moment, but it proved too late.

Sham's mouth came down on the swinging gate with an unnerving crunch, receiving full impact from the force of his thrusting hindquarters. Blood spewed from his mouth as two nearly severed teeth embedded themselves in the soft tissue inside his mouth. Thousands of electrified nerves must have exploded through his head like fireworks.

As his startled reflexes recovered from the sharp blow and he struggled to regain balance, his hind hoof clipped the back of his front. He jostled to the right and collided with Navajo breaking free of his gate, nicking that colt's left leg.

In midair, every horse scrambled to regain solid earth. Hooves struck the ground simultaneously, and the race was on. There was no looking back. Angle Light picked up the early lead from the second gate and settled in on the rail. Shecky Greene was breathing down his neck with a cluster of horses right behind. Secretariat got off to a slow start and dropped back to last, just behind Twice a Prince, Navajo, and My Gallant, who were all trying to regain control after bad starts.

Chic Anderson's voice echoed over the loudspeaker as he calmly called the race without knowing the full extent of the starting mayhem.

"They're by the stands for the first time. Shecky Greene is showing the way by a length-and-a-half. Royal and Regal now being moved to the inside, looking for room. Gold Bag is up on the outside, then on the rail it's Angle Light followed by Sham, Our Native, Restless Jet, My Gallant, then Forego. On the outside, it's Navajo followed by Secretariat, Warbucks, and, finally, Twice a Prince."[89]

Without indication, Sham struggled to regain composure as searing pain must have burned at his mouth. Pincay knew something was wrong from the light spatter of blood on his sleeve but couldn't assess the damage. Sham had fired off with the other horses—the intense pain distracting him. It undoubtedly gave him an ominous feeling of danger and false sense of security to stay in the middle of the field, but the sickly-sweet taste of blood on his tongue goaded him on.

Chic continued to call the race. "They're moving on the turn. The leader is Shecky Greene leading by two-and-a-half lengths. Gold Bag is second by a head. Sham now third on the outside by two lengths. Royal and Regal fourth, two lengths, then back to Angle Light in fifth. Secretariat has made a sudden move and is now sixth," Anderson's voice droned across the track.[90]

"They're into the turn and bunching for the lead, with Shecky Greene still the leader by half a length. On the outside and challenging is Sham, and he's now got a head in front. Now Shecky Green responds to the challenge, and those two are heads apart. Royal and Regal is third and holding on. Gold Bag drops back. Secretariat is fourth and moving up on the outside and is now third and moving at the leaders as they come for the head of the stretch," Chic continued.[91]

Pincay felt Sham's urge to take the lead and moved him off the rail. The horse broke to the outside of Shecky Greene coming out of the turn and lunged forward to pass. As Sham's dark shadow came into Shecky Greene's line of vision challenging him and forcing him to respond, that colt obliged. Dubbed the fastest in the Midwest, his courageous rally strove to prove it.

Pincay doubted Shecky Greene could hold that searing pace, but wasn't about to stick around and find out. The jockey knew the fast pace would only help him. He tightened up slightly on the reins and Sham responded instantly, leaping past his rival with ease. Sham's body stretched out as he eagerly sprang with the agility of a wild gazelle. Blood pumped through the rip in his gums as his heart beat faster and faster with the increased momentum of his stride.

As Shecky Greene faltered, Sham drew ahead. Larry Adams, Shecky Greene's jockey, felt the colt's hesitation and reached out with a hard, right-handed whip in an effort to regain lost ground, but Sham had proved his dominance.

Pincay's skin prickled with a cold rush and hair on the back of his neck stood on end as the taste of victory coursed through his veins. His mind sang out. *I know we have this race. Sham is running so easy. I know we are going to win the Kentucky Derby!*

As they moved to the final turn, Chic's excitement also grew, "They're at the head of the stretch, and Sham is the leader. He leads it by a length."[92]

Sham rounds the final turn at Churchill Downs in record time as he leads Secretariat by two-and-a-half lengths heading into the homestretch in the 1973 Kentucky Derby. Courier-Journal and Louisville Times photo; courtesy of California Thoroughbred Breeders Association.

Suddenly, out of nowhere, swinging wide on the turn, Secretariat burst onto the scene. Turcotte smacked Secretariat with a right-handed whip that sent his massive form flying forward like an arrow shot from a bow. His head immediately lowered as his front legs shot out, tipping his hooves to their maximum forward angle. The colt's leading leg punched the track with the determined force of a prizefighter. Powerfully cranking hindquarters threw his body into the air for a moment and recoiled on the arc of flight.

"Secretariat is in the center of the racetrack and driving! Shecky Greene now drops back. Coming on a bit is Forego. Our Native on the outside," Chic's voice was screaming across the track.[93]

In the stands Nack was mesmerized by Secretariat's move and flew out of his seat in the press box, shouting, "Ride him, Ronnie! Ride him!"[94]

Penny stood at a crowded rail with Lucien. Her binoculars hung loosely from her neck. Her left hand seemed to caress the rail as if petting her handsome red horse, while the other was clenched tightly into a fist. A frozen look petrified her otherwise attractive face in a trance.

Lucien stood at her side, head tipped low and lips pursed tightly. All ten fingers were interwoven into a tight ball as his arms rested on the rail.

Neither figure said a word. Neither moved.

Pincay sensed Big Red's ominous presence in their shadow and forged ahead, immediately calling on Sham's energy reserve. He heard the unmistakable pounding of Secretariat's hooves and knew the steed was gaining on them. His left arm flew, bringing the whip down harshly on Sham's side. The quick stinging sensation, coupled with the taste of blood on his tongue, made Sham accelerate with the instinctive fear of having a mountain cat on his back, ripping into his coat with razor-sharp claws.

The two horses forged together down the final yards and past the stands. They charged like bulls, stride for stride in unison, fighting for ground and pulling six lengths away from the field. The screaming crowd went wild!

Sham's burst of speed desperately held his hard-earned advantage, but Secretariat was accelerating. Turcotte raised his left arm, flashing the whip past the colt's line of vision. The colt immediately increased the intensity of his pace, unbelievably flying forward, thrusting violently as he left Sham's side. The pace was so fast he surely was airborne.

Chic's voice boomed out across the grandstand, increasing in tempo, "Now they're in the Stretch. It's Secretariat. Secretariat on the outside to take the lead. Sham holding in second. It's Secretariat moving away. He has it by two-and-a-half. Sham, then on the outside, Our Native."[95]

Pincay and Sham refused to give up and fought to regain control. They pulled away from the rest of the horses by another couple of lengths. The field desperately went to their final drive to try and catch the two. As Sham's hooves drilled, Secretariat flashed past the wire like a beacon on a lighthouse in a stark, black sky.

"At the wire it's going to be Secretariat!" Chic shouted with excitement. "He wins it by two lengths. Sham is second. Our Native third."[96]

Secretariat won the race, charging off with an unheard-of individual final-quarter fraction of 23 seconds. He officially took a two-and-a-half-length victory for the 99th running of the Kentucky Derby, setting a track record of 1:59 2/5 or 1:59.40, and beating the old record of 2:00 minutes

Secretariat at the wire breaking the record for the 1973 Kentucky Derby with Sham a close second. George Featherstone photo; courtesy of California Thoroughbred Breeders Association.

flat set in '64 by the Canadian superhorse, Northern Dancer. The Derby, theoretically, could not be referred to as *"the best two minutes in horse racing"* any more. The crowd was ecstatic.

Turcotte stood in his stirrups to slow the fiery copper colt and tipped his helmet to the crowd, which made the cheering fans roar all the louder.

The look on Penny's face transformed into unabashed elation and she cheered for Ron and Secretariat. Lucien seemed to still be in shock as he absentmindedly shook random hands reaching out to him. He turned to Penny and their eyes locked as they held hands and cheered. Instantly the prerace stress and haunting Wood drained from their minds.

Nack practically flew from the press box to the track and shouted to Turcotte, "What a ride!"[97]

Turcotte shouted back, "What did I tell you, Mr. Bill?"[98]

Sham regally trotted across the track, as Secretariat entered the winner's circle. While victory ceremonies began for Secretariat and his team, Sham stood patiently at the rail.

Governor Wendell Ford of Kentucky presented the five-thousand-dollar gold cup to Penny. When the traditional blanket of hundreds of red roses was ceremoniously placed across Secretariat's withers, he proved to the crowd he had more to spare. He tried to take off with Turcotte and drag Sweat along with them.

Reporters clamored to get pictures. Congratulations were given to Laurin and Turcotte, who continued to pose for cameras. Net to the winner was $155,050. It was also a record purse, an increase of $14,750 over the previous year for Riva Ridge. A record attendance of 134,476 grew to thousands more, when crazed celebrators outside the grounds stormed security, crashing gates and saturating the grounds.

Dehydrated, Turcotte struggled to get a drink at the track drinking water station while reporters mobbed him, shouting for his attention and a statement on the race. He answered quite frankly, "He [Secretariat] did all the running on his own until we challenged Sham.[99]

"Riders like Pincay or Baeza are so cool that they always will have some horse left, so you never know for sure what is going to happen until you challenge them," the jockey said.[100]

Turcotte had been concerned by Sham's ease at claiming the pace and even began to doubt Secretariat's ability to catch him. That's when the jockey used his whip and his horse "really got down to business." Turcotte added, "They were rolling, but I was flying."[101]

Sham's team was heartbroken. Human faces couldn't have looked more shocked or stricken. Viola clung to Sigmund's arm as the group gathered around Pincay and Sham. Each knew both horse and rider gave their all that day. Not one could utter a word, or even knew what to say.

Finally, Pincay managed to speak. He looked up at Pancho with incredulous eyes and said, "The only thing I did wrong was to move a little bit sooner than I would have liked."[102] He couldn't believe what had happened.

"I didn't think anybody would be able to catch him [Sham]. I knew we were going to win."[103] He was still in a state of shock.

They all knew they had an incredible horse, even if he crossed the wire second to Secretariat's furious charge. Sham conquered the field and led Secretariat on a progressively faster drive just to catch him. He forced Big Red into the fastest closing in Derby history, an estimated

23-second fraction. Incredibly, Secretariat never tired; instead, he increased his individual speed from 25 1/5, 24, 23 4/5, 23 2/5, to 23. Unbelievable numbers in a mile-and-a-quarter race, and a record that more than thirty years later would not be duplicated.

Gato and Pancho noticed blood trickling from Sham's mouth as Pincay removed his saddle. Pancho immediately examined the horse and discovered through the pink froth and blood that he had almost lost two teeth.

Second wasn't a bad thing that year. What an honor in such a prestigious race. Sham earned $25,000 and clearly dominated the rest of the field. Even Angle Light had steadily given up in a dull effort, finishing far back in eighth place.

Even though the official time is never really taken for a horse other than the winner, a general rule for handicappers is one length equals one-fifth of a second. Therefore, Sham's crossing the finish line two-and-a-half lengths behind Secretariat made him an unofficial record breaker, too. If Secretariat won in a record time of 1:59.40, then Sham crossed the wire with a record-breaking time of 1:59.90! Sigmund and Viola had the second-fastest horse to ever run the Kentucky Derby, an unofficial record that would remain unbroken into the twenty-first century. The only other horse that ran under 2:00 would be Monarchos at 1:59.97 in 2001.

Through the decades hundreds of Derby hopefuls ran in the Derby: crowd pleasers the likes of Barbaro (2:02.36), Smarty Jones (2:04.06), Funny Cide (2:01.19), Unbridled (2:02), Fusaichi Pegasus (2:01.12), Silver Charm (2:02.44), Sunday Silence (2:05), Spectacular Bid (2:02.40), Charismatic (2:03.29), and more. Even the past and future Triple Crown winners couldn't beat Sham's Derby: Sir Barton (2:09.80), Gallant Fox (2:07.60), Omaha (2:05), War Admiral (2:03.20), Whirlaway (2:01.40), Count Fleet (2:04), Assault (2:06.60), Citation (2:05.40), Seattle Slew (2:02.20) and Affirmed (2:01.20).

Much later, Pancho told newsmen, "My horse ran a perfect race. They both did, him and Secretariat. He had to break a record to beat us. He [Sham] did everything we asked. We'll try Secretariat again."[104]

While Pancho answered the reporters' questions, Sham's crew still worked to control the relentless bleeding in his mouth. Gato steadied the horse as the vet battled the clotting blood, but the color slowly drained from the groom's face and he succumbed to lightheadedness, falling to his knees. An assistant took over as he was carried off to the nearby tack room to recuperate. It took three-quarters of an hour to cauterize Sham's gums and remove the two teeth.

It was also discovered that Restless Jet, who valiantly finished in fifth place—just out of the money—fractured his right front pastern. That inevitably ended the rest of his sophomore season as he was fitted with a cast.

Twice a Prince was put on stall rest while the cuts he received from the starting gate healed. He would not be going to the Preakness.

Adams had taken Shecky Green to the front at the break, as expected. From there, he rated perfectly. That colt ran a great race.

Edward Bowen of *The Blood Horse* later wrote:

> *Shecky Green, which had cooked his field with six furlongs in 1:09 2/5 a week earlier in the Stepping Stone, went less torridly in the Derby. He clocked six furlongs in 1:11 4/5, as had Riva Ridge in his wire-to-wire act last year.*[105]

"Our Native got upset when Twice a Prince acted up," Brumfield said of his mount. "This was enough to make him harder to settle down, but he did settle down by the turn, and I had no other trouble."[106] Considering circumstances, the jockey believed his horse did well.

Resseguet, Our Native's trainer, shipped his colt home to Chicago but wasn't 100 percent sure he would stay away from the Preakness. It was too early to tell. He wanted to "think it over."[107]

After the race, Lucien told a writer for *The Thoroughbred Record,* "Well, I was mighty nervous going into that first turn. We were last again, and I said to myself, 'God Almighty, don't tell me it's gonna be another one of them!' So, naturally it was really nice when we got down the backside and I saw him start to go by those horses and I said, 'Well he looks awful good now.'"[108]

Penny turned to Lucien as she added her comments, "I think Lucien has done a fantastic job, to withstand the pressure of everything that's been said since the Wood and just keep his cool and do his job and get his horse ready and just stick to that one objective. I think he's marvelous.[109]

"And Ronnie rode him beautifully," she added. "He just kept his horse out of trouble, saved ground on the first turn, and only got into him when they hooked Sham."[110]

Turcotte strutted through the jockey's room puffing on a cigar, boasting, "Still think Bold Ruler can't go a mile and a quarter?"[111]

Upon witnessing Secretariat's furious charge in record time from last to first, other trainers and owners who held their horses from the Derby were undoubtedly reassured that their decision had just cause. *They weren't about to enter the Preakness.*

Arnold Kirkpatrick of *The Thoroughbred Record* summed it up by writing:

> *Sham is a fine individual and would outshine any other field which didn't include Secretariat. There are interesting days ahead.... Racing needs a superstar and now it may have two.*[112]

Secretariat and Sham had definitely whittled down the opposition. Of all the horses that ran in that grueling, fast-paced, record-breaking Kentucky Derby, no horse steadfastly dared challenge Secretariat in the Preakness except one—Sham.

CHAPTER FIFTEEN

Preakness Week, MD
May 1973

As Sham backed down the ramp of the trailer that shuttled him from the Maryland airport to Pimlico racetrack, the green-and-gold colors of his satin blanket shone and sparkled like precious stones under intense light. It was the day after his Derby duel with Secretariat, and he was a shimmering, dark-satin picture of health and stamina. Sham snorted, snaked his neck, and shot his front legs into the air, pawing the sky. To anyone passing, he looked fantastic. His magnificence made Gato regret pulling him back to earth.

"Easy 'der, boy! Let's keep all four o'dem feet on da ground. Ya don't wanna go gettin' yerse'f hurt. Not now. What'd Pancho do ta me 'den? I'd be hogtied. Dat's fo' shuh."

The groom quickly calmed Sham, though that horse's head moved in all directions while his ears played back and forth to catch any new sound. Sham felt so good, it seemed like he was looking for mischief after being cooped up in the airplane and then a cramped trailer.

As they walked toward Barn E, Sham picked up an energetic prance that rippled his muscles. At the receiving barn, he called out with inquisitive neighs to every horse he passed. Gato was exhausted when they arrived at the shed row and finally entered the frisky colt's stall. Relieved, they both settled into their routine.

The front of Sham's mouth was still sensitive but nimble lips quickly gathered up hay as he satisfied his hunger. It would take his mouth time to heal, but that didn't seem to bother him much, and he certainly received plenty of attention to make sure it didn't.

Pimlico racetrack was still being meticulously groomed and pampered in preparation for the Preakness Stakes on May 19. The grounds were always a fertile, verdant hue at that time of year, and when the sun shone, the infield resembled a velvety green carpet spread out in beckoning welcome. The Preakness has forever been argued the most exciting jewel of the Crown.

Traditionally, it began with a week-long party leading up to race day, the *Preakness Celebration*. Hot-air balloons dotted the sky, while parades of beautifully designed floats, huge helium-balloon characters, and firework displays enticed the crowd. The grounds came alive with lacrosse games, dance contests, rock bands and concession stands. The attending crowd's raucous shouts echoed its enjoyment of race-day celebrations as the day wore on. Now a casual atmosphere, years earlier during the days of the Maryland Jockey Club, it featured men and women impeccably costumed in height-of-fashion attire.

The 1870 building at Pimlico was destroyed by fire in June 1966. When rebuilt, a replica of the old clubhouse's cupola was constructed in the winner's circle on the infield. An annual tradition concluding the Preakness is the practice of a painter climbing the cupola to paint its weathervane the colors of the victorious owner's silks.

Another ritual since the 1920s, which grows more popular each year, is of a table in the old clubhouse nicknamed *The Alibi Table*. It's set up early Friday morning for hundreds of people to enjoy breakfast before the race. There, trainers, owners, racing officials, and numerous guests have historically swapped racing stories, giving the table its name.

Silent ghosts of the track repeatedly make their presence known to millions on Preakness day through flashes of the past as equine ears twitch in anticipation of the starting bell. It would be the same for '73—horses rounding the final turn with mouths foaming at the bits as they thundered past.

Rolling back the years, racing fans everywhere would remember great moments at Pimlico. Foremost, the famous 1938 match race where Seabiscuit upset War Admiral in a courageous battle holding the lead to the wire. Another champion, Native Dancer, after interference cost him the 1953 Kentucky Derby by a head, won the Preakness and never lost another race in twenty-two career starts. More recently, in '71, Canonero II stormed the field in 1:54 to set a new track record for the Preakness Stakes.

In the early hours before dawn on the day before the race, Pancho rested his elbows on the stall door and gazed into space. He wasn't focused on anything in particular. A far-off look in his usually keen eye was all anyone who glanced his way saw.

Gato observed him through guarded eyes as he gently polished brass nameplates on the horses' halters. With that one glance, he knew it was far too early to disturb the small measure of peace Pancho found that day.

Stress and pressure hadn't yet settled over the track that morning but the sun would be up in a couple of hours, and racing personnel knew both would descend on all of them shortly. The horses, just served their morning meal, munched contentedly, oblivious to any subliminal evil their human counterparts dreaded.

The clip-clop of aluminum shoes on the hard floor echoed through the shed row of Barn E while a groom led his equine charge down the long aisle to his stall. Sham, always having a strong social nature, nickered as the colt entered the stall next to his.

Pancho's eyes were disrupted from their trance as they glanced up to meet Sham's gaze. His horse was in peak condition, other than a slight indication of a kidney problem. Sham held a glow that radiated from his body through glimmering dapples and bright sparkling eyes. Pancho instructed staff to bring only bottled water as a deterrent to any chance of upsetting the colt's kidneys before the race.

Methodically, Pancho lifted the water bucket from the floor and fumbled with the stall door's latch. As his fingers worked the latch, he became lost in thought for a second time.

Sham was doing so well that Pancho didn't want to risk any hindrance to his fitness, not when his main competition was also at his peak. Just six days earlier, Secretariat worked five furlongs in 57 2/5 seconds, pulling up at the end of the sixth in 1:10. That was a good workout, but Pancho immediately negated that thought. He firmly believed in his fine colt, remembering that the following day, Sham ran five furlongs in 58 2/5 seconds, pulling up in 1:10 4/5 for six.

As he pondered the Derby again, his previous thoughts returned. *Boy, we really had that one until Secretariat flew down the final quarter like a demon possessed and snatched the race right out from under us. What strategy will work this time? Secretariat swings wide on his turns. Pimlico has tight turns. He typically breaks last, then methodically picks apart the field like swatting flies.*

This race is one-sixteenth of a mile shorter than the Derby. If Sham stays in front and on the rail, when Secretariat makes his move, Sham will have saved enough energy coming into that tight final turn. The horse will cooperate with whatever task we give him, and Pincay, he knows how to close in the stretch. With Secretariat swinging wide, we will have the advantage.

The trainer walked through Sham's stall and stopped at the water bucket hanging on the wall. Lifting the old bucket with one hand, he settled the other in place. Sham's nose found it. After playfully swishing his lips on the surface of the water, he greedily sucked the cool fluid through pursed lips, quenching his thirst and soothing his swollen gums.

Leaving the stall as quietly as he'd entered, Pancho settled into his chair surrounded by the stable's traditional maroon theatrical cords strung just outside the stall. He wanted no distractions and suddenly shouted orders that Sham was to have complete, undisturbed rest.

With that, Gato quickly entered the colt's stall and "toweled off a trickle of moisture from Sham's nostrils as he coaxed the horse to the back of his stall, where Sham remained through most of the morning."[113]

Pancho stared at the wall ahead through rakes, shovels and numerous wheelbarrows tipped up against it as if they were transparent. Cupped hands cradled his head, while his elbows rested on his knees. For the last time that morning, he was again in a trance, lost to thought. Was his confidence dwindling?

Penny, Laurin and Turcotte seemed relaxed while enjoying breakfast at The Alibi Table shortly after Secretariat's morning workout. Ed Bowen, of *The Blood Horse,* met up with them and struck up a conversation.

"Why had Secretariat gone wide in the final turn of the Derby?"[114]

Turcotte was more than happy to explain Secretariat's thrill of passing horses on the turns. He smiled and answered, "We were going so fast by that time that he just skidded around the turn...in measuring his stride (at 24 feet, 11 inches) this week, they noticed that his stride was even on the turns, too."[115]

Bowen continued, "Had he [Turcotte] hit him more than necessary to win?"[116]

Turcotte quipped, "I hit him just about enough, and not too much."[117] He was proud of his colt's response.

Lucien had been to the Preakness three times before with Amberiod, Jay Ray and Riva Ridge. When asked for his thoughts on that race, he replied, "I have been here three times before without winning. If I don't win tomorrow," Lucien said, "you've lost a customer."[118]

Much later, he admitted to a friend, "I really want to get by this one."[119]

Two other trainers happily added comments. Resseguet joked that Our Native would be "holding on to Secretariat's tail, so we at least will be second,"[120] while Buddy Delp humored that Ecole Etage "would be equipped with 'high-speed roller skates.'"[121]

Ben Cohen, a Pimlico representative, commented on the only scratch in the race, Larry Boyce's, The Lark Twist. "He put the horse in, for $1,000. Then, he found out Our Native was going, and he wanted out. I said, 'When you're in, you're in.' So, he scratched the horse. Then he decided on Friday that he wanted back in, but he already had scratched. So, for $1,000, he got in and then got out."[122]

Later that evening, at the Pimlico dinner, it seemed no one was one-hundred-percent sure of their chances, in all six entries. Secretariat's team had doubts due to Riva's loss the year before. Even though they believed the colt's failure was due to bad weather, Lucien explained his fears, "They go into the turn, and then they hit a little straight, and then another turn. Actually, it is two turns there. The other turn is okay. Last year Riva Ridge lost 10 lengths in that first turn. I may not win tomorrow, but I'll guarantee you I won't lose any 10 lengths in the first turn. And I'll make every one of them run every step of the way."[123]

Lucien wasn't about to fool around this time.

CHAPTER SIXTEEN

The Preakness Stakes, Pimlico, Baltimore, MD
May 19, 1973

As the sun's golden rays swept across the sky, filtered through tree branches and mottled the grass below, thousands of people began arriving at Pimlico racetrack. Parking lots swelled with slow-moving vehicles while the press swarmed shed rows, paddocks, jockey's quarters, and track grounds pursuing news-breaking stories.

Cars sporting "I'm For Sham" and "I'm For Secretariat" bumper stickers continued arriving all day, eventually spilling out onto nearby roads when the parking lots reached capacity. A record crowd of 61,657 fans arrived that day for the most talked-about race in recent years. Public interest in Thoroughbred racing was at a new high, thanks to Secretariat and Sham's battle in the Derby. Arnold Kirkpatrick's latest article in *The Thoroughbred Record* seemed to sum it up well. He wrote:

> *Give a superhorse a superrival, though, and the turnstiles will sing.*[124]

Secretariat remained the favorite at 1-5, with Sham, second, and Our Native, third. Along with the clear blue sky came the promise of a fast track and repeat of Derby day. Would that prove to be a good or bad omen? Only time would tell.

The jockey's room, located just over the finish line, was abuzz with nervous excitement as shiny silks of various stables glimmered on racks set up by the silksman. They were all neatly placed in order of the day's races. Valets worked like army ants busily adding finishing touches to fine leather riding boots and retrieving the silks for their jockeys.

Pancho stood by Sham's stall, waiting for the signal to proceed to the infield. On cue, Sweat and Secretariat left the barn, followed by Our Native and Sham. When Maryland's homebred, Ecole Etage, emerged, track employees shouted to his groom, "Go get 'em, Mo! Go out and get third money."[125]

With that, Mo replied, "Whatchewmean, third?"[126]

Torsion and Deadly Dream joined the line while trainers, owners and grooms nervously exchanged small talk along the way. The ever-present media bounded along beside them, moving from person to person and trying to get last-minute opinions.

Jockeys weighed in while horses were tacked up on the grassy turf course and indoor paddock area.

"Riders up."

After the command echoed over the track, grooms ushered horses to their jockeys as the call to the post trumpeted. The horses entered the track for the post parade and the crowd's nervous buzz droned over the park. The melodic sound of the track's theme song, *Maryland, My Maryland,* began to play. The crowd sang along as they watched the horses pass by.

In the box seats above the jockey's room, Penny and Lucien grew apprehensive with the commotion. Not far away, Seth's eyes were on Sham and Secretariat. He admiringly thought the two "looked like a picture," while admitting "[I am] not as nervous as I was before the Derby."[127]

When Secretariat appeared, cheers shook the rafters and shouts of encouragement reverberated across the track. The horses, sensing the excitement in the air, picked up the pace. Sham, Deadly Dream and Secretariat entered the first three gates, then Our Native, Torsion and Ecole Etage followed. All horses were in place. Eager to be free, the horses impatiently tossed their heads, fussing at the gates.

When the buzzer sounded, Secretariat broke clean while Sham unsteadily broke to the outside and bumped Deadly Dream. That colt stumbled slightly but immediately recovered and lunged ahead with Ecole Etage and Torsion, as Sham and Secretariat dropped back.

"On the early lead, that's Deadly Dream on the outside, Ecole Etage, then it's also Torsion on the outside."[128] Chic Anderson's voice echoed over the grounds, sending a chill of excitement through every fan.

Pincay was on edge. Something seemed very wrong. *What was it?* He braced himself, not moving, concentrating all his senses on Sham's way of going. *There it is again,* he thought. *Is it in the takeoff, flight, or landing?* He couldn't tell for sure, but Sham wasn't running freely. Something in the horse's stride was definitely different.

"They're coming by us. It's Ecole Etage getting it, and he's still moving away, about two-and-a-half as they pass the stands. Settling into second is Torsion. Sham has a good position third on the rail. It's another three lengths back to Deadly Dream, then Our Native, and Secretariat is last, again, as they move into the first turn."[129]

Suddenly, Sham lost his footing being crowded by Torsion's pulling ahead at the same time as Deadly Dream faded back. Pincay's heart skipped a beat as Sham slammed into the rail with a painful blow to his left shoulder that almost knocked Pincay off his back! They recovered quickly but lost their chance at second as Torsion angled in. Pincay hugged the rail to steady his horse. The leader, Ecole Etage, seemed to be slowing the pace as he prepared for that dreaded first turn.

"They're into the turn. Ecole Etage has it by two lengths, Torsion second by a length, and then Sham, third," Chic's voice droned.[130]

Turcotte's eyes were riveted on the horses in front as he started formulating a plan from the back of the field. He saw the horses begin to bunch up. *What's this?* he wondered. *They're slowing down, not speeding up! I'm not about to slow down if that's what they think I'll be forced to do. Lucien said to "ride my own race," and that's what I intend to do!* The jockey glanced to the outside and tipped the right rein.

As if Secretariat understood Turcotte's unspoken intentions, he took off! Lifting his front legs high over the heels of Our Native and Deadly Dream, he leaped to the right, going three wide as his determined head thrust outward.

In the box seats, Lucien blanched as he remembered his words at the celebration party. He vowed they wouldn't fall behind there, and here was his horse attempting to loop out—on that turn!

Nack's face emulated Lucien's as he watched from the press box. He, too, thought, "It had been considered suicidal to take the first bend too fast, but Secretariat sprinted full-bore around it!"[131]

Suddenly, Chic Anderson's excited voice increased in tempo. "Sham is under an easy hold right now, but here comes Secretariat! He's moving fast, and he's going to the outside! He's going for the lead, and it's *right now* he's looking for it! Ronnie Turcotte sends him alongside Ecole Etage."[132]

As if living a nightmare, Pincay glanced to the right to glimpse Secretariat storming past, his flashing copper hide like a flaming red gust of wind. The horse almost seemed to *grin* as he blew by.

Pincay had no idea that Secretariat would make his move so soon. Who would have thought the horse would try to drive from last place to first there? On *that* turn? It was unfathomable!

"Here we have it. Ecole Etage is the leader, but Secretariat is right alongside, then still farther back is Sham, now going to the outside in third."[133]

Feeling Sham had thoroughly regained his balance, Pincay momentarily blocked that worry from his mind. With a determined tug and a shift of weight, the jockey effortlessly moved more than one thousand pounds of equine power to the outside. Sham easily passed Torsion and was closing, just one length behind Ecole Etage.

There wasn't time to plan. Secretariat had the lead. The chase was on but Pincay remained dumbfounded. Muddled thoughts spun through his mind. *I don't believe it. This is unheard of. Even if I catch up with him, will my horse be able to hold that pace all the way to the wire? Will Secretariat? He's flying! I can't let him get away.*

Viola, Sigmund and Pancho watched through binoculars from their vantage point in the box seats. They also panicked as they sat transfixed in silence. Without a doubt, they weren't the only ones feeling that uneasy sense of trepidation. A quick rush of adrenaline coursed through Sigmund's veins as he continued to watch Pincay and Sham pursue the red horse.

In the first quarter-mile and through that unbelievable first turn, Secretariat had soared to first. Pincay knew he must stay close if he wanted any chance of overtaking him in the final furlong. He hardened his resolve.

"Now it's Secretariat the leader by one-and-a-half, with Sham moving into second, and it looks like Ecole Etage is dropping back in third. Coming on in fourth is Our Native, and he's pretty close. Torsion fifth, and a trailer way back is Deadly Dream."[134]

Sham's sleek frame stealthily moved in the wake of his rival. The horse summoned reserve strength as long legs reached out like switchblades released from safety catches. He blindly shot past Our Native and Ecole Etage as his eyes appeared glued to the glistening copper apparition ahead.

"We're moving down the backstretch. Secretariat holding it by a length-and-a-half. Here comes Sham second on the outside now! They're on the turn, and here's the race, folks. Secretariat trying to hold it, and Sham driving to get him. These two are beginning to open a few lengths as Our Native settles in third, and he has about three lengths on Ecole Etage."[135]

No matter how quickly Sham moved, Secretariat seemed to sense his gain and automatically compensated. That horse's powerful muscles undulated in perfect rhythm, mechanically moving on their own accord without effort.

"Head of the stretch. Secretariat two-and-a-half, Sham under a strong left-handed whip, and he's making his run now, but it's still Secretariat holding on!"[136]

The two horses rounded the turn for home. When the fans saw them battling together, they went wild. People on the infield scrambled to see them for the miniscule fraction of a second that they passed. With sheer mania overtaking common sense, fans jumped the inner fence and surged past security toward the rail, screaming, waving, and reaching for the horses as they neared.

Startled, Turcotte yanked Secretariat's head to the right to shield his view of the impending riot, but Secretariat clamped down on his bit. He didn't seem to notice, or care, and his powerful strides continued to pummel the earth. He was on a mission that nothing could stop.

Sham remained true on Secretariat's trail. Pincay went to the whip. He raised his left hand into the air. Sham seemed to anticipate the sting before it contacted his sweating flank and he ferociously dug deeper.

Turcotte heard the punishment and cringed, thinking, "Sham was trying to catch him (Secretariat). Laffit was whipping to beat Hell, and I kept hearing him. I'd 'a hated to be that horse!"[137]

Sham drove steadily faster and faster, his ears flattened against the back of his head. His eyes stung from the spray of dirt as did his flanks from the whip. Determination hounded him like a demonic spirit and he pulled away from the rest of the field—now ten lengths ahead of Our Native. It looked like a match race all over again.

Chic, unable to control himself, screamed into the microphone. "Secretariat by two lengths. Sham driving in second! There's a strong left-handed whip again by Pincay. He goes to it time and time again, but Ronnie Turcotte has his whip put away! Secretariat has them put away! He's beginning to draw away!"[138]

Sham's reserve was used up but he courageously stayed with Secretariat through the final furlong, a mere two lengths behind, as they approached the finish line. Oxygen fired through the exhausted colt's windpipe and lungs, engorging blood vessels and prickling frayed nerves under his skin.

Secretariat continued to pull away.

"It is Secretariat. He's coming to the wire. He wins it by two-and-a-half, almost three!" Chic shouted.[139]

With his head held low and his powerful neck stretched out straight, Secretariat stormed past the wire as the crowd's roar followed him. Two strides later, so did Sham.

Secretariat winning the 1973 Preakness at Pimlico with Sham, once again, a close second. Courtesy of California Thoroughbred Breeders Association.

The beginning of the race *had* been an omen. The final results were the exact margins of the Derby and were miraculously attained by the same horses—in order. Secretariat was first, Sham two-and-a-half lengths back in second, with Our Native eight lengths back in third. Never before in the history of the Preakness or Triple Crown had such a thing happened, nor was it likely to happen again.

In the press box, Nack could hardly contain himself. His head snapped around and he stared at his friend, Clem, whose excitement had cooled to a look of bewilderment. They stared at each other until Clem broke the silence.

"Horses don't do what he did here today. They just don't do that and win!"[140]

Nack knowingly nodded his head in agreement.

However, as victory celebrations began around the track, Frank Robinson shook his head, too. He looked at his stopwatch, then the infield tote board. The time was 1:55, one second slower than the track record set by Canonero II.

Dale Austin of the *Baltimore Sun* later told the story. "A guy named Frank Robinson, who was the clocker for the Daily Racing Form, was saying to some of his friends in the press box that the time was wrong, that he had a much faster time. The form guys got the story first, but right away it got around. I think [Gene] Frenchy Schwartz, who was the chief clocker for the Form, and had come down from New York for the race, had gotten the exact same time as Robinson, 1:53 2/5. That would have given Secretariat a new track record."[141]

To complicate matters further, Maryland racetrack's official timer, E. T. McClean, Jr., claimed he clocked it at 1:54 2/5 from the porch outside the jockey's quarters at the finish line. What should people believe? Though questions arose, Pimlico wanted to stick with 1:55 for the official time—as recorded by the Vis-U-Matic electric timer.

It was a controversial subject, and one that would fester for a long, long time. Journalists caused chaos with stories relaying anyone's version of events they could find.

The unrest forced a hearing in front of the Maryland Racing Commission. There, a recording of that race was simultaneously broadcast on CBS television frame-by-frame against the 1971 race. Purportedly, it proved Secretariat crossed the wire before the record-setting Canonero II. Then the 1973 race was replayed and once more Robinson clocked 1:53 2/5.

"The evidence was plain," said *Daily Racing Form* reporter Marty McGee, years later. "There'd been a mistake in timing Secretariat's race."[142]

Under pressure, Pimlico begrudgingly settled the dispute by acknowledging the hand-recorded time of Maryland's clocker, E. T. McLean, Jr., and the official time of the race was changed to 1:54 2/5. However, *The Daily Racing Form* adamantly publicized its own clocking, *1:53 2/5—New Track Record*, indicating its steadfast disagreement.

As the Secretariat team celebrated in the winner's circle, Turcotte relayed his story to the mob of reporters. "I never asked him to run at all, and he still won by two or three lengths, and I was thinking Belmont all the time I'm coming down the line. I'm saying, don't use him up too much, got another one to go."[143]

At the rail, Pincay told the press, "My horse ran a good race, made a fine try. The other horse is just too much. I kept waiting for Turcotte to hit Secretariat, but he never did. He went by us on the clubhouse turn like he was flying, and I attempted to keep close. I wasn't expecting his move. At the head of the stretch, I thought I might have had a chance, since Secretariat made a big move early, but he wasn't used up and kept going."[144]

"It was far too early for him to have been moved strategically. Ronnie wouldn't have asked him to run that soon in the race. It had to be what the horse wanted to do," Penny said, with a satisfied smile.[145]

"Once I got to the lead there, and I just dropped him on the rail, I just turned his head loose, and he went back to galloping his own self," a very proud Turcotte relayed.[146]

In the winner's circle, Maryland's Governor, Marvin Mandel, presented Penny with the trophy as her brother, Dr. Hollis Chenery, sister Mrs. Margaret Carmichael, Laurin, and Turcotte looked on. The traditional arrangement of the Maryland state flower, consisting of almost 2,000 black-eyed Susans, was draped across Secretariat's withers. He earned another $129,900 along with a reputation as the red-hot favorite for the upcoming Belmont and Triple Crown prospect.

The Woodland Vase trophy sparkled in the light, seeming to congratulate the winner as it had upon its presentation many times before. The 112-year-old twenty pounds of silver hadn't lost any of its charisma over the years and is still considered the most valuable trophy in American sports.

However, there were no special mentions for Sham with second place, no ceremonies at the track, and no swarming fans as he was led away. The horse was essentially forgotten as it passed the screaming crowd still pouring from the stands and cheering from the infield.

The meager two-and-a-half-length winning margins in those first two Triple Crown races had certainly proven that horse's ability to stand at the top with the superhorse. Both horses had the qualities of a champion, but there was room for only one winner. Of the 24,137 registered foals for 1970, Sham had outshone them all, except one.

Even though Sham's winnings were $30,000, his whole team felt a sad sense of dismay as they mechanically performed postrace motions before tackling the long walk back to Barn E.

What a day it had been. Physically draining for Sham as well as mentally draining for the team. When Sigmund and Viola met Pancho at the barn after the race, they stood and looked at Sham with grave concern. Pancho insisted Sham must have lost his momentum early in the race when he hit the inner rail. The owners just couldn't accept that as truth and didn't want to hear it.

Viola was more than a little concerned for Sham's welfare, and for good reason, remembering all too well her other champions that never made it to stud. She turned to Pancho and said, "I'll say one thing,

Secretariat surely was running easily."[147] Viola felt that Sham may have met his match and might be better off in the long run with a change in plans.

It seemed that Pincay agreed with her. He said, "I thought I had a good chance. At the three-eighths pole my horse was running pretty strong, and I hadn't really asked him to run yet, so I thought I had a chance to get him, but it turns out in the stretch that I kept hitting my horse left handed and kept looking at Turcotte and he looks like he never even cocks his whip. My horse ran a powerful race, but he just couldn't gain no ground on the other horse."[148]

After much consternation and very few words, the Sommers consoled themselves with the fact that their fine colt remained sound and fit. They invited everyone to meet in town for dinner that evening, one that would have been an unbelievable celebration under different circumstances.

Pancho adamantly held a different view. He felt his horse met with unfortunate circumstances in all of his last three races. The trainer seemed to cling to a silent plea as he shrugged, *They couldn't make me give up at the end of the quest, robbing me of the chance to prove the horse has more, could they?* Then someone mentioned Sham's collision with the rail again, and hearing that, Pancho abruptly concluded the discussion. "I don't want to make any more excuses—no more excuses," he said.[149]

When the Sommers said their good-byes, turned, and left, Pancho stared at the footprints in the dirt around him for a long time before looking up. He still didn't believe the turn of events and remained devoid of emotion. His mind recounted the race as he stood lost in thought. The situation became almost unreal as it replayed itself like a rerun of the Derby. *Secretariat finished two-and-a-half lengths in front of Sham, who gained eight lengths on Our Native—again! What were the chances of that? Was it fate? Would the Belmont end like that, too?*

Pancho's thoughts whirled, making it almost impossible for him to function. His fingers remained curled around the bridle in his hand, and when he looked up, Gato's eyes met his. The groom had patiently waited at Pancho's side for the bridle without uttering a sound. Finally, Pancho absentmindedly handed it to him, mumbling his thanks in an almost-incoherent voice.

He could hear the revelry at Secretariat's stall, not far away. Champagne glasses clinked as Secretariat was cooled out and tended to. Pancho could hear their small talk. Penny's husband, Jack

Tweedy, quipped, "Hill Prince used to just circle the whole field, too." Then changing the subject, he spoke of Laurin, "We'll take him out and party tonight, but by 1:30 he'll be worrying about what he is going to do Monday—if the horses are fit, if they are okay,"[150] and his voice gradually trailed off, suddenly overshadowed by others.

Turcotte hadn't yet tired of the story. He was so completely amazed with his horse's individuality it couldn't possibly grow old. Every time anyone asked why he moved Secretariat so soon, he once again repeated, "Passing under the wire the first time around, I started to draw behind them horses. As I looked ahead I seen they were all folded up on their horses and were backing it down. I eased him out a little bit so I wouldn't get trapped on the inside. But he just breezed by them. Went by everybody on the first turn, took the lead around the three-quarter pole and the rest was history."[151]

When asked if Secretariat could handle the Belmont, the jockey answered, "He sure seemed like it today."[152]

Dan Farley, a writer for the *Racing Post,* seemed to have a clear perspective of the race. He described how the red horse dealt with Lucien's *dreaded first turn.* "It's that *move* he made around the first turn. It was just shocking to see this horse go from last at about the 7/8ths pole to be on the lead a couple strides into the backstretch. It was a once-in-a-lifetime thing," Farley said in amazement.[153]

There would be no peace for Pancho that night. He heard the buzz of reporters moving through the barn. They'd finally turned to find him and he would be subject to all kinds of questions and scathing remarks. He hardened his resolve to avoid them. He would never cast a shred of doubt on his horse because he still believed in Sham. He never once doubted the colt's mettle, and would continue believing it, no matter what the *whole world* thought.

CHAPTER SEVENTEEN

Belmont Week, NY
June 1973

In the week before the Belmont, Secretariat was showered with attention. He appeared on the June covers of three national magazines—*Time, Newsweek,* and *Sports Illustrated*—each one proclaiming him a national phenomenon. Never before had any personality, human or other, been featured on all three in the same week! They flaunted his prowess with the hopes of establishing a new successor to the Triple Crown. While every magazine and newspaper exhibited Big Red as *a superhorse that could do no wrong*, Laurin and Penny had a hard time controlling their stress levels. Anything was possible!

In an interview with CBS reporters, Penny said, "It was just every day, one more day until race day. I had no idea whether or not he could do it, but I knew that he would be as fit as Lucien could possibly make him."[154] Penny's worst fear was the possibility of disappointing so many people.

Even many years after the race, in an ESPN special presentation, Penny would sum it up perfectly when she referred to that stressful week before the Belmont as "Hell Week."

"We were all under a lot of pressure. You talk about attention—when you're on the cover of three national magazines. It was really Hell Week. It was could I get through every day, and it was really terribly wearing. I wouldn't want to do it again."[155]

Nack was on pins and needles, too. He wouldn't have believed the results of the first two classics if he hadn't witnessed them himself. He called Lucien on Friday before the race and asked, "What is Secretariat going to do for an encore?"[156]

"I think he's going to win," Lucien answered, "by more than he has ever won in his life. I think he'll win by 10."[157] The trainer just knew his horse was ready and wished Nack could understand his gut feeling.

Later that night, Laurin and Turcotte had dinner together and discussed their chances. Both of them were so confident that they were willing to stake their careers on the colt.

"If this horse gets beat, I'm going to hang up my tack," said Turcotte.[158]

"I'm going to quit training if this horse gets beat," Lucien added.[159]

Only five horses were prepared to challenge Big Red in the big race: Sham, Knightly Dawn, My Gallant, Twice a Prince and Pvt. Smiles. The rest were definitely staying away. Trainers wanted their horses to *win*, not place, and with all the hype proclaiming Secretariat a "superhorse," they would rather try their luck elsewhere.

Pancho was devastated that John Campo was even considering running Twice a Prince. He still blamed that horse for Sham's trouble in the Derby, and, perhaps with reason. Campo's colt acted up at the gate again in his next start, finishing fourth in that race. Pancho was furious when Twice a Prince's name appeared on the card.

"They are giving that horse the same consideration as if he were Secretariat," he fumed. "You don't see him on the starters' list—at least not until he races. A horse like that should be sent to Lincoln Downs."[160]

Pvt. Smiles had only just broken his maiden on April 17, but in that short period of time seemed to prove himself worthy. That horse had charged from ninth place in the prestigious Jersey Derby to cross the wire a mere nose behind Knightly Dawn. The C. V. Whitney colt certainly seemed to be improving, and quickly, but was he ready for Secretariat?

My Gallant had bested older horses in a recent allowance and seemed to be well rested. However, considering the opposition, Goldfine confessed he thought it "a little like going after an elephant with a BB gun."[161]

An article by Kirkpatrick in *The Thoroughbred Record* read:

> *Like most superior athletes, Secretariat is a great crowd pleaser. As mentioned before he gives off an aura of crackling electric energy which seems ready at a moment's notice to transform him into a bolt of lightning streaking down the race track. His size, his stature, his exceptional conformation, his color, which is a sort of dark golden chestnut in the sunlight and a deep red chestnut in the shade, and his seeming disdain for everything that surrounds him, combine to give any onlooker the feeling that he is in the presence of something that is a little more than mortal.*[162]

The article quoted Penny as saying, "I am in absolute awe of him. His size, his good looks, his astounding speed—he must be frightening to other horses."[163]

Nack wrote his own comments about the magical equine flaunting Secretariat as a "cultural phenomenon."[164]

Pancho scattered the magazines across the desk. He was disgusted with the media's ranting and raving but realized he couldn't change the past. He had to focus on the immediate future if he wanted Sham to achieve his due recognition. There were many Triple Crown upsets in past years because of the Belmont and he still believed Sham could win.

He wanted to run Knightly Dawn in the Belmont but was undecided. That horse had recently won $131,200 in the Jersey Derby as the 7.2-1 favorite—on a rain-soaked track—beating Pvt. Smiles, Our Native, Warbucks, and Step Nicely. He was ready to go and certainly proved his ability to enter the Belmont.

Pancho formulated a plan. *If the race needed a speed horse, Knightly Dawn would run, otherwise, he'd be scratched. Knightly Dawn would go straight to the lead with Sham right behind so that slow horses couldn't hang him up. Secretariat will trail the field, but he won't surprise us this time. Not when Pincay is already out in front. Pincay will stay right with him all the way.*

Just before race day, Pancho scratched Knightly Dawn. Now only two questions remained. *How would Secretariat fare with the extra quarter-mile?* It was dubbed the Test of Champions for a reason. *Would Sham get his revenge in the Belmont?*

Pancho had it all wrapped up. *This will be the race where we find out who can go the distance and all questions will be answered once and for all!*

PART THREE

CHAPTER EIGHTEEN

Upshot — The Belmont Stakes Race
June 9, 1973

Sham's flanks began to lather, and sweat stained the beautiful raven coat on his neck and chest. Veins in his body visibly stood out as his chest heaved and nostrils flared, while blood pounded through him from head to tail.

The two horses sped together eye-to-eye, neither forfeiting an inch. Suspicions tormented their jockeys, eerily expressed in

Eddie Arcaro's words voiced years earlier, "No horse—I don't care who or how good he is—likes going head to head, eyeball to eyeball, with another. That kind of competition can gall the spirit, rub the horse the wrong way. You've got to attack early, gun 'em right from the start. One or the other—maybe both—will crack."[165]

Secretariat was at his peak and seemed to know it. Fully invigorated by Sham's challenge, he feigned interest in the combat and began to pull away.

Turcotte didn't flinch.

Pincay urged his thrashing mount on, remembering his promise to Pancho and feeling as if the colt had more to give.

Sham fought to oblige, but his heart appeared to break from fear of impending doom and the dark colt faltered as his rider asked for more. Sham desperately struggled to hold on to the figure pulling away as they approached the three-quarter-mile pole.

Chic Anderson's voice echoed across the track. "They continue down the backstretch and that's Secretariat now taking the lead. He's got it by about a length-and-a-half. Still Sham. Ten lengths back, My Gallant and Twice a Prince. They're moving on the turn now. For the turn it's Secretariat. It looks like he's opening. The lead is increasing—make that three, three-and-a-half. He's moving into the turn. Secretariat holding onto a large lead. Sham is second and then it's a long way back to My Gallant and Twice a Prince."[166]

Chic's voice increased in tempo and volume as his excitement grew. "They're on the turn and Secretariat is blazing along. The first three-quarters of a mile in 1:09 and 4/5ths!"[167]

Pincay's stubbornness began to soften as Sham's energy waned like a receding wave. His horse's body was helplessly drawn along in Secretariat's wake like a fish caught on a trolling line. The jockey knew Sham was fading as they reached the far turn. No other horse could possibly keep up with that record-setting pace. It just wasn't possible!

Trailing jockeys noticed Sham's wavering stride and instantly understood his dilemma. With the wind whipping their faces, they barked claims on second place, continuing to charge side-by-side like a pack of wolves targeting their prey.

Turcotte would tell reporters after the race, "I thought maybe he [Pincay] was going to take back and then run at me, and I went off there, real suddenly by two lengths. I looked back to see what he was doing, and then I knew I didn't have to worry about Sham anymore."[168] He added, "After three-quarters, I do not know what happened to Sham. All I can figure is that the 9 1/5 [furlongs] must have cooked him, because he suddenly just stopped...Yes, I knew we were going fast, but my horse was running so easily, I was not afraid. I never pushed him—he was just running on his own."[169]

Secretariat quickly opened seven lengths on Sham racing for the mile. Then he was alone. The mighty red horse out in front shone like burnished copper in the sultry afternoon sun. It appeared as if it had set him on fire as he burned away.

Chic screamed the race call as he couldn't believe what his eyes witnessed. "Secretariat is *widening* now. *He is moving like a tremendous machine!* Secretariat by twelve! Secretariat by fourteen lengths on the turn! Sham is dropping back. It looks like they'll catch him today as My Gallant and Twice a Prince are both coming up to him now. *But Secretariat is all alone*; he's out there almost a sixteenth of a mile from the rest of the horses. *Secretariat is in a position that seems impossible to catch!*"[170]

Pincay eased up on Sham, knowing they lost their chance and wanting to relieve the tremendous pressure on his determined mount. The other horses gained on them.

Secretariat continued ripping away furlongs in record time as Turcotte perched motionlessly above his back, riding but not moving.

In a state of shocked disbelief, Nack squirmed in his seat. Terrified, he began to wonder if Turcotte was still in control. He mumbled to himself, "What is he thinking about? *Has he lost his mind?*"[171]

Pincay and Sham floundered helplessly as Secretariat effortlessly gained ground in front of him. That horse drew farther and farther ahead while they helplessly faded farther and farther back, losing their hard-earned lead over the rest of the field. They struggled to remain in second place but couldn't hold ground after the duel. Sham dramatically fell another four lengths behind as My Gallant and Twice a Prince ardently began to compete for second.

"Secretariat leads this field by eighteen lengths. And now Twice a Prince has taken second and My Gallant has moved back into third. They're in the stretch. Secretariat has opened a twenty-two-length lead. *He is going to be the Triple Crown winner.*"[172]

Lucien and Penny were mesmerized. They couldn't look away for a second. Penny heard Lucien say, "Oh my God, Ronnie, just don't fall off! *Don't fall off!*"[173]

Every muscle, tendon, and bone in Sham's body trembled. Pincay knew his horse continued running on sheer will alone with an exhausted body that no longer felt thrusting legs punch the ground. As a final insult to that horse's injured ego, he was in last place behind Pvt. Smiles—six lengths behind Twice a Prince and My Gallant. Pincay refused to push his horse to the finish line. His brave mount was destroyed.

The other horses had saved energy for the final run down the stretch yet they could only compete for second because Secretariat reigned supreme. The 69,138 people at Belmont Park as well as millions watching on television reveled in the afterglow of his solitary hoofprints on the track.

A thunderous roar was heard for miles as Secretariat continued to pull away, twenty-four lengths ahead of Twice a Prince. He looked fantastic! It seemed he was thoroughly enjoying himself and wanting to prove his dexterity. He opened an incredible twenty-six-length lead and barely broke a sweat as he scorched the track to the wire.

The crowd's insanity shook the stands as his charging form flashed by. It was no longer the horse-and-rider form of Secretariat and Turcotte. Somehow they had vaporized into an almost supernatural blur of fire and ice blazing over the dark earthen track. It was a feat none could imagine. The fabled equine Pegasus couldn't surpass them.

People were jumping, cheering, whistling, shouting, laughing and crying. They waved arms and fists in the air, and tossed race programs to the sky. None could believe what their eyes witnessed.

They gave Secretariat a standing ovation for his performance as he passed the grandstand, now twenty-eight lengths in front and continuing to gain ground. Driving harder and harder, it seemed that he raced the wind down the homestretch for lack of challengers.

"The only place I ever really started riding him was in the last sixteenth or last eighth, when I see the time, and I want to be sure we get the record this time. But this horse really paced himself. He is smart: I think he knew he was going 1 ½ miles," Turcotte's thoughts would later be spoken aloud.[174]

Secretariat's legendary ride in the 1973 Belmont Stakes, setting a record that still stands today and becoming the ninth horse in history to win the Triple Crown. Courtesy of California Thoroughbred Breeders Association.

Chic was amazed at what he saw and quickly guessed at the winning margin. "*Here comes Secretariat to the wire. An unbelievable, an amazing performance! He hits the wire 25 lengths in front.* It's going to be Twice a Prince second, My Gallant third, Pvt. Smiles fourth, and Sham, who had it today, drops back to fifth."[175]

Turcotte glanced over to check his fractions on the infield teletimer and knew they had the Belmont record. Instinctively he turned his head and looked back at the field in total disbelief. *It was unheard of!* Stretched out in full stride to cross the finish line like a flashing bullet, Secretariat made history with a record time of 2:24 flat and an actual margin of thirty-one lengths.

The superhorse broke both the Belmont track, and stakes, record of 2:26 3/5 set by Gallant Man in '57 by 2 3/5 seconds for the one-and-a-half mile race, but it wasn't only the fastest race at that track. It was the fastest one-and-a-half-mile dirt race ever recorded in America, the record of 2:26 1/5 having been set in '64 by Going Abroad. He was two seconds, or just over eleven lengths, faster than the world record. A record the horse would hold into the twenty-first century.

"An amazing, unbelievable performance by this miracle horse. *And look at Mrs. Tweedy! She's having the time of her life.* She and Lucien Laurin who own this most magnificent animal who has today run the most sensational Belmont Stakes in the history of this race. Secretariat has accomplished the unbelievable task of breaking the mile-and-a-half record by 2 and 3/5 seconds. That is a record that may stand forever. The time of this race 2:24! Almost unbelievable!"[176] Chic's voice was hoarse from his uncontained excitement.

Big Red unofficially broke another world record as Turcotte pulled him up. Later, Hatton captured the feat in his column: "Secretariat pulled up the mile-and-five-furlongs in 2:37 1/5 which would have shattered that record held by Swaps, by 4/5[ths] of a second."[177] Ron Flatter also quoted Hatton as saying, "His [Secretariat's] only point of reference is himself."[178]

Heywood Hale Broun, a respected CBS commentator, said, "Every now and then some athlete is touched for a moment with a kind of higher level of greatness which they may never achieve again, but at that moment, they were more than life allows."[179]

Secretariat raced his way to superhorse stardom, while Sham staggered home in defeat. No other horse had ever disposed of Sham that quickly, thoroughly, and efficiently, and his competitive spirit appeared quelled. Witnesses to that race agreed that the talented dark bay horse could—and would—never be the same.

CHAPTER NINETEEN

After the Belmont
June 1973

As Sham was shuttled off the track, Chic said, "And there goes Sham. I don't think he'll ask for a rematch."[180]

If Sham could've answered, he most likely would have replied, *Ain't that the truth.* The horse looked exhausted. His mind and body had been severely tested. Even the other horses that hadn't joined in on the early speed duel with Secretariat were exhausted. The only lucky one that day was Knightly Dawn as he was scratched. It was a race no horse wanted to be part of. Not against the superhorse that captured all three classics in record time!

Secretariat strutted to the winner's circle, his proud bearing delivering him like a king receiving his shining crown and throne. The throng of the still-cheering crowd pulsated with a thundering echo through the park, reverberating into nearby city blocks. He was an incredible athlete. Some felt he did it for the thrill of knowing he could. It was the ground-breaking landmark that set him apart from the rest and proved his greatness to the world.

Chic's words continued to praise the copper colt and issue sympathetic statements of remorse for the losers. It wasn't much of a day for the second- and third-place horses as they left the track, unintentionally overlooked, while all eyes were on the winner.

The crowd realized that a miraculous feat in history was achieved that day. None could believe they were witness to it, but all knew they would never see that again.

Crazed reporters worried they wouldn't be the one to get the best picture, best story, best follow-up statement from owners, trainers, and jockeys—ultimately, the best scoop. Their press credentials afforded them entry to the jockey's quarters, stables, and paddocks, where the general public was not permitted. They swarmed everywhere hoping to get one last story.

Flashbulbs popped, questions soared, and microphones bobbed as the feelings of individual participants involved in the race slowly surfaced.

After Governor Nelson Rockefeller of New York presented the silver Belmont trophy to Penny, he also gave her the Thoroughbred Racing Association's Triple Crown trophy that had been presented just eight times before. The traditional blanket of hundreds of white carnations crowned Secretariat's withers. Lucien and Ron beamed with pride upon receiving their individual trophies, smiling for the cameras at every turn.

When Secretariat finally headed off the track, the crowd slowly began to get a grip. It was difficult coming down from such an incredible high. Eventually the thrill of the moment subsided into a warm, elated feeling of euphoria.

Later, recaps of the race were played for Turcotte on track monitors.

"He's just the complete horse," Turcotte beamed. "I let him run a bit out of the gate to get a position to the first turn. Once he got inside of Sham, he wasn't about to give anything away. He drew off on his own down the backstretch."[181]

The jockey admitted he hadn't taken Secretariat to the front at the break intentionally. It seemed the horse formed his own plan as he battled Sham through the first half-mile, covering the first quarter in 23 2/5 and the next in 22 3/5. After Sham's speed challenge, Secretariat's searing pace was faster than most horses went in a frenzied, all-out, last-ditched effort.

When Turcotte was asked if he did anything differently for that race, he believed it could be attributed to a longer warm-up than he gave before the Preakness or the Derby. He knew that they had to beat Sham whose intense desire would take him three-quarters of a mile in 1:09 anytime. The rider felt if they could get past Sham, the race would be over, and it was.

"When you're out alone like that," Turcotte summed up his thoughts during the race, "you know, you hear the crowd and you hear the announcer, and I kept hearing him say: 15 lengths, 20 lengths, and finally at the 3/16 pole I just looked back there and said, 'Hey, am I really that far in front?' After that, I couldn't hear anybody, and he [Secretariat] was, and when I got by the 8 pole I said, 'Pal, just don't fall down now.'"[182]

"Secretariat is a superhorse," Braulio Baeza said. "You can expect him to do more things better than any other horse."[183] He took second place on Twice a Prince and knew that losing by thirty-one lengths to

Secretariat was still something to be proud of, after coming in twelfth in the field of thirteen in the Derby.

"The winner, when he and Sham hooked up around the clubhouse turn, I thought I might have a shot to come on and get them both," Angel Cordero, Jr., My Gallant's jockey, said. "That feeling lasted only until Secretariat put Sham away and went off about his business. He is the best."[184] Even though My Gallant finished ninth in the Derby and third in the Belmont, he led from start to finish in a race just nine days earlier. That was the factor that made his owner, trainer, and jockey believe the horse had a good chance at the Belmont.

"How do I feel?" Laurin repeated the question, "Just great. I wondered a bit when I saw those early fractions—wondered if he wasn't going too fast. But I told myself that Ronnie knows the horse, and that made me feel better," he said proudly.[185]

He knew deep down the gut-wrenching terror of watching his horse blazing at that unbelievable pace, worrying to the point of sickness they were going too fast. As he watched them increase their speed through the final mile, he couldn't hide his momentary doubt of Turcotte's sanity, and told reporters, "I kept lookin' every time, 'cause I thought the thing [timer] was broken. It was impossible to run that fast...." Then he added, "How's he gonna' last? He's only half way and he's going that fast! There's no way in the world he can run a mile in 34-and-3. He ran a mile-and-a-quarter in 1:59 flat which would have been a record... nobody broke it yet, never even came close to it...going a mile-and-a-half—that's unbelievable."[186]

Penny was extremely proud of her horse. She later said, "I was afraid when Sham went with him, that this was going to be the time that Sham was going to get his revenge, and a little part of me said 'Go for it, Sham' because I had great respect for Sham and felt really sorry that he happened to have raced the same year as Secretariat, because he was a wonderful horse. But then Sham did draw back and I was just in awe. I couldn't believe that he [Secretariat] was just going on, and I kept hearing in my mind Chic Anderson's call 'Secretariat is moving like a tremendous machine, he's out there all alone.'"[187]

Laffit Pincay, Jr. at the weigh scales. Copyright © Bill Mochon Photography. Used by permission.

Pincay knew the pace had become suicidal at the three-quarter-mile pole and felt something was wrong when Sham let Secretariat pass. Pincay wasn't about to dishearten such an outstandingly brilliant colt by asking for more than he could physically give. It was as if the courageous colt had looked at his rival and said, *Enough is enough. I can't possibly stay with him through another grueling three-quarter-mile stretch*, and so the jockey backed off.

"I was following the trainer's [Martin's] instructions in attempting to go to the front," Pincay told the media. "However, I couldn't get past Secretariat. Sham didn't seem to be the same horse he was in the Kentucky Derby and Preakness."[188]

It would be a long afternoon and evening for all, especially the horses after striving to keep up with Secretariat. Not one of the horses in that race would leave the track untouched by the events, and none of the people who saw it would be untouched, either. Not many of the two-dollar tickets to win placed on the 1-10 favorite would be cashed in at the ticket stand. How could anyone give up such a memento—proof of witnessing *history in the making* for a meager $2.20 payoff?

It had been twenty-five years since the Triple Crown was taken by Citation for Calumet Farm in '48. However, the only other horse in history that came close to winning by such an incredible margin as Secretariat's was Count Fleet, who won the Belmont by twenty-five lengths during his 1943 Triple Crown.

Much later, to the extreme relief of the trainers, the heat of the day subsided and the busy humming of crickets began to fill the night air. The horses had long since finished their evening meal and were contentedly settled in their stalls for the night. The staff blocked the path of any further intrusion. No one could take any more questions. It began to feel like an interrogation to employees who were just trying to do their chores, and the trainers were becoming irritable from all the interruptions.

Pancho couldn't come to grips with how severely Sham had been beaten. It started out exactly the way he wanted, but ended all wrong. The trainer knew in his heart Sham would have been the Triple Crown winner if not for Secretariat.

With that final thought, he refused to give in to defeat and end his colt's career. He would give Sham some well-deserved time off, then gradually bring him back to peak and continue his sophomore campaign elsewhere. The four races Sham was destined to run against Secretariat were over, but Sham's future still looked bright. Pancho knew there would be plenty of time and reason to celebrate Sham's triumphs later.

CHAPTER TWENTY

The Peril of Fate
July 6, 1973

Pincay was concerned about Sham's overall demeanor during and immediately after the Belmont. He thought Sham's very soul had been irreparably damaged. Sham seemed delicate, ready to snap, which was certainly uncharacteristic. Something was bothering the horse. Pancho saw it too, but couldn't explain it. No one could, and in the few weeks since the race, sportswriters voiced their concerns. Arnold Kirkpatrick told his story in *The Thoroughbred Record.*

> *To digress briefly, the one distressing facet of this year's Belmont to me was the damage to Sham's spirit… a horse of great beauty, speed, and heart, who was, far and away, the best of the others of his generation…. Secretariat had broken his heart like a twig, and Sham was fading to finish last, beaten by 42 lengths. Whether he will have the fortitude to return from this trouncing after a layoff, or if his spirit is broken altogether will remain to be seen, but it was indeed a sad thing to see the magnificent Sham come back an ordinary horse.*[189]

Pancho was reluctant to pressure Sham to resume his training program after that grueling race, but he couldn't give the horse too much rest lest he lose the peak conditioning the trainer worked so hard to achieve. He gave Sham four weeks of almost-complete rest, had him examined by the vet, and carefully observed when he went to the track for a workout. He watched for signs of physical or mental breakdown. There weren't any—except that the horse wasn't exactly the same. Pancho was torn. He knew it was too early in the season to take a competent horse like Sham out of competition.

Secretariat's career hadn't slowed. He was in such high demand that racetracks across the nation sent Penny bids for her horse to race at their tracks. Together, she and Lucien formulated a plan. Secretariat would run five more races, and then he and Riva would both retire to stud on

November 15. Penny certainly had her hands full that summer with her two equine champions, though it was Secretariat who stole the show.

"He was so good-looking, had such great presence," that even Penny's other horses seemed envious.[190] Penny would laugh and tell the media how Riva Ridge seemed to sulk and act like he was jealous of Secretariat.

Indeed, the horse's charisma *had* taken over. Just six days earlier, on June 30 at Arlington Park in Chicago, he easily won the mile-and-an-eighth Invitational. The colt ran wire-to-wire in 1:47, missing another track record by just 1/5 of a second, and distancing the field by nine lengths! He spellbound the country. His posters adorned bedroom walls alongside national idols such as Elvis Presley, The Beatles, and, years later, even Farrah Fawcett. He bumped President Nixon, Hollywood celebrities, top music entertainers and leading sports figures from televised nightly news spots.

Invitations from Las Vegas casinos and even *The Sonny & Cher Show* begged the horse's appearance. Photographers, artists, writers, reporters, racing officials and trainers, *literally everyone,* all wanted to get close to the horse. Overwhelmed, she hired a public relations firm, the William Morris Agency, to help manage Secretariat's fame.

Immediately, Penny was thrust under the scrutiny of the public eye and admitted, "I had to get my hair done just to go to the grocery store. People recognized me on the streets," as the superhorse's owner.[191] She told the media, "I respond to the crowd in moments of victory with greater abandon than other members of the clubhouse. I think I do it, though, for myself. I also buy more clothes because I feel I'm on exhibition so much more. My one regret is racing's intrusion of my family life."[192]

Veteran trainer D. Wayne Lukas would later tell a reporter for the *Denver Post* that he couldn't "think anyone has ever done more for racing than Secretariat."[193]

Another famous trainer, Bobby Frankel, would admit he thought Secretariat was "the best horse" ever.[194]

Pancho stewed about all the publicity the red horse had captured since his last race. He still believed it should have been Sham. *Surely Sham was ready to get back into training, wasn't he?* Before the break of day Pancho was at the barn. He knew he couldn't wait forever and needed to get on with it.

At 6:00 a.m., he summoned Gato. "I want you to get Sham ready for a workout. I think he's as ready as he'll ever be. I want to clock 'im. Call me when you're ready," Pancho dictated then left for the barn office.

Soon, Sham stood tacked up and Gato summoned the trainer. As the horse was led out, Pancho gave instructions on what he wanted. With a leg-up, the rider settled familiarly into the well-worn leather saddle on Sham's back. He wondered why Pancho seemed so edgy and tense that morning. The instructions he issued were handed out in military fashion. *What was the big deal?* He rode Sham in plenty of workouts before.

Dawn was breaking. A typical July morning embellished with the sparkle of dew. The moisture would quickly burn off as the sun's hot rays transformed it into a humid, misty haze.

The horse walked down the shed row and stopped at the path's entrance to the paddock. From that vantage point, the colt could see horses negotiating the track.

A strange premonition filled the jockey's mind. Sham's ears pricked forward as if sensing that hesitation, and then flicked back, waiting for a cue. He gave the horse a slight nudge with his calf and Sham enthusiastically stepped into motion. The colt appeared to welcome the cool, fresh air.

Pancho followed them to the track and positioned himself at the rail. A stopwatch was poised in his hand. The second Sham sprang into action, Pancho's thumb hit the button and the stopwatch began ticking. Sham took off as his rider encouraged him to pick up speed. A cloud of churning dirt followed like a swarm of angry bees.

Pancho knew Sham was frustrated with his confinement and would want to run unchecked, so he told the rider to rate him only if he felt hesitation or instability. He hoped, beyond hope, that Sham's spirit was back.

Suddenly the color drained from Pancho's face as he helplessly watched events unfold.

Sham seemed to miss a step coming into the turn, which unbalanced him. His rider heard a sickening crack, like the snap of a stick. Instantly, his body tensed as if preparing for an unseen assault.

The force of well over 3,000 pounds of landing pressure had thrust Sham's right front leg into the ground at an unnatural angle, snapping it like a piece of chalk. His rider paled and desperately tried to pull the horse up, knowing the danger of another step. He stood in the stirrups, leaned back, and pulled hard with successive tugs.

"No, no, *nooooo*! Whoa! Sham, *stop!*" he shouted as he did everything possible to pull the horse up while desperately struggling to stay on.

Sham panicked, undoubtedly sensing his rider's anguish coupled with a searing pain shooting through his splintered bone. His rear legs bounced up into the air and his front legs drilled into the dirt driven by his body's impulsion.

Sham's awkward thrashing movements finally slowed to a nervous jitter. Still holding the reins, the rider sprang to the ground in a desperate attempt to immobilize the horse.

Instantly, Pancho was there with the track ambulance. He was in shock. Stupefied, he quizzed himself: *What happened? Was it a bad step? A soft spot on the track? Or, had the leg weakened from his battle with Secretariat?*

Pancho's body moved while his mind reeled, taking in the scene. Attendants desperately tried to immobilize the leg and save Sham's life. For support, the cannon bone was encased in a temporary splint. The horse was loaded into the ambulance and shuttled to the barn. Alerted to the disaster, Dr. William O. Reed was on his way.

Pancho couldn't force himself to believe the X-rays Dr. Reed showed him. Sham fractured his right front cannon bone.

It was a trauma undoubtedly caused by a twist that popped the bone into two pieces, creating a fault line following an oblique direction of force.

The severity of the fracture would no doubt determine stabilization and chances for successful healing. Infection and circulation issues were additional worries.

The prognosis on Sham's racing career, and his life, was questionable. All Dr. Reed could do was relay the facts. It would be up to the owners to decide an outcome.

"Even if he survives surgery, recovery will be a long, perilous journey. We can attempt it, or he will need to be euthanized."

Pancho didn't know how to tell Sigmund and Viola. They had such high hopes for Sham and would be crushed. He wondered, *Was there a chance after surgery?* No one knew. No one wanted to be the one to shatter hopes and dreams. Pancho was heartbroken. Dealing with similar hardships and accidents over the years, he knew the chances of a horse surviving a fracture were slim.

"Sigmund? It's Pancho."

"Hi, Pancho. It's pretty early in the day for a call from you. What's on your mind? You don't sound too happy."

"No, Sigmund. I'm not. I've got bad news for you and Viola. It's gonna hurt. Sham fractured a front cannon in his workout today," he said matter-of-factly, trying to get it over with as quickly as he could. "The vet's here, and I've seen the X-rays. Not good. He says we have to decide immediately what we want to do."

"Oh, no! How'd it happen?"

"Just one of those things. Nobody knows what happened, exactly. He was out for a gallop, and he broke down on the track. A fluke. I can't believe it myself—and I was there. The vet says we go ahead with surgery or put him down. It's up to you."

"What do you think we should do?" Sigmund asked, growing increasingly alarmed.

"I think he has a good chance to recover because of his determined nature, but I don't see any chance of future racing. Sorry, Sigmund. I can't tell you how sorry I am." The trainer's voice sounded strained. Pancho couldn't stand the thought of Sham never having another chance. It was destroying him.

"Surgery," Sigmund said grimly. "Viola will agree with me. Don't make him wait. Tell the vet to get started immediately. We'll come right away."

Standing nearby, Viola instinctively knew what happened. Her cheeks were already streaked with tears when Sigmund turned to her.

Pancho hung up the phone and quickly relayed the message to the vet. "Surgery. Let's get him back on the van and to the clinic. Fast!"

Dr. Reed performed the two-hour major surgery at his equine facility a few blocks from Belmont. He told journalists, "The operation was apparently a success. The injury will be protected by a cast. We also have some hopes that he may race again."[195]

Just as an earlier Triple Crown favorite, Hoist the Flag, recovered from a fractured rear cannon bone in '71, Sham would, only two years later, be subject to a similar ordeal. Hoist the Flag's life was saved by a surgical technique called internal fixation, whereby a metal device was affixed with screws directly on the cannon bone to stabilize the bone ends. That horse's surgery, the first high-profile one of its kind, was an incredible success and he was able to continue a second career as a successful sire at Claiborne.

Jacques Jenny, a Swiss-born professor of veterinary surgery at the University of Pennsylvania, couldn't save Hoist the Flag's racing career, but he did save the horse's life. Ironically, Jenny didn't get a chance to hear of Hoist the Flag's accomplished career at stud. Sadly, the professor succumbed to cancer in November, not long after. Without his successful breakthrough surgery leading the way, Sham's chances would have been slim.

Sham's surgery proved a success. During the operation, any small bone fragments were meticulously removed, the jagged bone ends secured by a pin in the bone, and displaced tissue repaired. The fractured limb was stabilized with a cast and, after additional antibiotic was administered, left to heal naturally.

Since a horse with a bad limb will be forced to shift extra weight to its three remaining legs, all were protectively padded and wrapped. That offset the unease of the cast limb and ensured prevention of founder or bowed tendons.

Thus, the horse began his inevitable confinement and tried to adjust to his new inactive life while recuperating. The healing process would be carefully inspected as the bone remineralized, and by six months, the bone would show little sign of the surgery or initial fracture.

While Sham healed in the first month after his injury, Dr. Reed continued to monitor his condition and after each examination was impressed with his improvement.

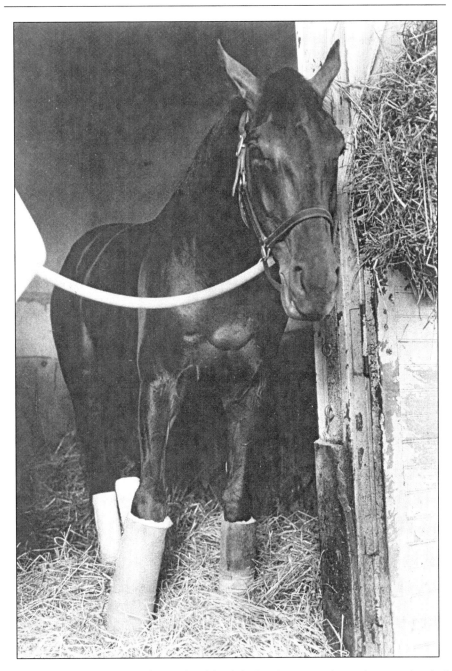

Sham on stall rest after fracturing his right front cannon bone in a workout at Belmont Park. Courtesy of California Thoroughbred Breeders Association.

CHAPTER TWENTY-ONE

A Test of Time

Sham's future was determined for him. He would be forced to retire early with a lifetime total of thirteen starts. Pancho felt he could not ask any more of the courageous colt—not after Sham had come perilously close to losing his life. The trainer would approach the Sommers to see what they intended to do, knowing they would be in agreement.

Sigmund and Viola decided to retire Sham immediately. They concluded that if Sham could no longer prove his worth at the track he would get the chance to prove himself at stud. They contacted Leslie Combs II at Spendthrift Farm to discuss the possibility of syndication. The horse would enter stud at Spendthrift Farm soon after his leg mended at Claiborne. Their courageous colt would race no more.

Spendthrift Farm was one of the nation's top commercial breeding operations. The original 127 acres expanded to nearly 4,000 acres at the farm's peak in the 1960s and 1970s. The owner, Leslie Combs II, had been a prominent, successful salesman at Keeneland and for fifteen consecutive years he topped all sellers at the July yearling sales.

Combs trained and raced many of Spendthrift's high-quality Thoroughbreds under its orange and blue silks, but most of the foals were sold and went on to race for different owners. As time passed, Leslie's health began to falter, so his son, Brownell, became involved in the operation.

On the thirteenth day of July, after much negotiating, Leslie announced that Brownell had completed the syndication of Sham for $2,880,000. All thirty-two shares were valued at $90,000 each, and the Sommers retained three, hoping beyond hope that some day they would once again have another horse as special as Sham. The syndication hinged on confirmed fertility tests, as well as the horse's complete recovery of his broken leg.

In the July 14 issue of *The Racing Calendar,* the same week that Sham was syndicated, the Jockey Club reported the death of War Admiral, the 1937 Triple Crown winner. It also noted that only two Triple Crown winners survived him—Count Fleet and the newest champion, Secretariat.

Then on July 21, *The Thoroughbred Record* announced that Sham's sire, Pretense, would be moved from Claiborne Farm to Spendthrift for the 1974 breeding season forward. It seemed appropriate that his sire should join him at stud. Two days later, Dr. Reed advised Brownell that since Sham was recovering so quickly, he would allow the horse to be moved to Spendthrift the following month.

The orange glow of the sun filtering through the sky seemed to light the surrounding clouds on fire. Post lamps flickered on one-by-one, casting intermittent light on ancient oak trees. Their swaying shadows danced through the twilight and across the lawns. Dampness penetrated the air as the temperature fell.

Sham was jostled awake when the van's tires unexpectedly hit a low spot in the gravel where the pavement met the driveway and the horse's head raised to the window. There were so many new scents on the breeze that seemed to pique Sham's senses.

The vehicle passed the main gate, where two massive statues of eagles on either side stood guard on cement pillars. It entered the intersection known as the Lion's Circle. A statue of a proud, stalking lion watched their approach amongst ornate cement planters sitting high on stone pillars surrounded by hedges.

That circle was one of the cemeteries where, over the years, many famous mares and stallions were buried. From there, the circle branched out in different directions. One drive led to the Green Hills Mansion, another to the breeding facility where the broodmares were stabled, and the last led up to the stallion's quarters.

The most prominent stud at that time was Nashua, who first took up residence at the magnificent farm in '57, when Combs bought him for a then-record price of $1,251,200. Nashua and his loyal groom, Clem Brooks, were a huge tourist attraction in Kentucky, and a life-sized statue of them walking together has forever dominated the cemetery near the stallion barn. The van stopped on the drive outside the facility.

When Sham arrived at the barn, he was met with squeals of interest along with a few of displeasure at his intrusion into the current stallions' domain. His cast all but forgotten, he proudly bobbed down the aisle past resident champions: Nashua, Majestic Prince, Gallant Man, and Raise a Native.

Upon entering his stall, Sham spun circles in the fresh straw. His head lowered and he pawed the deep bedding while he surveyed his new home. As soon as his injury was fully healed, he would join the other stallions at the breeding facility. For the next eighteen years,

Sham would stand stud at Spendthrift. The brave horse's life settled into a peacefully relaxing routine—a royal one, befitting a king.

Secretariat's career went on as planned. In an unfortunate upset at Saratoga racetrack, appropriately nicknamed "The Graveyard of Champions," he was defeated in the Whitney Handicap on August 4. Recovering from a fever, the colt weakened in the stretch and lost the race by a length to Onion. That horse's trainer, Allen Jerkens, would later be nicknamed "The Giant Killer" for his notoriety of defeating champions with unknowns.

The Marlboro Cup followed on September 15, pitting Secretariat against Riva, along with some of the best horses in the country: Key to The Mint, Big Spruce, and Cougar II. With Big Red's loss in the Whitney and Riva's loss just three days earlier, stress levels quickly soared for Penny and Lucien. However, their worries quickly vanished when Secretariat crossed the finish line in 1:45 2/5, three-and-a-half lengths ahead of Riva, setting a new world record. Secretariat also got revenge on Onion who finished twelve lengths behind the red meteor carrying an eight-pound advantage for that race.

Afterwards, Turcotte told reporters, "I believe I got more satisfaction out of winning this race than I did out of the Derby or the Belmont Stakes—or the Preakness—because nobody seemed to believe us after we got beat in the Whitney."[196]

Knowing that Big Red's races were numbered, he also expressed remorse, saying, "I think he's [Secretariat] growing every day. It's just too bad he has to go to stud at the end of the season."[197]

Eddie Maple managed to pilot Riva to the lead but realized they were doomed when Secretariat decided to take over. "I took a peek over my shoulder at the three-sixteenths pole. My horse was running as hard as any horse ever ran but this big red body was coming right at us. It was a helpless feeling," he said.[198]

That day, Secretariat became the youngest Thoroughbred millionaire at $1,132,089, which included his $150,000 earnings from the Marlboro. Riva earned $55,000 by placing second, raising his career earnings to $1,077,027. Always one to support charities, Penny told reporters that she had decided to donate the Meadow's share of the $205,000 purse.

On a sloppy track at Belmont on September 29, Secretariat filled in for his stablemate in the one-and-a-half-mile Woodward Stakes. Another one of Allen Jerken's underdogs, Prove Out, bested him by four-and-a-half lengths, while Secretariat distanced the field by eleven.

His only excuse was lack of preparation. Riva had been prepped for the race, not Secretariat, and when the track turned up wet, Big Red was his replacement.

Coming back just nine days later in the Man o' War at Belmont, his first race on the turf, Secretariat broke first, ran wire-to-wire and beat the Eclipse Award winner and world record turf runner, Tentam, by five lengths. His time was 2:24 4/5, which broke the track record by 3/5 of a second! Tentam distanced the field by another seven-and-a-half lengths.

While Secretariat shattered records, politicians seemed to defy laws. On October 10, Spiro T. Agnew resigned as vice president, later pleading no contest to immoral income tax evasion charges.

Political affairs were deplorable and, Judge John Sirica, presiding on the Watergate case, was contemplating a contempt of court charge against Nixon for his refusal to submit the ill-famed Watergate tapes.

It was a time when newspapers around the globe covered Nixon's scandal. They headlined calls for his resignation after he had the special prosecutor, Archibald Cox, dismissed on October 20. The press quoted politicians expressing some very dire concerns.

In a convention speech at Bal Harbor, Florida, Senator Daniel Inouye said, "I most respectfully call upon the president to place our national interest and welfare above all other concerns and to resign from the office of the presidency."[199]

"One of the most disturbing aspects of the intense constitutional crisis into which the nation has been plunged...," Senator Edward Kennedy stated, "is the evidence now beginning to accumulate that Mr. Cox may have been fired for reasons that originally had nothing to do with the tapes, and that the tapes compromise was a sham, a pretext to fire the special prosecutor because Archibald Cox was too hot on the White House trail."[200]

The future vice president, Gerald Ford, voiced his opinion, saying, "The president had no other choice after Cox—who was, after all, a subordinate—refused to accept the compromise solution to the tapes issue."[201]

Illinois Republican John Anderson gave his prediction, "Impeachment resolutions will be raining down like hailstones."[202]

Robert Drinan, Massachusetts Democrat, added, "I think Nixon will be out by spring."[203]

"The roof is caving in," California Democrat Fortny Stark said. "It won't take many more acts like this before the republic will rise up in arms and Congress will act."[204]

Michigan Democrat John Conyers, Jr. gave his summation with one uneasy comment. "I believe it puts us in the deepest crisis that this country has been in."[205]

It was a political nightmare the populace desperately wanted to escape, but knew not where to turn.

On October 22, *The Toronto Star,* a Canadian newspaper, boasted, "$6 Million Horse Comes Here to Run Last Race."[206] Secretariat had created a diversion from the disgrace of government. The following day, "Superhorse Is Here"[207] headlines appeared below a close-up photograph of the horse walking down a ramp as he exited the plane.

He settled in nicely at Woodbine's Barn 8 amid the buzz of security. Though not accompanied by his own, The Canadian Jockey Club police force assigned nine guards, three per eight-hour shift, to protect "the world's most expensive piece of horseflesh around the clock."[208] No one was taking any chances. Another "bit of special attention given the big red horse," was the unloading ramp, driven up from Kentucky.[209]

"Usually horses are unloaded with an elevator," Richard Bennett, the driver, told the press. "But Mrs. Tweedy prefers this rig. If he [Secretariat] should take a fit while being unloaded, all you have to do is lead him straight down the ramp. With the elevator you have to wait until it stops."[210]

Five days later, on October 28, Secretariat ran his final race, the Canadian International Championship Stakes at Woodbine racetrack in Toronto, Ontario. Woodbine named it *Big Red Day,* and it would be the colt's second turf race. Unleashed publicity spanning two nations compelled Canadians and Americans alike to converge on Woodbine for the big red horse's final race. The Constellation Hotel on Dixon Road advertised a "Special *Secretariat* Sunday Brunch" from 10:00 till 2:00 in their Burgundy Room before the race.

That year the Canadian International seemed to hold many deep meanings, one being the fact that Man o' War, the other *Big Red,* ran his last race in Canada, too. Penny single-handedly tackled an immense amount of distress arranging the race. She did it for her Canadian friends. It was a special tribute for two people who meant the world to her, Laurin and Turcotte. It was also her personal thanks to one of Secretariat's syndicate owners, E. P. Taylor of Windfields Farm.

"I remember asking him [Taylor] to swap the services of one of my sires, Sir Gaylord, with his own Northern Dancer, which he did as a favor to me. This was at a time when you just couldn't get to Northern Dancer. So I sent our best mare, Somethingroyal, to Northern Dancer and from this consideration came Somethingfabulous, which is aptly named."[211]

Penny's horse would run against the Canadian Queen's Plate winner and future Canadian Horse of the Year, Kennedy Road. That colt had been syndicated for $1.5 million and was slated to retire to stud at Spendthrift.

Big Spruce was also trying Secretariat again after finishing third to him in the recent Man o' War race. Allen Jerkens' entry, Triangular, would be the last horse *The Giant Killer* would pit against Secretariat.

Unexpectedly, things began to sour when Turcotte received notice the day before the race that he was suspended for five days due to an October 24 careless riding charge in New York. Fortunately Riva's jockey, Eddie Maple, was available—if only somewhat ready. Maple was extremely nervous after a loss the day before on Riva at the Jockey Club Gold Cup in New York. That race was Riva's final, too.

"He [Riva] didn't seem to be himself," Maple explained to reporters. "He didn't feel quite right to me, almost from the start."[212] He couldn't understand Riva's bad loss, but his horse struggled through most of the race in a tumultuous battle with Secretariat's foil, Prove Out, who won it.

Maple dreaded the thought of both horses going to stud off a loss—with himself the rider. "I felt a certain amount of pressure," Maple said. "I mean I've rode in big races before, but this horse [Secretariat] here, he's a little special. It was his last race and everything. I mean he's the greatest piece of horseflesh I'll ever see, let alone get up on."[213]

Turcotte harbored fears too. He said, "I had only one concern. I figured Kennedy Road would set the early pace and I was afraid Eddie might go head-and-head with him. That would have been a mistake because Kennedy Road is a sprinter, who'd come back to you anyway."[214] Turcotte added, "It wasn't my job to tell Eddie what to do. That's for the trainer to do."[215]

Penny and Laurin would be happy to have it all over with. They were worn out, and now with the wet, cold, near-dusk race time, it was all they could possibly endure. They felt as though they were playing a dangerous game with someone else's priceless possession. Anything could happen in horseracing, and it unnerved them knowing the combined value of the two Meadow champions totaled about $11,000,000—all syndicate members' property!

"Every one [race] is a big one," Lucien explained, "especially this one. Probably the biggest of all because that's his last one, and I'd certainly hate to see him get beat. I'd like to send him home a big winner."[216]

With chins held high, they smiled for the crowd and graciously answered questions. Lucien and Penny put their trust in the big, red horse. *Secretariat wouldn't let everyone down, would he?*

"If he runs like he did the last time," Ed Sweat said before the race, "I don't think there'll be no contest."[217]

It was the eighth race on the card that day, and, through the foggy autumn gloom, Secretariat emerged from a dark tunnel into the brilliant lights on the mutual board.

Laurin began to fret, "Secretariat has never seen lights shining as brightly as that before. You could tell that by the way his ears were twitching."[218]

Secretariat proved the lights hadn't been an issue. He stayed close to the pace set by Kennedy Road through the first half of the race. The copper streak took command after the far turn and from there, no horse could even get close. Tired after running head-and-head with Big Red, Kennedy Road ended up exhausted and finished ninth.

Big Spruce, Golden Don and Presidial finished second, third and fourth. In spite of the deplorable weather conditions, Secretariat missed breaking the track record by just 4/5 of a second. His time was 2:41 4/5, and he finished six-and-a-half lengths ahead of the field.

After the race, Maple told reporters for *The Toronto Star,* "I figured Kennedy Road would be on the front end, like he was, and I kind of kept an eye on him while Secretariat was getting ready. You know. I didn't want Gomez to get too far ahead. But then when Secretariat turned it on, well, it was no contest, was it?"[219]

Avelino Gomez, Kennedy Road's jockey, had but one comment. He said, "I tried to go as far as I could, and then maybe steal it,"[220] but that tactic had proven futile.

Turcotte watched the race from the crowded infield winner's circle and was relieved when he got a glimpse of the horses as they passed. He had been stewing about Eddie's whereabouts, "But when he [Secretariat] went past us, which was with less than a mile to go, I said 'beautiful' Eddie wasn't pushing him at all, just letting him run his own race. I thought he had it won right then, the way he was going."[221]

"I'm so pleased Secretariat went out a winner," said Penny as a smile lit up her beguiling face. "I'm thrilled with the way he ran. He was running on a different type of turf and he handled it perfectly."[222]

John J. Mooney, president of The Ontario Jockey Club, added his comments that day, saying, "I was thoroughly convinced after the

Belmont. There was no question in my mind that this was the greatest horse I'd ever seen, and perhaps the greatest ever."[223]

"In the tradition of champions," sports columnist Jim Coleman wholeheartedly relayed, "Secretariat climaxed his career with a smashing triumph. It was an unforgettable moment. That great crowd's thundering acclaim as Secretariat smashed his way across the finish line in the final race of his career. What more fitting climax could there have been for the most brilliant and successful season in the long history of Canadian horseracing?"[224]

Right up to the hour of 7:00 p.m., fans battled parking lot lineups in Woodbine racetrack's "worst-ever traffic jam, heightened by a deluge after the last race and a rash of home-going accidents," Bob Pennington wrote in *The Toronto Star* the following day.[225]

Secretariat would return home with a total of sixteen wins, three seconds, a third and a fourth from his twenty-one starts. With his final purse of $92,775, he retired the fourth-richest Thoroughbred with a career total of $1,316,808. Kelso held the number one spot at $1,977,896, with Round Table and Buckpasser following.

Penny had mixed feelings about her champions going to stud. She told Pennington, "Ideally I would not have syndicated either Secretariat or Riva Ridge with a deadline. I would have waited until their racing careers were logically finished…This is something I regret. No, I am not disappointed. At least they have allowed us to pay the death duties and retain our breeding farm…. I have faced the fact that I will have to hand him [Secretariat] over. It's very sad and I'm going to miss him terribly."[226]

Later Penny would talk about her horse and the energetic sport of Thoroughbred racing in general. "Secretariat loves to run, and this should be communicated to the world. This is a vital sport, an exciting sport. It's not exploitation of horses. There are horses like Secretariat, who are sound and able, and think running is thrilling. He knows when he wins. He knows when people notice him. It's been a great experience for him, too."[227]

With his return to the United States, Penny and Laurin arranged Secretariat's *final curtain call* for his adoring public. It was a last chance for fans to see the superhorse on a track, this time in the United States. On November 6, at Aqueduct, 33,000 people came to see him off on a midweek, non-racing day. Not many were prepared for the good-bye and the farewell song, "Auld Lang Syne," brought a flood of tears.

"I was unprepared for how badly I'd feel," Penny later admitted, "I've seen the film of it and I was on the edge of tears, other people were crying, 6,000 people came out just to see him gallop up and down the stretch there, and he felt he hadn't done his job.... It was a hard day, but it was a heartwarming day cause so many people came out just to say a personal good-bye to him."[228]

One spectator felt badly in a different sort of way. That individual was Pancho. Nack bumped into him at the paddock that afternoon and made note of his parting words. "I'm just sorry it's not Sham," the despondent trainer uttered as he turned and left shaking his head.[229]

Arriving at Blue Grass Airport in Kentucky on November 11, Penny later remembered the painful separation at the airport as the horse left for stud. "That was sad. I guess I only took the plane ride because I was trying to make it not end. The Claiborne people took him right from the plane, put him in their van, and off he went. It was just terribly hard."[230]

Lawrence Robinson was there to meet the plane along with several hundred other well-wishers. A tower communications employee joked that Secretariat drew a larger crowd than the state governor. Nack was on the plane that day and chuckled when he heard the pilot's reply.

"Well, he's won more races than the Governor," said Dan Neff.[231]

Nack would forever hold a great amount of sentiment in his heart for the copper horse. At the end of the trip, he watched Robinson walk away from the police-escorted van to settle Secretariat in Bold Ruler's stall. As he watched, he recounted precious memories he would later set to paper as the "most exhilarating time of my life."[232]

Secretariat was presented with the 1973 Eclipse Awards for Champion Horse of the Year, and Champion Male Turf Horse. In 1974 he was inducted into the National Museum of Racing's Hall of Fame. A spectacular bronze sculpture of him was placed at Belmont Park. Its inscription reads:

> Secretariat belongs to history, to the romance of the turf, and to the people.

Years later, on October 3, 1989, Nack arrived at Claiborne to interview Seth. The sportswriter couldn't understand the morbid, tear-streaked faces he met that day. As he tiptoed through the building, he met John Sosby who told him that Secretariat had contracted laminitis on Labor Day. The degeneration and inflammation in the horse's feet had quickly been diagnosed and monitored, but to no avail. Nack was devastated when Sosby added that Secretariat had recently taken a turn for the worse, and then panicked when told the horse's time had run out.

"How do you think I feel?" Seth asked him, "Ten thousand people come to this farm every year, and all they want to see is Secretariat. They don't give a hoot about the other studs. You want to know who Secretariat is in human terms? Just imagine the greatest athlete in the world. The greatest. Now make him six foot three, the perfect height. Make him real intelligent and kind. And on top of that, make him the best-lookin' guy ever to come down the pike. He was all those things as a horse. He isn't even a horse anymore. He's a legend. So how do you think I feel?"[233] Seth had tears welling in his eyes.

The next day, Bobby Anderson, Secretariat's groom, led the suffering horse to a van parked outside. To Bobby, it was as though time stood still. The scene was heartrending as the weeping man coaxed the magnificent stallion to follow.

"Come on, Super Red, Big Bum. Attaboy, Red. You can do it. Please, Red, just a little further," Bobby wailed. The man ignored his male ego and begged piteously. His grief was impossible to conceal.

The stallion looked at him. Where once a pair of warm sherry-brown eyes reflected a stoic *look of eagles,* there remained only an eerie, haunting stare. For Bobby, minutes seemed like hours as he anguished over each laborious step the great champion managed, yet the pain wasn't about to stop the horse. Secretariat bore the pain and struggled on.

The farm's vet, Dr. Walter Kaufman, stood awaiting their arrival as if he were a statue carved of ice. While Kaufman prepared the concentrated barbiturate, not one in attendance remained in control of traumatized emotions. There wasn't a dry eye in the group. Secretariat stood bravely, his muscular body only slightly wavering as he searched for relief from the pain.

At 11:45 a.m., Kaufman issued orders to stand back and grabbed hold of the stallion's muscular neck. As quickly and efficiently as a wasp's sting, the needle entered the stallion's jugular vein and Kaufman quickly moved away.

For a moment, the magnificent copper-colored animal stoically stood his ground while a strange, sickly, dizzy-faint feeling undoubtedly consumed his chest and brain. Secretariat's heart failed to beat. Seconds later, his massive body pitched forward, crashing to the ground—never to rise again. His suffering had ended. The stallion was now at peace.

The vehicle immediately pulled down the drive en route to the University of Kentucky for the necropsy. Secretariat revealed the true meaning of heart when it was found that his heart was two-and-a-half-times the normal size of an equine heart. It weighed just over twenty-one pounds—compared to the average horse's eight-and-a-half. In all respects, Secretariat's heart was as awe-inspiring as the stallion himself—unbelievably perfect.

In an ESPN documentary, many years later, Nack voiced his opinion concerning this discovery, "He [Secretariat] had a larger motor and he was able to crack up oxygen and synthesize it faster and more efficiently than any other horse I've ever seen."[234]

Penny added, "He just had a superior power pack and he was showing it to the world. I wonder what he felt? He must have had a sense of accomplishment."[235]

When the oak casket was encased by earth, not far from where his ancestors—Bold Ruler, Nasrullah, and Princequillo—lay, his human counterparts grieved. Through diverse media, the entire populace sympathetically listened to their laments and shared their pain.

"It was a terrible day for all of us," Seth told reporters. "We just couldn't stand to see him suffer."[236]

Sweat had one last parting sentiment for his equine friend, "Thank you, Big Red, for all the things that you have done for me and for the public, the people."[237]

"All I did was went along for the ride," said Turcotte. "You know, he was the most horse. He was so great. He done everything himself so I take no credit for what Secretariat has done...I loved him."[238]

Someone asked Laurin if there would ever be another Secretariat, and he answered, "Not in my time. I'll guarantee you. Not in my time."[239] Laurin also said, "I just think he was the greatest of all horses, bar none."[240]

"People all over the world are missing the horse that represented a wonderful dream," Penny said. "A dream of success and accomplishment....Just something special is gone."[241]

While Sham stood at Spendthrift, time took its toll. Several years after it incorporated in '77, Spendthrift went public. By 1985, Leslie and Brownell Combs sold all their interest in the farm. Brownell moved on to other pursuits, and Leslie passed away in 1990. Spendthrift fell on hard times, and a few years after Leslie's death, the farm filed for bankruptcy.

The once-massive breeding and training facility was sectioned off into two tracts to be sold at auction, along with many of the remaining horses, to try to cover the financial loss. The main mansion and stallion facility were on the smaller tract. The stallion barn, nicknamed the Nashua Motel, stood proudly adorned with huge memorials in honor of the great champions who had, over the years, graced its stables. Majestic Prince, who died in '81, Nashua in '82, Gallant Man and Raise a Native in '88. They all held the honor of being named on those memorial plaques. The once-immense acreage would eventually be whittled down to 636 acres by 1994.

On a bitter cold December night in the late winter of 1992, with snow falling mercilessly from the sky casting a frigid white solitude, Sham was unceremoniously transferred to Walmac International to spend his final days at stud. At twenty-two years old, he certainly felt the test of time as he trudged up the ramp that would lead to the new life awaiting him.

Spendthrift had suffered to endure the hardships of the '80s, and the harsh realities of life had been cast upon man and beast at the struggling farm. Many unfortunate changes had been made as the original farm carried on through those difficult years as best it could. By 1992, Sham's stud fee had dwindled to $3,500 for a live foal.

He received no special recognition. He seemed only as important as a claimer or an also-ran, carelessly discarded by the media when his chance at fame had been quelled on the racetrack in '73. Even though he proved a capable sire by siring forty-seven stakes winners, there was still no true respect given him.

The stallion's humble existence continued to falter after his arrival at Walmac that December and slowly sifted away like sand passing through an hourglass until it was ultimately lost in time and flickered out.

CHAPTER TWENTY-TWO

Walmac International, Lexington, KY
April 3, 1993

In Sham's own naïve aspect of the animal kingdom, he took each day as it came, not worrying whether there would be more. Walmac had proven beautiful, peaceful, and relaxing for the horse over the past three months, and his spacious corral was a welcome spot, especially that morning after a seemingly troublesome night in his stall. Sham had been restless all night, as his dam had been almost twenty-three years earlier in the predawn hours of April 9, 1970, when Sham's little form struggled to burst into the world.

Sham's groom had developed a soft spot for him in the little over three months Sham stood at stud for Walmac. He loved how full of life Sham was, always eager for his morning grain, nickering the instant he heard the feed cart. Sham beckoned his groom with quick, successive nods of his head as if he would reward him for haste.

That morning, the horse seemed different. The groom noticed that Sham was on edge and couldn't seem to relax. The horse's body intermittently twitched uncontrollably as if trying to tell him something.

The sun was warm and inviting. A light breeze drifted through the oak tree in the corral and rustled newly budded leaves on gently swaying branches while it combed through the grass below. After Sham's groom turned him loose in the corral, the horse ambled to his favorite spot near the base of the oak tree.

The groom watched as Sham scanned the horizon to make sure nothing was out of place. Joints in the stallion's legs locked to brace his frame, ears lopped out to the sides, and his eyes closed. Seeing all was well, the groom headed back to the barn and daily chores.

Sham's weary muscles relaxed as his head drooped lower and lower toward the ground until sleep overtook him. There was no indication as to how long the horse slept before he suddenly stirred.

Without warning, his muscles began trembling and twitching uncontrollably, and his eyes sprang wide open, drawing him from deep sleep. The horse was suddenly in a visible sweat caused by nauseating heart palpitations and an abnormal, uncoordinated twitching that left his body shaking. A raw basic instinct prepared him for flight as it brought idle senses to life.

The stallion fought the pressure in his chest as his massive body reared straight up, hooves flailing the sky and pawing the otherwise motionless air. An eerie neigh pierced the silence.

Sham's groom burst through the open barn door. He saw Sham's massive body sliding and falling in slow motion, as if a tide of warm water were engulfing him, effortlessly drawing him along as it slowly cascaded downward and trickled away.

The groom hopped the fence, raced across the paddock to the foot of the oak tree, and knelt beside the horse. He bent down and cradled the horse's head in his arms.

"It can't be," he lamented. "Sham...Sham.... Come on, old boy. Let's git ya up and in'ta yer stall."

He touched the middle of Sham's forehead in a calming gesture. There was no movement. Not a sign of life in that once-proud, energetic body, just a blank, glassy look in his eyes as they stared up to the Heavens. White clouds in the azure sky cast ghostly shadows on the ground around him.

The groom frantically searched for any sign of a pulse, placing three fingers on either side of Sham's face below the cheekbones where an artery ran horizontally across his face. Failing to find any, he gave a last attempt to apply pressure with one hand to the front of Sham's chest, as if willing his heart to revive.

"Oh, Sham, old boy, ya never gave me no warnin'. No time for g'bye...." He didn't want to believe it as he stroked the dried sweat on the dark coat of Sham's proudly crested neck.

Even in death, Sham looked determined and unwilling to give up, his long legs curled as if in the perpetual motion of a proudly rearing stallion challenging an unseen opponent—ready to respond courageously.

Memories reminded the groom of how Sham would twist his body back and forth, extending his neck and twitching his lips, when rubbed with the currycomb. How the horse nuzzled his pocket each morning, looking for a hidden treat, and, after finding it, impatiently pushed him out the door toward the beckoning corral.

He remembered the way Sham pranced toward the breeding pen, his neck tightly arched and his head proudly drawn toward his chest, always driven by a deep male instinct to continue his line.

After a long time, the groom despondently walked into the barn and came out with Sham's stall blanket. He quietly draped it over the horse, turned, and walked down the path to the main office to inform the owners. Sham lay motionless in an abnormally crumpled position in the sand near the gnarled trunk of the oak tree. The earth had already begun to claim his dark form by creating ridges of wind-blown sand around his body.

That night, phones rang informing the syndicate owners of Sham's passing. Viola Sommer, who held a special place in her heart for Sham, sat quietly on the overstuffed linen armchair beside the telephone in her living room. Suddenly, she was deeply saddened by memories of the past and her late husband, Sigmund. Sham brought such joy and excitement into their lives. Fond memories resurfaced after so many years as tears slowly filled her eyes and spilled down her cheeks.

A strange scene played in her mind, slowly at first and then increasing in tempo until it was little more than brief flashes. She imagined Sham flying through a lush, green grassy field as a young foal, kicking up his heels and rearing in playful challenge to his dam as she reached out with a warning nip. The long hours he must have endured while learning to accept the as-yet-unfamiliar demands of his human handlers, and the many workouts where he strove to better himself.

She remembered how he proudly strutted to the winner's circle to claim his prize after an exhilarating race well run. Viola pictured her brave colt's Derby race and the swinging gate that sent him galloping off with the wind as if pursued by a demonic spirit. In her mind, Sham remained a regal picture of a promising young colt in a race against time, leading a field of horses at breakneck speed—only to see a flash of copper at his side, racing neck and neck with him, challenging him, pushing him, then breaking away and leading him. All the while, his courage to win drawing him helplessly along a never-ending path with his lungs bursting and a stabbing pain in his heart.

Viola knew it was the last time his heart would break.

Sham was buried the following morning. It wasn't a grand procession, nor were there acquaintances or fans from his past to see him off. As earth was cast into the grave, landing lightly and settling on Sham's wrapped body, his groom bid him a last farewell.

His final resting place was under the swaying branches of a row of giant oak trees just outside the farm's office, alongside the racehorse Brent's Prince who was buried there years earlier.

Ironically, in only five years, Secretariat's greatest son, Risen Star, would be buried near Sham, seemingly as the superhorse's final peace offering to his courageous dark opponent—*forever*—through eternity.

The simple, pale-gray gravestone read, *Sham, 1970–1993.*

EPILOGUE

Through the years 1973–2003, many great achievements were attained by many of the people involved in Sham's racing life. However, only a few horses survived the era of the superhorse.

To those of us who watched Sham run, bravely challenging Secretariat, his courage will forever be remembered. Sham's brilliant run in the 1973 Kentucky Derby afforded him a place in history and our hearts.

At two, Sham started in only four races, winning one, placing second in two, and third in one. His three-year-old sophomore campaign allowed him only nine starts. Sham's intense, courageous will to succeed in that fateful Belmont Stakes weakened him and ultimately cost him his career—almost his life.

His racing career earnings totaled $204,808. He sired 625 foals, with 70 percent of them that started in races being winners and bringing in total overall earnings of $16,727,862. Some of his famous offspring included such stakes winners as Outlaw's Sham, winning $265,300; Shamgo, winning $348,735; Diabolotain, a champion in Mexico; Safe Play, a stakes winner earning $393,085; Arewehavingfunyet; and Defensive Play. Among Sham's offspring as a broodmare sire were some twenty-five stakes winners. They raced on through the years, trying to achieve success and continue his proud, courageous line.

Recognition for the great racehorse he once was came in the form of a stakes race for three-year-olds at Santa Anita Park. Now held annually on the first Saturday in February, it was named the Sham Stakes in commemoration of the 1973 California track star.

In June 2006, a successful photo exhibit in the McBean Gallery at Saratoga entitled "California Images: The Racing Photography of Bill Mochon" included pictures of the great horse.

Dr. Thomas Swerczek also performed a necropsy on Sham. To his amazement, Sham's heart weighed nineteen pounds, a record in keeping with his career—second-largest heart size to Secretariat's. It beat Key to the Mint's third-place record of sixteen pounds and Phar Lap's heart weight of fourteen.

Sigmund Sommer passed away in 1979, leaving his wife, Viola, to continue their mutual love of the sport of Thoroughbred horse racing. Viola didn't disappoint him. She went on to win the Eclipse Award in

1982 as Outstanding Owner and placed second in 1997 among owners of New York race winners. Some of her stakes winners included Machine to Tower, Cracked Bell, Cold Execution, and Ring of Light. By 2003, Viola still held prestigious ties to the world of horse racing as Trustee Emeritus of the New York Racing Association, Incorporated; Trustee of the National Museum of Racing and the Racing Hall of Fame; and as a member of the Jockey Club.

Frank Martin enjoyed a wonderfully prosperous career while being honored by the New York Turf Writers Association ten times and presented with the Outstanding Trainer award for 1971, 1974, and 1982. Pancho led the nation in purse earnings in 1974, which totaled $2,408,419. His achievements also included New York's Champion Trainer award for 1971, 1973, 1976, 1977, 1978, 1979, and 1981, a total of ten straight New York trainer titles between 1971 and 1982. He was inducted into the Thoroughbred Racing's Hall of Fame in 1981. As of the fall of 2003, he still continued to train racehorses at Belmont Park in his hometown of New York, and his son, Jose, and grandson, Carlos, are also well-known trainers.

Laffit Pincay, Jr., went on to enjoy a hugely successful career and retired in April 2003, after a serious racing injury on March 1. He held a record 9,530 wins, making him the "World's Winningest Jockey" of all time (which remained unbroken until 2006), and he was the first jockey to ever reach the 9,500-win milestone. He and Willie Shoemaker, whose record of 8,833 wins Pincay broke in 1999, were good friends throughout their racing careers. Shoemaker continued to attend Pincay's races even after being confined to a wheelchair after an auto accident in 1991.

Included in Pincay's career achievements are six Eclipse Awards for the years 1971, 1973, 1974, 1979, 1985, and 1999. Pincay won more Eclipse Awards than any other jockey. He's the all-time leader in victories at Hollywood Park, Santa Anita, and Del Mar racetracks, and he won the honorable George Woolf Memorial Award in 1970. There is a statue tribute to him, a large bronze bust, situated between the saddling ring and racetrack at Santa Anita Park. In 1971, he led the nation in victories with a total of 380 in that year alone. He was the Leading Money-Winning Jockey for the years 1970, 1971, 1972, 1973, 1974, 1979, and 1985, and was inducted into the Racing Hall of Fame in 1975, and that year, he and Linda had a son they named Laffit III.

Statue at Santa Anita Park commemorating Laffit Pincay, Jr. as the World's Winningest Jockey and All-Time Leading Jockey at Santa Anita Park. Susan Fletcher, photographer. Used by permission.

In 1984, after eleven unsuccessful attempts, Laffit won the Kentucky Derby. Later he would remember, "In the 1984 Derby I rode Swale. For some reason, I knew that that was probably my last chance to win the Derby. I had a lot of pressure. My wife was very sick at the time. So many things were going wrong, and for me, you know, I wasn't doing that great. When I remember this particular day, I say to God, 'If you can give me a little push then I would really appreciate it. If you can do anything for me, just do it today.'"[242]

His life wasn't always enjoyable and he met with hardship many times. Laffit suffered numerous injuries: a broken back; broken collar bone—twelve or thirteen times; broken ribs—both sides; broken toes, ankle and leg. He continuously struggled with his efforts to control his required jockey's weight in a five-foot-one-inch muscular frame. In December 1984, Linda suffered a ruptured appendix and became very depressed. Laffit endured the tragic loss of his wife on January 21, 1985, when she died of a self-inflicted gunshot wound. For many years his grief held his career in jeopardy, but his extreme willpower eventually brought him back to the top.

Willie Shoemaker, Laffit Pincay, Jr. and Sandy Hawley holding the Santa Anita Handicap trophy in 1976. Copyright © Bill Mochon Photography. Used by permission.

On March 14, 1987, for the first time in Santa Anita history, Pincay rode seven horses to victory on a seven-race card. They were Polly's Ruler, Texas Wild, Traction, Fairway's Girl, Lookingforthebigone, Integra and Bedouin.

He remarried in 1992, and in 1993, he and his lovely second wife, Jeanine, had a son they named Jean-Laffit. Every jockey, past and present, will always admire Pincay's stamina and achievements. All would agree that he rose above and beyond the title of champion jockey. Some of his best mounts included Affirmed, John Henry, Landalucie, Genuine Risk, Susan's Girl, Desert Vixen, Bayakoa, Gamely, Swale, Cougar II, Medaglia d'Oro, Autobiography, and many others including Sham. To many adoring race fans, he became a superjockey. A documentary honoring him entitled *Laffit, All About Winning,* produced by Jim Wilson/Six Furlongs LLC, was released in the summer of 2005.

Claiborne Farm continues to be the home of many of the world's premium Thoroughbreds. True to his father's wishes, Seth Hancock returned to breeding to race, raising and training their own homebred yearlings. Claiborne still holds the leading position of the world's Thoroughbred breeding and training facilities, while many outstanding champions rest in their cemeteries.

There are unforgettable names engraved on the pages of *The Blood Horse*'s Top 100 list of racehorses for the twentieth century, including Secretariat (#2), Bold Ruler (#19), Gallant Fox (#28), Buckpasser (#14), Round Table (#17), Riva Ridge (#57), Ack Ack (#44), Easy Goer (#34), and Damascus (#16), along with such giants as Princequillo, Nasrullah, Nijinksy II, Mr. Prospector, Reviewer, Swale, and Hoist the Flag. Claiborne's champion filly, Ruffian (#35), was buried at Belmont Park racetrack where she tragically ended her unbeaten career. Buried facing the finish line, it remains a legendary story that she is still racing in her final, fateful race, courageously charging toward the wire.

Belmont Park statue of Secretariat commemorating the historical superhorse. Copyright © Tracy Gantz, photographer. Used by permission. Courtesy of California Thoroughbred Breeders Association.

Secretariat will forever be remembered for the numerous records he set, some still standing today. He sired 653 foals, fifty-seven of them being stakes winners, and was given the title of Leading Broodmare Sire for 1992. Included in his offspring was Risen Star, a champion three-year-old Preakness and Belmont Stakes winner. He also sired Lady's Secret, champion Handicap Female Horse of the Year and 1992 Hall of Fame inductee.

From his first crop of colts, one sold at Keeneland's 1976 July yearling sale for the then record price of $1.5 million. He was also the grandsire of future champions, Storm Cat, A. P. Indy, Summer Squall, Gone West, and Secreto. Even Smarty Jones carries his blood.

Upon his passing, a blue-and-white wreath was placed on his statue at Belmont Park, symbolizing his achievements as a superhorse. The Virginia Thoroughbred Association named him Horse of the Century.

His picture appeared on a thirty-three-cent U.S. postage stamp, which was unveiled in Keeneland Race Course's winner's circle on October 16, 1999. ESPN honored him by naming him the thirty-fifth athlete in their program *The Century's 50 Greatest Athletes.* The *Blood Horse's* choice of the Top 100 Thoroughbred Racehorses of the 20ᵗʰ Century named him second only to the historically immortal Man o' War, who at all distances proved his superhorse ability in 1920 by retiring with twenty wins out of a career of twenty-one starts and placing second in just one. He sired sixty-four stakes winners, including Triple Crown winner War Admiral.

Secretariat is an immortal legend that will always be remembered. Numerous documentaries and books rehash his life and fame. He was symbolized once again in 2004 when a new bronze statue was erected at the Secretariat Center, an equine adoption facility run by the Thoroughbred Retirement Foundation at the Kentucky Horse Park, honoring his greatness of thirty-one years earlier. The addition of his statue to the grounds where Man o' War's statue and grave already stand entwines the memory of the two superhorses of the century and honors both with their heroic-sized likenesses as two symbols of equine perfection.

Arnold Kirkpatrick would remember Secretariat's greatness in a 1973 *The Thoroughbred Record* article. He wrote:

> *Physically, Secretariat is the most striking horse I've ever come across. One cannot be entirely impersonal in evaluating his conformation because of the charisma and intense sense of energy generated by the horse…. It is really sort of humbling to be in the presence of such a remarkably handsome horse and one which seems to have such disdain for his opposition.*[243]

In 1972 and 1973, Christopher T. Chenery received the Eclipse Award for Outstanding Breeder. There was no Eclipse Award for Outstanding Owner in 1972 and 1973, but for many it is clear who would have won.

Penny Chenery, always considered the warmth and charm representing Secretariat, continues to help support his memory through the website www.secretariat.com. Her contagious smile will always be a special reminder of her gift to the sport.

"I'm very grateful to have had Secretariat in our lives," Penny would later say. "My father spent thirty years in racing and developing his broodmare band, and to have something like this come out of your own breeding is a tremendous thrill and a great sense of accomplishment. The children are crazy about this horse. I hope all of this lasts and inures to the benefit of racing."[244] She also would later say, "Sometimes little girls will come and burst into tears and say: 'You're Secretariat's mother!'"[245]

From 1976 to 1984, she was president of the Thoroughbred Owners and Breeders Association, and president of the Grayson Foundation in 1985 and 1986. She is a longtime member of The Jockey Club and a leading advocate for the Thoroughbred Retirement Foundation (TRF), the Secretariat Foundation, and the Kentucky Horse Park Foundation, backing numerous foundation endeavors to protect Thoroughbreds and their jockeys. Unofficially titled the "First Lady of Racing," Penny is renowned around the world for her heartfelt involvement with charitable causes, and she received the prestigious Eclipse Award of Merit for 2005.

Lucien Laurin's skill along with Riva Ridge's and Secretariat's winning streaks pulled Meadow Stables from its financial slump. By 1973, Lucien had trained thirty-one stakes winners.

Lucien enjoyed his greatest fame at sixty years of age, alternating between work and interviews. He received the Eclipse Award for Outstanding Trainer in 1972 and was inducted into the National Museum of Racing's Hall of Fame in 1977 and the Canadian Horse Racing Hall of Fame in 1978. After Secretariat won the Derby, Lucien was hailed as the fourth trainer in history to saddle back-to-back Derby winners.

He retired for a second time in 1976; however, he just couldn't give up his love of horses and, in 1983, returned as trainer and part owner of Evergreen Stable. While living at his home in Key Largo, Florida, Lucien passed away due to complications after hip surgery in 2000. A few of his great success stories include Secretariat, Riva Ridge, Quill, Amberoid, and Kike & Drone. His favorite horse to train was, of course, Secretariat.

Ron Turcotte was born on July 22, 1941 in New Brunswick, Canada, and began his career as a lumberjack. At nineteen, he relocated to Toronto, Ontario and began working as a hotwalker at E.P. Taylor's Windfields Farm. His first victory in 1962 was on Northern Dancer. He moved to the United States after being proclaimed Canada's best jockey for the years 1962 and 1963. By 1970 he had already amassed numerous awards and trophies. By riding Riva Ridge and Secretariat to victory in 1972 and 1973, he was titled leading stakes-winning jockey of North America and became the second jockey in history to ride consecutive winners in the Kentucky Derby—something that hadn't been done in seventy years.

Unfortunately, Ron was denied the 1973 Eclipse Award for Outstanding Jockey, as Pincay stole the show that year by being the first jockey in history to win over four million dollars in prize money. However, Turcotte did receive the highest Canadian award, the Order of Canada, presented to him by her majesty, Queen Elizabeth II. Along with receiving such prestigious awards as The Paul Harris Fellowship Award, The George Woolf Memorial Award, The Avelino Gomez Memorial Award, The Canadian Sovereign Award, and The Big Sport of Turfdom Award, he was inducted into numerous Sports Halls of Fame.

Ironically, the same racetrack that brought him lifelong fame through his winning the 1973 Belmont Stakes retired him as a paraplegic a short five years later due to a bad racing accident. He returned to Canada to retire with his wife, Gaetane, and their four daughters. In 1979, Turcotte was inducted into the National Museum of Racing's Hall of Fame.

In 2003 the Meadow Stables property, then owned by the Virginia State Fair, was planned for a 340-acre "Museum of the Horse" and fairground facility to pay special homage to Secretariat. Besides generous private donations, a project by Maker's Mark on the issuance of commemorative bottles celebrating the three Triple Crown winners of the '70s—Secretariat, Affirmed, and Seattle Slew—contributed a portion of their proceeds to the center's construction costs.

The state of Virginia took orders for license plates featuring Secretariat's image to help fund the project in 2004. Called the TRF Secretariat Center, it is operated by the Thoroughbred Retirement Foundation (TRF), and the facility's office, barn, arena, and paddocks safeguard retired Thoroughbreds. It also welcomes horses from other rescue groups to retrain them for adoption.

From the 1970 crop of colts, it seemed the only other true champion was Forego. He never raced against Secretariat again after placing fourth to him in the Kentucky Derby. His trainer, Sherrill Ward, spared him from further competition against Secretariat. He finished his three-year-old sophomore season with a total of eighteen starts, winning nine, placing second in three, and third in three.

Martha Gerry, Forego's owner, wanted to show the world that her Lazy F Ranch's born and bred gelding could go the distance and would prove to be an excellent handicap runner. Martha and Sherrill were right. Through the ages of four to six, Forego proved to the world that he was a heavyweight champion by carrying handicap weights of up to 140 pounds.

Only a few horses ever excelled in America at carrying the record weight of 136 pounds, those being Tom Fool, Native Dancer, Kelso, Gun Bow, Buckpasser, and Dr. Fager. An outstanding gelding named Phar Lap raced primarily in Australia and was a heavyweight champion that consistently won races while carrying weights in excess of 140 pounds. As a five-year-old, under an impossible 150-pound handicap in the Melbourne Cup, he courageously struggled to finish eighth.

Sherrill Ward's illness in 1976 forced Martha Gerry to assign a new trainer to her six-year-old champion, and Frank Y. Whiteley was appointed to the position. With strenuous handicap weights, Forego managed to win six of his nine starts, placing second in one and third in another. Throughout the years after his 1973 Derby loss to Secretariat, Forego went on to win the Eclipse Awards for Horse of the Year three times in a row, for 1974, 1975, and 1976. He also won the award for best Older Male successively for 1974, 1975, 1976, and 1977.

Proving he was a well-rounded horse, he also took the award for Best Sprinter in 1974. For his lifetime fifty-seven starts, he won thirty-four, placed second in nine, and third in seven, retiring in 1978 at the end of his eight-year-old season with total earnings of $1,938,957. He was inducted into the Racing Hall of Fame in 1979. On August 27, 1997, at the grand age of twenty-seven, he was euthanized after fracturing his right hind pastern in his paddock. The Blood Horse's choice of the Top 100 Thoroughbred Racehorses of the 20th Century ranked Forego #8.

Forego's last regular jockey, Willie Shoemaker, had been to jockeys what Secretariat was to racehorses before Pincay overtook him. He knew horses and could make almost any horse win with his quiet expertise. He rode many great champions, such as Gallant Man, Round Table, Sword Dancer, Northern Dancer, Damascus, Dr. Fager, John Henry, Swaps, Spectacular Bid, and Forego.

He earned an Eclipse Award in 1981 for Outstanding Jockey and was inducted into the Racing Hall of Fame in 1958, only nine years after he started his jockey career. He retired in 1990 with the "World's Winningest Jockey" title for the then-record 8,833 wins and began training horses. In 1991 a devastating automobile accident left him restricted to a wheelchair.

That didn't stop him from attending the Santa Anita racetrack, where he went every day to talk to young riders about his riding tricks. Shoemaker died in his sleep in October of 2004, still holding the second-place record for "World's Winningest Jockey." He only relinquished first place to Laffit Pincay, Jr., on December 10, 1999.

Sherrill Ward and Frank Whiteley were ironically both inducted into the Racing Hall of Fame in the same year, 1978. Ward received the Eclipse Award for Outstanding Trainer in 1974.

Ancient Title, a California-bred competitor of Sham's, never challenged Secretariat. After Sham left for the East Coast, Ancient Title's owners, Mr. and Mrs. William Kirkland, and his trainer, Keith Stucki, continued to run him in California, where he raced through the age of three. In a total of fifty-seven starts, he won twenty-four, took second in eleven, third in nine, and retired with total career earnings of $1,252,791. He held twentieth place on the official All-Time California-Bred Money Winners List, courtesy of The Jockey Club Information System Inc.

Shecky Greene was another competitor that went on to win seven of the ten stakes and feature races he entered in 1973, placing second in one and fourth in two. Like Forego, he never raced Secretariat again after placing sixth to Big Red in the Derby. His winnings for 1973 totaled $160,939. Shecky Greene was awarded the 1973 Eclipse Award for Best Sprinter. Upon retirement, he had accumulated total career earnings of $317,654 with fifteen wins, four seconds, and one third out of twenty-nine starts. He sired thirty-four stakes winners and died in 1984.

Forever remembered for defeating Secretariat in the '72 Champagne Stakes by default, Stop the Music also set two career track records at Belmont: 1:03 4/5 for five-and-a-half furlongs, and 1:33 3/5 for the mile. He challenged Secretariat many times and ranked second as a two-year-old to the copper colt on the 1972 Experimental Free Handicap. The bay colt, son of Hail to Reason, won eleven of thirty career starts and retired with earnings of $448,922. At stud, the stallion sired 409 winners, including Temperance Hill and Cure the Blues. He was broodmare sire of the 2005 Kentucky Derby winner, Giacomo. On July

8, 2005 at Gainesway Farm, the then thirty-five-year-old stallion was euthanized due to complications of old age.

Linda's Chief's career ended with total earnings of $490,571 and fifteen wins, places, and shows out of thirty starts. He raced against Secretariat as a two-year-old and beat most rivals at some point, except for Big Red. Linda's Chief finished his three-year-old campaign in California at Hollywood Park where he met an unfortunate end. For a horse that had once been considered unbeatable as a two-year-old, his racing career and life tragically ended with a broken leg.

Our Native's racing career earnings were just under Linda's Chief's, totaling $426,969 with fourteen wins, four seconds, and seven thirds out of thirty-seven starts. He went on to challenge Secretariat again, though he had no success beating Big Red. He was pensioned in 1992, sired forty-nine stakes winners, and was euthanized at the age of thirty-one on August 26, 2001, as a result of severe arthritis.

Out of the East retired with racing career earnings of $246,105 through a total of forty-six starts with only nine wins, thirteen places, and ten shows.

Knightly Dawn, retired with earnings of $233,483 from twenty-seven starts, giving him eight wins, never placing second, and five shows.

Angle Light never won a race again after the Wood Memorial. He lost more often than not. Out of twenty-one starts he won four, placed second in four, and third in three. His racing career earnings upon his retirement to stud in Kentucky were only $196,986. However, with his fame after winning the Wood Memorial over Sham and Secretariat, along with the fact that he was Secretariat's stablemate, his days at stud were renowned.

Sham and Secretariat's other competitors including Restless Jet, My Gallant, Royal and Regal, Gold Bag, Twice a Prince, Ecole Etage, Deadly Dream, and many others, never excelled.

It was indeed a challenge to all to race against the superhorse.

BIBLIOGRAPHY

1. *The Daily Racing Form Chart Book* (Triangle Publications, Inc., 1972 and 1973).
2. *The American Racing Manual* (1972 and 1973).
3. Zeh, Lucy. *Etched in Stone: Thoroughbred Memorials* (The Blood Horse, Inc.).
4. The Blood Horse. *Thoroughbred Champions, Top 100 Racehorses of the 20th Century* (The Blood Horse, Inc.: 1999).
5. Nack, William. *Secretariat: The Making of a Champion* (Da Capo Press, Inc.: 1975).
6. Georgeff, Phil. *And They're Off!* (Taylor Trade Publishing).
7. Heller, Bill. *Graveyard of Champions* (The Blood Horse, Inc.).
8. Shulman, Lenny. *Ride of Their Lives: The Triumphs and Turmoil of Today's Top Jockeys* (The Blood Horse, Inc.).
9. Simon, Mary. *Racing through the Century: The Story of Thoroughbred Racing in America* (BowTie Press).
10. Shoop, Robert. *Down to the Wire: The Lives of the Triple Crown Champions* (Russell Dean and Company: 2004).
11. Schwartz, Jane. *Ruffian: Burning from the Start* (The Ballantine Publishing Group: 1991).
12. Hillenbrand, Laura. *Seabiscuit: An American Legend* (The Ballantine Publishing Group: 2001).
13. Price, Steven D. *The Greatest Horse Stories Ever Told* (The Lyons Press: 2001).
14. Nack, William. "Pure Heart"; "Pure Heart – II"; "Pure Heart III"; "Big Red (1970–89)" (ESPN.com online: 2006), www.smythe.nb.ca/class97/fanjoy/pure%20heart.
15. Peace, Michael and Lesley Bayley. *Think Like Your Horse* (David & Charles Publishers: 2001).
16. Rashid, Mark. *Horses Never Lie* (Johnson Books: 2000).
17. Spaulding, C. E., DVM, *A Veterinary Guide for Animal Owners* (Rodale Press, Inc.: 1976).
18. CBS national broadcast on public television. *The Kentucky Derby Call of the Race (in its entirety) May 5, 1973; The Preakness Stakes Call of the Race (in its entirety) May 19, 1973; The Belmont Stakes Call of the Race (in its entirety) June 9, 1973.* Used by permission.

19. ESPN SportsCentury special national broadcast on public television. *The Century's 50 Greatest Athletes (of the 20th Century)*, #35 Secretariat.

20. *The Life and Times of Secretariat: An American Racing Legend* (Secretariat.com: 2006 video).

21. *Laffit, All About Winning* (Six Furlongs LLC; www.laffit.net: 2005 video).

22. Rice, J. Timothy. *Derby Choice Journal 2000 – 21st Edition* (Online, Innisfree Farm. www.innisfree.org: 2000).

23. "Pincay Breaks Tie with Shoemaker" (ESPN online, 12/17/99, http://sports.espn.go.com).

24. Wolfe, Raymond Jr., Rhonda Turman, ed. *A Thoroughbred Vision: The Origin and Inspiration of the Virginia Thoroughbred Association* (Online, http://www.vabred.org/history.cfm).

25. McNamara, Ed. *Pincay's Ride to Record Was Never Easy* (ESPN online: 2003, http://espn.go.com/horse/s/1999/1203/210611.html).

26. *Equus* (PRIMEDIA Enthusiast Publications, Inc.).

27. *Horse Illustrated: The Magazine for Responsible Horse Owners* (Fancy Publications, Inc.).

28. *The Western Horse* (Frontier Publishing Co.).

29. *The Thoroughbred Record*, now *Thoroughbred Times*, (Lexington, KY).

30. *The Blood Horse* (The Blood Horse Publications, Lexington, KY).

31. Bowen, Edward L. "Resumption of a Legend." *The Blood Horse* (Lexington, KY: May 14, 1973).

32. Bowen, Edward L. "At the Threshold of Giants." *The Blood Horse* (Lexington, KY: May 8, 1973).

33. Bowen, Edward L. "Joining the Giants." *The Blood Horse* (Lexington, KY: June 18, 1973).

34. Rudy, William H. "The Hatton Angle." *The Blood Horse* (Lexington, KY: April 30, 1973).

35. Casale, Mike. "Strictly Fourteen Carat." *The Thoroughbred Record* (Lexington, KY: November 4, 1972).

36. "Belmont's Biggest Sale." *The Thoroughbred Record* (Lexington, KY: December 2, 1972).

37. Rasmussen, Leon. "Point, Counterpoint." *The Thoroughbred Record* (Lexington, KY: April 7, 1973).

38. Casale, Mike. "New Light on the Derby Picture." *The Thoroughbred Record* (Lexington, KY: April 28, 1973).

39. Bowmarr, Dan III. "Clocking the Candidates." *The Thoroughbred Record* (Lexington, KY: May 5, 1973).

40. Kirkpatrick, Arnold. "Doubts Dispelled." *The Thoroughbred Record* (Lexington, KY: May 12, 1973).
41. Kirkpatrick, Arnold. "Secretariat's Stride." *The Thoroughbred Record* (Lexington, KY: 1216-B).
42. Kirkpatrick, Arnold. "The Name of the Game Is Class." *The Thoroughbred Record* (Lexington, KY: May 26, 1973).
43. Green, Ashbel. "A Threat to Secretariat." *The Thoroughbred Record* (Lexington, KY: June 2, 1973).
44. Kirkpatrick, Arnold. "Secretariat, the Ultimate Superlative." *The Thoroughbred Record* (Lexington, KY: June 16, 1973).
45. Flatter, Ron. "Secretariat Remains No. 1 Name in Racing" (Online, Special to ESPN.com: 2006).
46. Schmitz, David. "Stop the Music Dead at 35." *The Blood Horse* (Lexington, KY: July 23, 2005).
47. *The Toronto Star Newspaper* (Toronto, Ontario, Canada).
48. *The Denver Post* (Denver, CO).
49. *The Rocky Mountain News* (Denver, CO).
50. Cathro, Morton. "The Derby Restaurant Ranks with Racing's Foremost Museums." *The Blood Horse* (Lexington, KY: 01/06/01; Online: www.thederbyarcadia.com).
51. Reed, William F. "The Iceman's Watering Hole." 10/18/93 (Online: www.thederbyarcadia.com).
52. *Secretariat. The Free Lance-Star* (Online, Fredericksburg.com: 07/20/2002).
53. Votaw, Richelle. Short bio on Laffit Pincay, Jr. (www.geocities.com/Colosseum/Loge/8074).
54. www.nyra.com.
55. www.pbs.org.
56. www.secretariat.com.
57. www.espn.com.
58. www.msnbc.com.
59. www.perfecthorseracing.com.
60. www.brisnet.com.
61. www.thoroughbredtimes.com.
62. www.jockeyclub.com.
63. www.drf.com.
64. www.thoroughbredchampions.com.
65. www.pedigreequery.com.
66. www.equibase.com.
67. www.equineline.com.
68. www.laffit.net.

69. www.horseracing.about.com.
70. www.wikipedia.org.
71. www.kypost.com.
72. www.nmr.com.
73. www.dmtc.com.
74. www.racingmuseum.org.
75. www.santaanita.com.
76. www.simulatedsports.com.
77. www.vabred.org.

ENDNOTES

1   Phil Georgeff, *And They're Off!* page 27
2   CBS national sports broadcast, the call of the race, recorded live June 9, 1973, at Belmont Park
3   *Ibid.*
4   *Ibid.*
5   *The Life and Times of Secretariat,* Secretariat.com [2006 video]
6   "The Wow Horse," online, http://www.geocities.com/SouthBeach/Coast/9039/racehorses/Secretariat.html
7   Penny Chenery remembering her father "dynamic." Clay Latimer, "Down Memory Lane for Penny," *Rocky Mountain News,* 6/10/06
8   Eddie Sweat's start, "Mr. [Lucien] Laurin's farm..." Rick Matsumoto, "Groom Sorry to See 'Big Red' Go," *The Toronto Star,* 10/27/73
9   Eddie Sweat, "The first thing I..." Rick Matsumoto, "Groom Sorry to See 'Big Red' Go," *The Toronto Star,* 10/27/73
10 Eddie Sweat, "By the time they..." Rick Matsumoto, "Groom Sorry to See 'Big Red' Go," *The Toronto Star,* 10/27/73
11 Eddie Sweat, "Then around 1:30..." Rick Matsumoto, "Groom Sorry to See 'Big Red' Go," *The Toronto Star,* 10/27/73
12 Penny Chenery doubts, "but racing?" Clay Latimer, "Down Memory Lane for Penny," *Rocky Mountain News,* 6/10/06
13 Penny Chenery doubts, "supportive role." Clay Latimer, "Down Memory Lane for Penny," *Rocky Mountain News,* 6/10/06
14 "Secretariat Story," *The Free Lance-Star,* Fredericksburg.com, 7/20/02
15 *The Life and Times of Secretariat,* Secretariat.com [2006 Video]
16 Eddie Sweat's start, "I was away on holidays..." Rick Matsumoto, "Groom Sorry to See 'Big Red' Go," *The Toronto Star,* 10/27/73
17 William Nack, "Pure Heart," ESPN.com online, http://www.smythe.nbcc.nb.ca/class97/fanjoy/pure%20heart
18 *Ibid.*
19 *Ibid.*
20 *The Daily Racing Form Chart Book,* Triangle Publications LXXVII, 8 Aug/72
21 *A Day at the Races,* online http://www/pbs.org/wgbh/amex/seabiscuit
22 *Laffit, All About Winning,* Six Furlongs LLC [2005 Video], www.laffit.net
23 Advertisement, *The Thoroughbred Record,* November 1972

[24] Mike Casale, "Strictly Fourteen Carat," *The Thoroughbred Record,* 11/04/72, para. 1, page 1401

[25] Mike Casale, "Strictly Fourteen Carat," *The Thoroughbred Record,* 11/04/72, para. 5, page 1401

[26] *Laffit, All About Winning,* Six Furlongs LLC [2005 Video], www.laffit.net

[27] *Ibid.*

[28] *Ibid.*

[29] *Ibid.*

[30] *Ibid.*

[31] Laura Hillenbrand, *Seabiscuit: An American Legend,* page 108

[32] Arnold Kirkpatrick, "Secretariat's Stride," *The Thoroughbred Record*, 1973, para.1, page 1216-B

[33] "Notes," *The Thoroughbred Record,* April 14, 1973, page 902

[34] Lenny Shulman, *Ride of Their Lives,* page 185

[35] *Ibid.*

[36] *Laffit, All About Winning,* Six Furlongs LLC [2005 Video], www.laffit.net

[37] *Ibid.*

[38] *Ibid.*

[39] Lenny Shulman, *Ride of Their Lives,* page 187

[40] *Ibid.,* page 190

[41] *Laffit, All About Winning,* Six Furlongs LLC [2005 Video], www.laffit.net

[42] *Ibid.*

[43] *Ibid.*

[44] J. Timothy Rice, *Derby Choice Journal 2000,* 1971 interview, Innisfree Farm online, http://www.innisfree.org/2000.html

[45] Lenny Shulman, *Ride of Their Lives*, page 199

[46] *Ibid.*

[47] *Ibid.*

[48] Phil Georgeff, *And They're Off!* page 159

[49] William F. Reed, *The Iceman's Watering Hole,* online 10/18/93, http://www.thederbyarcadia.com/review_101893.php

[50] Morton Cathro, "The Derby Restaurant Ranks with Racing's Foremost Museums," *The Blood Horse,* online January 6, 2001, http://www.thederbyarcadia.com/review_010601.php

[51] William Nack, "Pure Heart – II," online [2006], http://www.smythe.nbcc.nb.ca/class97/fanjoy/pure%20heart

[52] *Ibid.*

[53] Leon Rasmussen, "Point, Counterpoint," *The Thoroughbred Record,* page 819

[54] Leon Rasmussen, "Point, Counterpoint," *The Thoroughbred Record,* para. 4, page 819

[55] *Ibid.*

[56] Dan Bowmar III, "Clocking the Candidates," *The Thoroughbred Record*, 1110

[57] William Nack, *Secretariat, the Making of a Champion,* page 217

[58] *Laffit, All About Winning,* Six Furlongs LLC, [2005 Video], www.laffit.net

[59] Lenny Shulman, *Ride of Their Lives,* page 192

[60] William Nack, *Secretariat, the Making of a Champion,* page 216

[61] William Nack, "Pure Heart II," ESPN online 2006, http://www.smythe.nbcc. nb.ca/class97/fanjoy/pure%20heart

[62] William H. Rudy, "The Hatton Angle," *The Blood Horse,* April 30, 1973, pages 1478–79

[63] *Ibid.*

[64] *Ibid.*

[65] *Ibid.*

[66] *Ibid.*

[67] Dan Bowmar III, "Clocking the Candidates," *The Thoroughbred Record,* 1110

[68] *Ibid.*

[69] *Ibid.*

[70] Mike Casale, "New Light on the Derby Picture," *The Thoroughbred Record*, 1070

[71] William H. Rudy, "The Hatton Angle," *The Blood Horse,* April 30, 1973

[72] *Ibid.*

[73] Ron Turcotte E-mail, regarding "Horse of the Century," Secretariat.com online 2002

[74] *The Life and Times of Secretariat,* Secretariat.com [2006 Video]

[75] William H. Rudy, "The Hatton Angle," *The Blood Horse,* April 30, 1973

[76] *Ibid.*

[77] *Ibid.*

[78] *Ibid.*

[79] Edward L. Bowen, "Resumption of a Legend," *The Blood Horse*, 1662

[80] Arnold Kirkpatrick, "Doubts Dispelled," *The Thoroughbred Record,* 1160 05/12/73

[81] Arnold Kirkpatrick, "Doubts Dispelled," *The Thoroughbred Record*, 05/12/73, para. 1, page 1160

[82] Edward L. Bowen, "Prologue to the 99th Running," *The Blood Horse,* 1592

[83] *Ibid.*

[84] *Ibid.*

[85] William Nack, "Pure Heart II,",para. 24, online 2006, ESPN.com, http://www. smythe.nbcc.nb.ca/class97/fanjoy/pure%20heart

[86] Arnold Kirkpatrick, "Doubts Dispelled," *The Thoroughbred Record,* 05/12/73

[87] William Nack, "Pure Heart II," online 2006, ESPN.com, http://www.smythe. nbcc.nb.ca/class97/fanjoy/pure%20heart

[88] *Ibid.*

[89] CBS national sports broadcast, the call of the race, recorded live May 5, 1973, at Churchill Downs

[90] *Ibid.*

[91] *Ibid.*

[92] *Ibid.*

[93] *Ibid.*

[94] William Nack, "Pure Heart II," online, ESPN.com, 2006, http://www.smythe. nbcc.nb.ca/class97/fanjoy/pure%20heart

[95] CBS national sports broadcast, the call of the race, recorded live May 5, 1973, at Churchill Downs

[96] *Ibid.*

[97] William Nack, "Pure Heart II," online 2006, ESPN.com, http://www.smythe. nbcc.nb.ca/class97/fanjoy/pure%20heart

[98] *Ibid.*

[99] William Nack, *Secretariat, the Making of a Champion,* page 271

[100] Edward L. Bowen, "Resumption of a Legend," *The Blood Horse,* 1660

[101] William Nack, *Secretariat, the Making of a Champion,* page 271

[102] Edward L. Bowen, "Resumption of a Legend," *The Blood Horse,* 1666

[103] Ron Flatter, "Secretariat Remains No. 1 Name in Racing," online 2006, ESPN.com, http://www.espn.go.com/classic/biography/s/Secretariat.html

[104] Joe Hirsch, "Secretariat Smashes Record in Magnificent Derby Score," *Daily Racing Form,* online, Secretariat.com

[105] Edward L. Bowen, "Resumption of a Legend," *The Blood Horse,* para. 9, page 1666

[106] Edward L. Bowen, "Resumption of a Legend," *The Blood Horse,* 1666

[107] Arnold Kirkpatrick, "Doubts Dispelled," *The Thoroughbred Record,* 1164

[108] Arnold Kirkpatrick, "Doubts Dispelled," *The Thoroughbred Record,* 1162

[109] *Ibid.*

[110] *Ibid.*

[111] Ron Turcotte on Bold Ruler, "Still think Bold Ruler…" Jim Armstrong, "Big Red Remembered," *Denver Post,* 5/02/03

[112] Arnold Kirkpatrick, "Secretariat's Stride," *The Thoroughbred Record,* para. 15, page 1216-B

[113] Edward L. Bowen, "At the Threshold of Giants," *The Blood Horse,* 1834

[114] Edward L. Bowen, "At the Threshold of Giants," *The Blood Horse,* 1832

[115] *Ibid.*

116 *Ibid.*

117 *Ibid.*

118 *Ibid.*

119 *Ibid.*

120 *Ibid.*

121 *Ibid.*

122 *Ibid.*

123 *Ibid.*

124 Arnold Kirkpatrick and Ashbel Green, "The Name of the Game Is Class," *The Thoroughbred Record,* 05/26/73, last paragraph, page 1261

125 Edward L. Bowen, "At the Threshold of Giants," *The Blood Horse,* 1834

126 *Ibid.*

127 *Ibid.*

128 CBS national sports broadcast, the call of the race, recorded live May 19, 1973, at Pimlico

129 *Ibid.*

130 *Ibid.*

131 William Nack, "Pure Heart III," ESPN.com, online 2006, http://www.smythe. nbcc.nb.ca/class97/fanjoy/pure%20heart

132 CBS national sports broadcast, the call of the race, recorded live May 19, 1973, at Pimlico

133 *Ibid.*

134 *Ibid.*

135 *Ibid.*

136 *Ibid.*

137 *The Life and Times of Secretariat,* Secretariat.com [2006 video]

138 CBS national sports broadcast, the call of the race, recorded live May 19, 1973, at Pimlico

139 *Ibid.*

140 William Nack, "Pure Heart III," ESPN.com, online 2006, http://www.smythe. nbcc.nb.ca/class97/fanjoy/pure%20heart

141 *The Day Time Didn't Stand Still,* Secretariat.com, online 2006, http://www. secretariat.com/races/preakness_popup.html

142 *Ibid.*

143 CBS national sports broadcast, the call of the race, recorded live May 19, 1973, at Pimlico.

144 Joe Hirsch, "Secretariat Adds a Victory in the Preakness," *Daily Racing Form.* online, Secretariat.com

145 ESPN's national broadcast of *The Century's 50 Greatest Athletes [for the 20th century],* [video]

146 *Ibid.*

[147] Edward L. Bowen, "At the Threshold of Giants," *The Blood Horse*, 1840

[148] Arnold Kirkpatrick, "The Name of the Game Is Class," *The Thoroughbred Record*, 259.

[149] *Ibid.*

[150] *Ibid.*

[151] *The Day Time Didn't Stand Still,* Secretariat.com, online 2006, http://www.secretariat.com/races/preakness_popup.html

[152] Edward L. Bowen, "At the Threshold of Giants," *The Blood Horse*, 1840

[153] *The Day Time Didn't Stand Still,* Secretariat.com online, http://www.secretariat.com/races/preakness_popup.html

[154] CBS national sports public television broadcast

[155] ESPN's national broadcast of *The Century's 50 Greatest Athletes [for the 20th century],* [video]

[156] William Nack, "Pure Heart III," ESPN.com, online 2006, http://www.smythe.nbcc.nb.ca/class97/fanjoy/pure%20heart

[157] *Ibid.*

[158] *The Life and Times of Secretariat,* Secretariat.com [2006 Video].

[159] *Ibid.*

[160] Edward L. Bowen, "Joining the Giants," *The Blood Horse*, 2078

[161] *Ibid.*

[162] Arnold Kirkpatrick, "Secretariat, The Ultimate Superlative," *The Thoroughbred Record,* para. 6, page 1439

[163] Arnold Kirkpatrick, "Secretariat, The Ultimate Superlative," *The Thoroughbred Record*, 1439

[164] William Nack, "Pure Heart III," para. 5, ESPN.com online 2006, http://www.smythe.nbcc.nb.ca/class97/fanjoy/pure%20heart

[165] Phil Georgeff, *And They're Off!* page 229

[166] CBS national sports broadcast, recorded live June 9, 1973 at Elmont, NY

[167] *Ibid.*

[168] Edward L. Bowen, "Joining the Giants," *The Blood Horse,* 2077

[169] *Ibid.*

[170] CBS national sports broadcast, the call of the race, recorded live June 9, 1973, at Belmont

[171] William Nack, "Pure Heart III," online ESPN.com 2006, http://www.smythe.nbcc.nb.ca/class97/fanjoy/pure%20heart

[172] CBS national sports broadcast, the call of the race, recorded live June 9, 1973, at Belmont

[173] *The Life and Times of Secretariat,* Secretariat.com [2006 Video]

[174] Edward L. Bowen, "Joining the Giants," *The Blood Horse*, 2076

[175] CBS National sports broadcast, the call of the race, recorded live June 9, 1973, at Belmont

176 *Ibid.*

177 *The Life and Times of Secretariat,* Secretariat.com [2006 Video]

178 Ron Flatter, "Secretariat Remains No.1 Name in Racing," ESPN online 2006 http://espn.go.com/classic/biography/s/Secretariat.html

179 *The Century's 50 Greatest Athletes [for the 20th century],* ESPN documentary

180 CBS national sports broadcast, recorded live June 9, 1973, Elmont, NY

181 Joe Hirsch, "Secretariat Achieves a Triple," *Daily Racing Form*

182 *The Life and Times of Secretariat,* Secretariat.com [2006 Video]

183 Joe Hirsch, "Secretariat Achieves a Triple," *Daily Racing Form,* online 2006, Secretariat.com

184 *Ibid.*

185 *Ibid.*

186 *The Life and Times of Secretariat,* Secretariat.com [2006 Video]

187 *Ibid.*

188 Joe Hirsch, "Secretariat Achieves a Triple," *Daily Racing Form,* online 2006, Secretariat.com

189 Arnold Kirkpatrick, "Secretariat, the Ultimate Superlative," *The Thoroughbred Record,* para. 7, page 1440

190 Penny Chenery on Secretariat, "He was so good looking…" Clay Latimer, "Down Memory Lane for Penny," *Rocky Mountain News,* 6/10/06

191 Penny Chenery on publicity, "I had to get…" Clay Latimer, "Down Memory Lane for Penny," *Rocky Mountain News,* 6/10/06

192 Penny Chenery on publicity, "I respond to the…" "$6 Million Horse Comes Here to Run Last Race," *The Toronto Star,* 10/22/73

193 D. Wayne Lucas on Secretariat, "think anyone has…" Jim Armstrong, "Big Red Remembered," *Denver Post,* 5/02/03

194 Bobby Frankel on Secretariat, "the best horse." Jim Armstrong, "Big Red Remembered," *Denver Post,* 5/02/03

195 "Things and People: Surgery for Sham," *The Blood Horse Weekly Magazine,* July 1973

196 Ron Turcotte, "I believe I got…" Milt Dunnell, "Even the Ghost Is Slowing Up," *The Toronto Star,* 9/17/73

197 Ron Turcotte, "I think he's…" "Secretariat Improves Commercial Appeal," *The Toronto Star,* 9/17/73

198 Eddie Maple, "I took a peek…" Milt Dunnell, "Even the Ghost Is Slowing Up," *The Toronto Star,* 9/17/73

199 Senator Daniel Inouye, "I most respectfully…" "Cox Was 'Too Hot on White House Trail,'" *The Toronto Star,* 10/23/73

200 Senator Edward Kennedy, "One of the most…" "Cox Was 'Too Hot on White House Trail,'" *The Toronto Star,* 10/23/73

201 Gerald Ford, "The president had no…" "Legislators Line Up to Impeach Nixon After Cox Fired," *The Toronto Star*, 10/22/73

202 John Anderson, "Impeachment resolutions…" "Legislators Line Up to Impeach Nixon After Cox Fired," *The Toronto Star*, 10/22/73

203 Robert Drinan, "I think Nixon…" "Legislators Line Up to Impeach Nixon After Cox Fired," *The Toronto Star,* 10/22/73

204 Fortny Stark, "The roof is…" "Legislators Line Up to Impeach Nixon After Cox Fired," *The Toronto Star*, 10/22/73

205 John Conyers, Jr., "I believe it puts…" "Legislators Line Up to Impeach Nixon After Cox Fired," *The Toronto Star,* 10/22/73

206 Newspaper headlines, "$6 Million…" "$6 Million Horse Comes Here to Run Last Race," *The Toronto Star*, 10/22/73

207 Newspaper headlines, "Superhorse…" "Superhorse Is Here," *The Toronto Star,* 10/23/73

208 On Secretariat's security, "The world's most…" Rick Matsumoto, "Secretariat Looks Ready for Last Race," *The Toronto Star,* 10/23/73

209 On Secretariat's security, "Bit of special attention…" Rick Matsumoto, "Secretariat Looks Ready for Last Race," *The Toronto Star*, 10/23/73

210 On Secretariat's security, "Usually horses are…" Rick Matsumoto, "Secretariat Looks Ready for Last Race," *The Toronto Star*, 10/23/73

211 Penny Chenery, "I remember asking him…" "$6 Million Horse Comes Here to Run Last Race," *The Toronto Star*, 10/22/73

212 Eddie Maple on Riva Ridge, "He [Riva] didn't…" Jim Proudfoot, "Race as Easy as Pie, Says Stand-in Jockey," *The Toronto Star*, 10/29/73

213 Eddie Maple uncertainties, "I felt a certain…" Jim Proudfoot, "Race as Easy as Pie, Says Stand-in Jockey," *The Toronto Star,* 10/29/73

214 Ron Turcotte concerns, "I had only one…" Jim Proudfoot, "Race as Easy as Pie, Says Stand-in Jockey," *The Toronto Star,*10/29/73

215 Ron Turcotte about Maple, "It wasn't my…" "Ron Turcotte: Maple Just Let Him Run His Own Race," *The Toronto Star,* 10/29/73

216 *The Life and Times of Secretariat,* Secretariat.com [2006 Video]

217 *Ibid.*

218 Lucien Laurin, "Secretariat has never…" "Perfect Finale for 'Big Red' and His Lady," *The Toronto Star,* 10/29/73

219 Eddie Maple post race, "I figured…" "Race as Easy as Pie, Says Stand-in Jockey," *The Toronto Star,* 10/29/73

220 Avelino Gomez about mount, "I tried to go…" Al Nickleson, "Secretariat: A Magnificent Finale," *The Toronto Star*, 10/29/73

221 Ron Turcotte post race, "But when he…" "Ron Turcotte: Maple Just Let Him Run His Own Race," *The Toronto Star*, 10/29/73

[222] Penny Chenery post race, "I'm so pleased..." Al Nickleson, "Secretariat: A Magnificent Finale," *The Toronto Star*, 10/29/73

[223] *The Life and Times of Secretariat,* Secretariat.com [2006 Video]

[224] *Ibid.*

[225] On postrace traffic concerns, "worst-ever traffic jam..." Pennington, "Perfect Finale for 'Big Red' and His Lady," *The Toronto Star*, 10/29/73

[226] Penny Chenery on retirement, "Ideally I would not..." "'Wow!' She Said at First Sight of Secretariat," *The Toronto Star*, 10/22/73

[227] "Canadian International Stakes Race," article on Secretariat.com [online 2006]

[228] *The Life and Times of Secretariat,* Secretariat.com [2006 Video]

[229] William Nack, *Secretariat, the Making of a Champion,* page 337

[230] *The Life and Times of Secretariat,* Secretariat.com [2006 Video]

[231] William Nack, "Pure Heart," ESPN.com online 2006, http://www.smythe. nbcc.nb.ca/class97/fanjoy/pure%20heart.

[232] *Ibid.*

[233] *Ibid.*

[234] *The Century's 50 Greatest Athletes [for the 20th century],* ESPN video

[235] *Ibid.*

[236]   *Ron Flatter, "Secretariat Remains No. 1 Name in Racing," ESPN on- line 2006, http://expn.go.com/classic/biography/s/Secretariat.html*

[237] *The Life and Times of Secretariat,* Secretariat.com [2006 Video]

[238] *Ibid.*

[239] *Ibid.*

[240] *Ibid.*

[241] *Ibid.*

[242] *Laffit, All About Winning,* Six Furlongs LLC 2005 Video

[243] Arnold Kirkpatrick, "Doubts Dispelled," *The Thoroughbred Record,* 1164

[244] *The Life and Times of Secretariat,* Secretariat.com [2006 Video]

[245] *Ibid.*

Printed in the United States
105224LV00004B/193-195/P

9 781593 305062